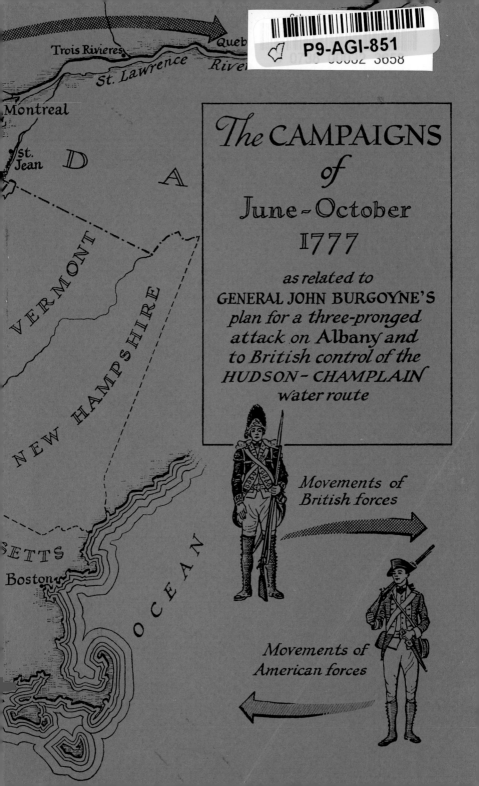

Trois Rivieres

St. Lawrence River

Queb[ec]

Montreal

St. Jean

CANADA

VERMONT

NEW HAMPSHIRE

[MASSACHU]SETTS

Boston

OCEAN

The CAMPAIGNS
of
June ~ October
1777

as related to
GENERAL JOHN BURGOYNE'S
plan for a three-pronged
attack on **Albany** *and*
to British control of the
HUDSON ~ CHAMPLAIN
water route

Movements of
British forces

Movements of
American forces

March to Saratoga

March to Saratoga

General Burgoyne and the American Campaign

1777

HARRISON BIRD

New York Oxford University Press 1963

In grateful memory

of

Sir George and Lady Langton

whose friendship sustained me

1940–1945

Preface

Lieutenant General John Burgoyne's "Thoughts for Conducting the War from the Side of Canada" developed an idea that did not originate with that officer. As early as 1642, the French in Canada had appreciated the tactical value of the Champlain-Hudson Pass through the Appalachian mountain barrier and had commenced the building of a chain of forts to the south from the St. Lawrence outlet of Lake Champlain. The ultimate French fort was at Ticonderoga, which Burgoyne was to capture from its rebel owners in July 1777. In the year 1666 a tactical plan brought European soldiers marching from "the side of Canada" through the natural gap made by the lake and river valley in an invasion that was a North American projection of European rivalries. During the next century and a half, when European wars were fought in the New World, the Hudson-Champlain Valley was the classic invasion route between the rich coastal plain of the Atlantic seaboard and the arterial St. Lawrence and Great Lakes, giving access to the heart of the continent. The Hudson-Champlain

Pass ranks with the great invasion routes of the world: the Belfort Gap, the Low Countries, the Great Grass Bridge out of Asia, and the Khyber Pass. Its defiles and crossroads at Ticonderoga and West Point stand with Gibraltar and Verdun.

In planning either for invasion or defense, the minds of rulers and their cabinets and generals invariably turn to the old routes. This is not for want of boldness or imagination, but because these are the only roads for the supply and transport of invasion armies, or for effective defense by forts and forces. The Mongol Horde marched where their ponies could graze, and in the nineteenth century armies advanced along the newly developed railroads which followed the easiest way through the mountains and along the rivers, while today an army is geared to the requirements of the airplane, the helicopter, and the parachute drop zone. In 1777 General Burgoyne's "thoughts" were dictated by the requirements of his transport and supply. The validity of these thoughts rested on the fact that Lake Champlain, the Hudson, and the westward-branching Mohawk River, in his time and given his transport of boats and horse-drawn carts, constituted the only clear way through the mountain barrier dividing the rebellious colonies on the Atlantic seaboard and the loyal colony of Canada on the St. Lawrence. The Hudson-Champlain Pass was the short crossbar that marked the letter "A" across the geography of British North America, making it the controlling factor in the alphabet of British colonial aspiration.

This book is the story of John Burgoyne and his "thoughts," and of the stalwart men and women who had a part in putting those thoughts into action along the old invasion route.

General Burgoyne himself, and many of his comrades-in-arms, helped in the writing of this story through their own accounts of their adventures and of what befell as they made their way up Lake Champlain, across the long portage, and along the southward-flowing Hudson River. Their efforts are appreciated on every page and in every episode related in the book; their written work is acknowledged in the Book List (p. 290).

My appreciation is sincere and my thanks are due to those who introduced me to the "contemporary sources" mentioned above, and who by their research, generously shared, into the conditions and events of the exciting year of 1777, provided the basis for much of this book. I am ever in the debt of the Fort Ticonderoga Museum, its first director, Stephen H. P. Pell, and its present president, John H. G. Pell, for a lifetime of interest and inspiration engendered in me by that place. I wish particularly to thank Eleanor Murray, of Fort Ticonderoga, for giving me of her research and knowledge in connection with the troops under General Burgoyne. Information on the Tory troops and the Loyalist corps was generously provided by Henry I. Shaw of the Company of Military Collectors & Historians. Through the courtesy of the National Park Service, operating the Saratoga National Historical Park, I obtained a listing of the American units of General Gates's army, for which I am grateful. With unfailing generosity, Mrs. John Nicholas Brown, of Providence, Rhode Island, permitted an unrestricted selection of military prints from her great collection, adding greatly to the interest of my book and increasing an already substantial indebtedness which it gives me pleasure to acknowledge.

In conclusion, I wish to mention by name some few of the many persons who have helped me in many divers ways: W. Gillette Bird, John R. Cuneo, John J. Demers, Dr. Alfred Emerson, Mrs. Lorentz Hansen, Richard B. Harrington, Edward Mann, Rolland Miner, Mrs. Doris Morton, Robert E. Mulligan (Senior and Junior), J. Y. Shimoda, Miss Claribel Snody, and Earl Stott.

For my wife, Harriette Jansen Bird, who typed and otherwise worked with me on the manuscript, I have no adequate word of praise; only, in retrospect, wonder.

Huletts Landing, New York   H. B.
December 1962

Contents

Illustrations

Maps

Maps

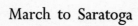

March to Saratoga

1

The New Year

1777

The music of the processional died away quickly, as if fleeing into the darkest and highest reaches of the great vault of the cathedral. In its wake a chilled hush swept down the long nave to settle on the shoulders of the packed congregation; some shivered.

No head turned to look, as the eight forlorn penitents began their slow walk to the distant altar rail, where the magnificence of the archbishop of Canada, robed in his richest garments, awaited their approach. In almost military array, the eight lined themselves with bowed heads outside the altar rail, to supplicate the mercy of the Church under whose anathema they had existed for almost a year. Around the neck of each man hung a length of navy rope, tied into a hangman's noose. The rope signified the secular crime of treason, to be expiated or forgiven on this first anniversary of 31 December 1775.

The sentences of the eight men would be forgiven only when the ceremonies of Church and State had been completed, and the full measure of warning drawn from the spectacle of Public Penance. On this

last day of 1776, the British government of this Canadian colony could afford to be magnanimous to
traitors. That a Protestant king chose to punish and
forgive his French Canadian subjects through their
own Roman Catholic archbishop was due entirely to
the good sense, political acumen, and loyal efforts of
the governor general of Canada, Guy Carleton.

Twelve months earlier, on 31 December 1775, the
eight penitents now standing humbled before the
altar rail had joined the American rebel army in
the assault on the City of Quebec. That attack by the
heretical Puritan "Bostonais" had been the high-
water mark of the attempt by the thirteen united
American colonies to wrench Canada from her political loyalty to Britain.

General Guy Carleton had stood firm, on that night
of the swirling blizzard, and Fortune as well as the
prayers of the archbishop had favored his defense of
Quebec. As the defense of the western barricade had
wavered in the face of attack, a sailor had clapped a
lighted linstock onto the breech of a primed and
loaded cannon. The blast of grapeshot had ended the
life of the American general, Richard Montgomery,
and with his death, the will of his followers. At the
eastern barricade a musket shot had struck the leg
of Brigadier General Benedict Arnold, throwing him,
helpless, into the snow. He was carried back out of
the line of fire by his ardent followers (Arnold
seemed always to inspire ardor when he led men into
battle). Behind an angle of a building, Colonel
Daniel Morgan rallied Arnold's soldiers and led them

in vengeance against the barricade held by the British and the Canadians. In the melee of the snowy night, Dan Morgan got himself "cooped" in a warehouse by General Carleton's sortie, and in the morning gave himself up a prisoner.

As Carleton had beaten back the assault of Montgomery and Arnold and Morgan during the first hours of 31 December 1775, so he had withstood the winter-long investment of Quebec, the last place in all of Canada firmly under his viceregal suzerainty. In May 1776 reinforcements for Carleton came out from England, and with the British fleet of men-of-war and transports came Major General John Burgoyne, "Gentleman Johnny," as he was referred to with affection by his soldiers. In the same convoy came Major General Baron Friederich Adolf von Riedesel, like Burgoyne a cavalry colonel of experience and capability.

With eight fresh regiments of good British infantry and the competent battalions of Brunswickers and Hesse-Hanauers hired for the occasion, General Guy Carleton soon drove the tardily reinforced Americans out of the St. Lawrence Valley. At the foot of Lake Champlain, Carleton was forced to pause through the high summer months in order to build a battle fleet before pushing south along the classic invasion route up Lake Champlain and Lake George, down the Hudson River to Albany, and thence to the Atlantic Ocean at New York. By the end of October 1776 Carleton had gained naval command of Lake Champlain, and stood with part of his army before

the walls of Fort Ticonderoga. There, under the gridiron flag of rebellion, General Horatio Gates and
Benedict Arnold (limping now) awaited him.

Burgoyne wished to give spur to the British army
and ride roughshod over the American rabble, but
Carleton held him back. The latter had a staff officer's
eye to his supply line, and many years of experience
with the northern seasons. Carleton knew the contrary temper of the autumn winds and the insidious
forming of the ice, either of which could trap an in-
cautious army caught up the lake too far from its
supply base. Then, too, Carleton did not share the
contempt of his second in command for the American
soldier and for the strategic fort at Ticonderoga which
he held. The season was advanced and the enemy
stanch. Early in November Carleton withdrew down
Lake Champlain, made his fleet secure against the
ice, and sent his army into winter quarters. Ever restless, ever active, Burgoyne sailed back to England.

Now, in the bright warm sunlight of a winter's
morning, General Guy Carleton stood talking with
the archbishop as the congregation filed out of the
cathedral. The eight penitents were nowhere to be
seen. All solemnity was over.

Close behind Carleton on the cathedral steps were
his officers, gray-cloaked British from as far away as
Montreal, and German officers in their blue capes or
white Canadian coats, some with mitre caps as tall
and as flashing bright as the bishop's. All waited the
departure of the personages, so they could hurry off
to prepare for the first of the festivities that were to
begin the new and wonderful year of 1777.

The Thanksgiving Service at the cathedral had started at nine o'clock in the morning. The reception at Government House, which was a "parade" for all officers, was scheduled for ten o'clock. Those commanding troops were excused early so that they could fall in with their detachments for the military review called for eleven. They were bidden to lunch with the governor and his lady at three o'clock, and in the late afternoon all would be confusion in the quarters that the visiting officers shared with the officers of the Quebec garrison, as everyone dressed for the great ball.

By six o'clock the winter's night had drawn in. Amid a silvery jingle of bells, sled after sled drew up to the door of the *auberge,* and the high-born of Quebec threw aside their fur lap robes to dash between the pine torches lighting the doorway and into the warmth of the party rooms. As was to be expected in a city swollen by an army, there were two gallants for every lady — the odd man being, of course, an officer. Only two English ladies were present, and these, being the governor's lovely young lady and her sister, married to the governor's nephew, were too exalted for more than the most formal flirtation. The British grenadiers regretted particularly the absence of their commander's wife, the sharp-witted, sharp-featured Lady Harriet — herself, like the two Carleton ladies, the daughter of an earl. But Major John Acland was down sick in his wretched quarters on the bank of the Richelieu River, and the devoted Lady Harriet nursed him. So no Quebec lady went unnoticed through the evening of the New Year's ball, though she be so provincial as to speak her French, to awkward-tongued English or German officers, with the accent of her native Indian tongue.

A concert filled the hours to midnight, and there was dancing, too, of a desultory nature. The party was at supper when the magical moment struck, and the year was 1777.

For the officers the festivities continued for two more days and nights. There seemed to be so much for them to do and say, so much to plan for this new year. The year just closed had carried most of them from towns along the Rhine or the sleepy little rivers of England to the walls of Ticonderoga on Lake Champlain, and they were confident, for the most part, that 1777 would take them full cycle down the Hudson and, the futile rebellion having been quashed, home to shire and dorf.

Colonel Barry St. Leger, a man of the kidney of the absent Johnny Burgoyne, was host at a stag dinner, and a sleigh ride took his guests singing through the night to the country house of a doctor, whose reputation as the Lucullus of Quebec was found to be justified. They made the acquaintance, too, of the fabulously rich bachelor, Monsieur de la Naudière, who, in the lodges of the Indians, was the son-in-law of the monumental Chevalier St. Luc de la Corne. At sixty-seven, St. Luc could still call up and lead to war a thousand savage Indians, and rumor had it that already his messengers had gone to the western tribes beyond Montreal and far out on the Great Lakes to rally the warriors for the approaching campaign.

At last the parties came to an end. The officers returned to their billets and their troops scattered in a hundred villages from Quebec to Montreal and up the Richelieu as far as Ile aux Nois, where the Lake Champlain fleet lay waiting for the thaw.

Baron Riedesel commanded his Germans from Trois Rivières, and out of loneliness, wrote fond and longing letters to his wife, asking her to join him. The British troops stationed in and around Montreal were under the command of Major General William Phillips, a proud man — "the proudest man of the proudest nation on earth," according to Thomas Jefferson, who knew him. Phillips was proud of being a gunner, even more than of being a general officer, and he was especially proud of the military band of the Royal Regiment of Artillery, which he himself had created. On the other hand, plump, little Colonel St. Leger, who commanded at Quebec, was an infantryman, light of foot, the master of maneuver and attack, either in the field or on the ballroom floor. Commanding them all and in command of all Canada was Guy Carleton.

With all the British in Canada, scarcely anyone took notice of the Yankees. The soldiery trained and paraded, drank when they could, gossiped interminably, and fought among themselves; they seized upon any excuse for a party or sat by the fireside at their billets, and, whenever possible, kept out of the way of their corporals and sergeants and captains and colonels and generals. Only the displaced Tories, driven from their homes in the Atlantic colonies, were venegeful. One of these, Samuel McKay, re-

cently escaped from a Connecticut jail, on 3 April
1777 made a raid on the American supply route. The
ambush he laid at Sabbath Day Point on Lake
George killed four rebels; and their captain, wounded
and a prisoner, was carried back to Canada by the
tall, pale Tory ranger.

McKay's raid was the beginning of the campaign.
The winter had been mild and spring came early to
rot the ice on the lakes, where each new patch of
open water increased the apprehension of the Americans, watching anxiously to the north from the
bastions of Ticonderoga.

On 6 May, His Majesty's Frigate *Apollo* dropped
anchor among the last ice floes lingering in the roadstead at Quebec. She was the first ship of the year to
arrive from England, and aboard her was the express
passenger, Lieutenant General John Burgoyne. It
was the general's third trip across the Atlantic to the
North American theater of war. One of a pack of
major generals sent to help General Thomas Gage
run the hare of rebellion to ground in 1775, Burgoyne
had arrived at Boston aboard the *Cerberus*. There,
Sir William Howe and Sir Henry Clinton took care of
all the duties requiring the attention of a major
general, so Burgoyne, as junior, employed his time
in writing letters describing the military operations
around Boston. He also wrote a play, in which he
ridiculed the prudery of the Bostonians. In November he returned to London and the House of Commons, where he held the seat for Preston.

The following year Burgoyne came out to Canada in HMS *Blonde,* to be commander of troops under Guy Carleton, the commander in chief in Canada. Again, the month of November saw Burgoyne on the stormy Atlantic on his way to the House of Commons and to the Ministries where plans would be made for the 1777 campaign in North America.

Now, while the sailors secured the *Apollo* at her anchorage, Burgoyne stood on the quarterdeck with the captain, politely taking his leave as he watched the government barge pulling out from the quay to fetch him. He was cloaked, booted, and ready to ride. Slung over the shoulder of his aide who was waiting in the waist of the ship, were saddle bags containing orders, dispatches, and instructions for Carleton. During the long haul up the St. Lawrence the *Apollo* had been in touch with shore, and everyone on board knew that the governor general was upriver with the army. Burgoyne must hurry to him. The meeting between the two gentlemen was bound to be somewhat awkward, for the news must be broken to Carleton that he had been superseded as commander of the invasion army by Burgoyne himself.

As commander in chief of the expedition designed as the maul that would split in two the rebellious Atlantic colonies down the natural fault of the Montreal–New York waterline, John Burgoyne stood, his legs firmly braced, to swing that maul for the highest stakes of his already brilliant career. He was fifty-four years old, with strong features and a decided jut and clench to his jaw. The weight that he had put

on in recent years became him, and limited him only
in the choice of horses that could carry him. As a
slim youth he had been accustomed to the heavy
dragoon charger of his regiment. It was not until
1759, when he raised his own regiment of light
dragoons, that he found in the agile animal required
for that new cavalry service the mount to match his
spirit and his image. If he now needed a sturdy
hunter to carry him, it would make little actual difference, for in Canada a horse fit for a gentleman to
ride was nowhere to be found.

John Burgoyne's career in the cavalry was a logical
one in view of his background: that of an old county
family with good, if modest, patronage. His early
elopement with a daughter of the Earl of Derby, a
step which he assured that important Whig family
had not been dictated by opportunism, nevertheless
widened considerably the range within which he
could develop his capacities. First and foremost was
his military life, through which he was in the ken
of the sovereign owing to the high standard maintained by his 16th ("Queen's") Light Dragoons, as
well as to a brilliant campaign as brigadier general
in Portugal.

He was a hard campaigner and an adroit politician,
who, lacking the ambition to attain cabinet rank, was
free of the constraint of normal party lines. In 1773
Burgoyne had stood as accuser at the impeachment
trial of Robert Clive for the alleged misdeeds of that
soldier-empire builder while in India, and had won
his case. His military career kept him away for long

periods from his seat in the House of Commons, which he entered in 1761, but when in the House John Burgoyne was a conscientious member of parliament, who voiced his opinions in fine rhetorical speeches.

Burgoyne's gifted use of words and of resounding phrases of wit and elegance gave him more than a passing vogue as poet and playwright. In his varied pursuits, he epitomized the English gentleman of the eighteenth century, and that he was successful in three fields of endeavor — the military, the political, and the literary — proves him to have been more than the casual dilettante, and marks him as one determined to excel.

In his vices, too, John Burgoyne excelled. He gambled more successfully than had his father; he drank with greater discrimination and capacity than most officers and gentlemen; and he wenched within the boundaries of his own class, without prejudice to his devotion to his own wife.

Thus, it was in admiration of a completely rounded man of the eighteenth century that his soldiers on the Peninsula dubbed Burgoyne with a ribald nickname and bestowed upon him the truer accolade of "Gentleman Johnny," which, in 1777, epitomized the new lieutenant general in Canada.

Guy Carleton, too, was a gentleman and, commensurate with his rank in the army and in the colonial service, a politician. His removal as commander in chief of the northern striking force was a political setback, and the promotion of John Bur-

goyne to replace him an intentional rebuke. But the
insult came from the minister in London, not from
the gentleman whose embarrassing duty it was to
deliver it. The orders Burgoyne produced from his
saddle bag, therefore, could be accepted by Carleton
with all the grace of one gentleman losing to another
at cards.

Burgoyne was the logical person to carry out the
campaign as ordered from London. The plans were of
his own devising. They were based upon a fact as old
as the geography of North America itself. When the
great glacier receded it left one geological fault
through the mountain barrier which, in the eighteenth
century, held the thirteen American colonies to the
Atlantic coast. Furthermore, the melting ice left a
chain of lakes in the northern half of the corridor
through the mountains, and in the southern half of
that corridor the glacial freshet had gouged out a
wide river basin. To Burgoyne, and to the exalted
gentlemen pouring over maps in a Whitehall office,
these waterways seemed expressly created to carry
the heavy baggage of a British army. Nor would
the land which divided Lake Champlain and Lake
George, the northward draining lakes from the
Hudson River, flowing to the south, hamper the
passage of a well-equipped expedition. It had been
crossed by the British armies that had conquered
Canada, and even the rabble army of the Americans
traversed its roads freely to supply the fort at Ticonderoga.

Twice Burgoyne had prepared for the British cabi-

net plans based on the strategical importance of the
Lake Champlain–Hudson River gap. On his return
from Boston in November 1775 he had written and
presented his "Reflections upon the War in America."
The campaigns of 1776, during which Howe had occupied New York City and the lower Hudson Valley
while Carleton, with Burgoyne as his second in
command, had reconquered Canada including Lake
Champlain, were a part of these "Reflections." On
his return to London in November of 1776, Burgoyne
had written out his "Thoughts for Conducting the
War from the Side of Canada." These thoughts
formed the basis for the orders which Burgoyne was
now delivering to Guy Carleton.

The orders called for a three-pronged advance on
Albany, set midway between New York and Montreal, the largest and most important inland city in
the American colonies. General Howe, or his second
in command, General Clinton, was to move northward up the Hudson, perhaps with the British fleet,
and would provide a solid British block. Burgoyne
was to be the axe, cleaving swiftly through the American army which awaited the blow at Ticonderoga,
and falling lightly on the block. Like a split balk of
fine wood, the American revolution would then fall
apart, its shattered armies to be gathered up at
leisure. The third force, as outlined in Burgoyne's
"Thoughts," would immediately begin on the tidying
up. Colonel Barry St. Leger would take a small
force, made up for the most part of loyal Americans and Iroquois Indians, and proceed in a wide

swing around the mass of the Adirondack Mountains
through the Mohawk River Valley which had been
their homeland, to fall on Albany from the west.
Burgoyne expected that St. Leger would draw off
some of the rebel army facing him, and that there
would be a general rising and return to loyalty by the
people of the Mohawk Valley.

The tactical plan of the campaign was reminiscent
of Jeffrey Amherst's final and masterful stroke in the
conquest of Canada in 1759, when, with perfect tim-
ing, he had converged three armies, from three distant and different directions, upon Montreal. Burgoyne's campaign, like Amherst's, depended for its
success upon the concerted movement in time and
space of three separate forces: the forces of Howe,
of St. Leger, and of Burgoyne himself. Specific orders
to Howe, covering this vital aspect of the plan and
his part in it, were drawn up by Lord George Germaine, who, as Colonial Secretary, was responsible
for the conduct of the American war. These orders
were to be sent direct to General Howe, wintering
comfortably with his mistress in New York.

Germaine's orders to Carleton, though less important to the success of Burgoyne's plans, were more
specific. They called on him to prepare the Champlain
fleet, furnish artillery and stores, recruit a large number of Canadians and Indians, and, while aiding his
successor in every way, defend all of Canada against
invasion or revolt. This last was to be accomplished
with 3000 soldiers chosen from the "odds and sods"
of the expedition's regiments, and with the remains

of existing regiments from which the elite had been drafted to Burgoyne and St. Leger. As a soldier Carleton had no alternative but to comply. This he did, though he doubted his ability to supply the Canadians and Indians in the quantity or quality expected of him. He also doubted the claims of the Tory refugees as to the number of their fellow sympathizers who would co-operate with the "liberating" army. Carleton knew the vast extent of forest distances, as he knew the deceptive seasons of the north country. He knew the long chance a messenger took in coming from New York to Montreal, whether by sea or through the lines of the able Continental army or the militia watch in each isolated town. Perhaps Guy Carleton was wisely relieved of the responsibility of leading an expedition based upon estimates with which he was at variance. Hope for the success of Burgoyne's venture lay in the infectious enthusiasm and the bright spark of that gentleman's gay conviction. The displaced Carleton was unstinting in his aid.

2

On Your Markers; Fall In!

Ten days after landing at Quebec, Gentleman Johnny made his entry into Montreal, where he took command of the right (or British) wing of his army.

On his arrival, there was a formal reception, a pretty affair of fine uniforms and of musicians playing behind a screen of evergreen boughs, and on the fourth day, which was 21 May, a Grand Review of the British line. The massed bands played before the reviewing stand as Major General Phillips made the formal presentation of the two brigade commanders. With each of them in turn Burgoyne walked the length of their lines, inspecting, exchanging a word with a subaltern, ramrod-stiff in front of his platoon, or questioning a sergeant about the food or billets.

The appearance of these men had changed in the year since Burgoyne had brought them to Canada. The conventional smartness of their uniforms was gone. No new clothes had come out to them from England, so their old long coats had been cut short and the tails used as patches. The wide-brimmed tricorne hats had been cut down into jaunty small

caps, to which each regiment had added a distinctive plume of feathers or horsehair. Though these were the battalion companies, they now looked like light infantrymen, representing the British army's compromise to meet the challenge of American rangers and riflemen. It was this new appearance of the men that would cause Burgoyne to publish a general order reminding them of the British soldier's traditional reliance on the bayonet, and stressing their superiority in open space and hardy combat.

Not all of the new commander in chief's first days in Canada were occupied with froth and show. On the way up from Quebec he had seen the German troops of his left wing, and now his orders routed the regiments out of their billets around Lake St. Pierre. From his headquarters in the prelate's fine house at Trois Rivières, Major General Riedesel pulled his battalions together again after the long winter. He worked with an eye to the east, hoping against hope that from that direction his little baroness would arrive before he had to set out once again on field service. Otherwise, he had made arrangements for her to pass the summer, with their children, in the hospitable household of the prelate.

The day before the Grand Review, Brigadier General Simon Fraser's advance corps, which was to lead the army all the way, assembled in cantonment at Longeuil, across and downriver from Montreal. Across the river, too, well away from the gay city, the Indians in their village of Caunawaga, and their savage brothers from up the Ottawa in their temporary camps, made preparations for the campaign in their own ominous way. They were to go ahead even of the advance corps, exploring the woods, eyes for Burgoyne, blinding the eyes of the enemy, and casting their dark shadow before the bright battalions of the British regulars.

The forest road from Longeuil to St. Jean, at the foot of navigation on Lake Champlain, was still deep in mud at the end of May, and Fraser had to lead most of his advance corps around and up the Riche-lieu in order to reach his final muster point. As he passed through St. Jean, he saw that all was in readi-ness there. Captain Skeffington Lutwidge, Royal Navy, had launched his new ship, the *Royal George,* and was slinging aboard its battery of twenty-four iron 12-pound cannon. In the roadstead, tugging at her anchor cables, rode the veteran *Inflexible,* twenty guns, bows on into the swift spring current. In line behind her, with white canvas furled, was the stately fleet of Britain's inland navy: the *Lady Maria* and the *Carleton,* named in compliment to the governor gen-eral and his young wife; the *Loyal Convert;* and the three prizes taken the previous October, the *Wash-ington,* the *Lee,* and the gondola *New Jersey.* Anchored off the fort was the square, blunt radeau *Thunderer,* a vessel of the royal artillery, her mast restepped this year to make her into a bomb ketch for the expected siege of Fort Ticonderoga, almost a hun-dred miles up the lake.

Before it sailed, the battle fleet would lose three of its number to the transport service — the *Wash-*

ington, Lee, and *Loyal Convert.* Even the mighty *Inflexible* and the *Royal George* would become tows for the ungainly pontoon-bridge-boom that Lieutenant John Schank, engineer and sailor, had designed to bridge the narrows between Crown Point and the east shore of the lake. As May gave place to June, it became known that the Yankees had not rebuilt their fleet, so there would be no naval battle in 1777. Then, too, as the staff officers checked and rechecked their lists, and once more figured their estimates, the necessity for additional transports became apparent. More and more food would be needed, for the hungry mouths of men and horses, and for the guns of both siege and field trains of artillery. Supplies of all kinds, and in vast quantities, must be built up in the first great depot, to be established at Crown Point, for the siege and the dash across the land divide and down the Hudson River.

With the decision in favor of transport, Lieutenant Schank left unassembled the timbers of the new style gunboats, brought in pieces from England. He had enough work in hand, caulking and repairing the gunboats of '76 and the five hundred bateaux which would carry the soldiers and their equipment up the lake, then return for the barrels, kegs, boxes, and bales. These last were accumulating slowly, due to the persistent mud on the roads from Montreal and from Chambly, up around the rapids of the Richelieu.

In Montreal, Lieutenant James Hadden of the Royal Artillery waited long enough to see the illumination of the city in honor of the king's birthday.

After dark, bonfires were lighted by every house-
holder in his front yard, and the streets were filled
with youthful revelry, the enthusiastic celebrants
smashing the windows of anyone whose fire did not
seem sufficiently large or patriotic to match the glory
of King George and the omnipotence of his army,
so soon to set out to victory. The convoy which
Hadden was to take did not leave Longeuil for St.
Jean until 6 June, the second day after the illmuina-
tions. It was a hard journey. Mud dragged at the
wheels of the newly made carts, and the plunging
horses, straining into their collars to free a mired
wagon, broke the axles fashioned of too green wood,
the iron shoes working loose from the wheels. Not
until nightfall did the carts, worn and battered after
their first day's journey, reach St. Jean. Extensive re-
pairs were needed before they could be sent up the
lake to ply the portage from Ticonderoga to Lake
George, and further on, from Lake George to the
navigable Hudson at Fort Edward.

When possible, dinner began in the early after-
noon and continued course after course until late in
the day. At St. Jean, on 12 June, General William
Phillips was the host. His troops were ready to em-
bark; those of General Fraser were up ahead, and the
Germans were staged all the way down the Richelieu
River to its mouth at Sorel, on the St. Lawrence
River. All the generals were Phillips's guests: Bur-
goyne and Riedesel and the brigadiers. Sir Guy
Carleton, too, had come up for the farewell dinner

and for his official part in the formal leavetaking on the morrow.

Confidence in the success of the expedition was borne in with the *potage au Canadien;* congratulations flowed out of the wine bottles, from the madeira through the Rhenish wines of Germany to the champagne that accompanied the sweet. With the port, came a messenger from Quebec with the news of the arrival of a convoy from England, bearing supplies, reinforcements for regiments, three companies of Hesse-Hanau Jägers — and three small girls with their mother, the Baroness Friederika von Riedesel. Brandy, obviously, was the drink with which to toast the major general from Brunswick and his good fortune. Riedesel was excused, for though theirs was an army on the move, Burgoyne, a widower for the past year, knew and could well understand the feelings of his subordinate. Furthermore, the lady herself had ignored the arrangements made for her at Trois Rivières and was on her way to the Richelieu. It was best for the morale of all concerned that Riedesel should have a few days' reunion with his family, while his regiments moved up under their own competent officers. The indomitable little baroness might then settle down to wait in Canada with the other ladies of the army. Burgoyne knew the limits of his leadership, and halted at the perimeter of a hoopskirt!

On 13 June, in front of all the troops, with full regimental bands playing, and in the presence of the habitants of St. Jean and the surrounding country-

side, Sir Guy Carleton took the salute in the name of
His Majesty King George the Third. Out in the river,
flying from the high mainmast of the radeau *Thunderer,* was the royal standard, emblazoned with the
heraldry of England, Scotland, Hanover, and ancient
France. In the gentle wind, it billowed lazily and
confidently, for all to see and know where true
loyalty lay. The bateaux of the first brigade were
moving out from shore and forming up in fours, their
oarblades flashing in the sunlight as they hurried
after the vessels of the fleet, already lost to view
beyond the first bend of the river.

Burgoyne and Phillips stepped into their respective
pinnaces, doffed their hats to the royal standard of
their sovereign and to his representatives on shore.
Canada left behind; the expedition was under way.
In full command, John Burgoyne was charging down
the summer fields of glory with seven thousand
veterans at his back.

In actual fact, Burgoyne himself did not leave St.
Jean until 17 June. He watched his regiments as they
went by. He made a point of seeing every soldier of
the main body, and made sure that every soldier
in the army saw him, standing in the stern of his
pinnace as the bateaux rowed past, on the foreshore
as the regiments landed to make camp for the night,
or wandering casually through the company lines
while the cook-fires yet burned. On these occasions,
his orders expressly forbade the formalities due his
rank. Burgoyne stood with Riedesel as the German

division marched up from Chambly, every rank dressed, the interval an exact eighteen inches, every man chanting the somber songs of the Rhineland, which sound so lugubrious to English ears.

With the plan rolling smoothly on the well-greased axle of discipline, General Burgoyne could turn to his field desk, which had been taken aboard the *Lady Maria* for the journey up to the advance elements of his army.

High Command called on Lieutenant General Burgoyne to prepare the way ahead and to strike with strategy, like a billhook clearing brush from an untended cart road. With his army moving forward in a pageant of might, Gentleman Johnny, the playwright, penned a *Proclamation to the American People*. Trumpets blared from the wings, "numerous" armies and fleets moved across the stage; the "good" Americans were cosseted; the "Assemblies and Committees" were scorned, abhorred, and cast out. Finally, in a crescendo of rhetoric, this Thor of the northern armies let loose his threat to "give stretch" to his savage Indian horde.

The proclamation embodying this threat was only the prologue of the drama. On 20 June, General Burgoyne made his carefully staged entrance upon the scene.

The *Lady Maria* anchored in the mouth of the Bouquet River. The commander in chief went ashore, where an escort of officers — Englishmen, Germans, Loyal Americans, and Canadians — awaited his landing. Burgoyne and his aides wore their full-dress

regimental uniforms. The officers on shore had had
their servants working through the night, brushing
and polishing away the stain of the forest from their
service dress. In all the ruck of uniforms, one man
stood out by dint of his appearance: he was the
Chevalier St. Luc de la Corne, the leader of Burgoyne's "Indian horde."

St. Luc was now an old man, a relic of New
France and of all the Indian Wars of those earlier
days. In 1777 he was a Canadian, and though he
wore his Order of St. Louis, as he stood among the
British against whom he had won the Order with
tomahawk and scalping knife, he was a loyal, art-
ful, and ambitious subject of King George. He
controlled the Ottawa Indians; his name and reputation were known, and his influence felt, in many
more distant lodges.

With all the dignity of an Indian warrior, the
grace of a courtier, and the ease of a gentleman,
St. Luc greeted his general and guided him up a
short trail to the council place. In a clearing, the
old Indian leader had gathered his warriors, who —
like their brothers, the white warriors — were be-
decked for this ceremonious occasion.

Burgoyne rose to speak. His opening words of
greeting, put together to resound in praise of the
Indians' loyalty to their king, lost nothing in transla-
tion. The chief and the warriors approved. Warming
to his audience, Burgoyne made his first point: as the
rebels had abused the clemency offered them, the
Indians were now granted "stretch" against the "par-

ricides of State." Continuing, Burgoyne modified this
license to a certain extent by pointing out that there
were many loyal and good Americans who were
allies, and therefore inviolate, as were the English
and German officers ranged behind him at the solemn
council. Unfortunately, the British general concluded
his oration in weakness. He forbade the Indians to
kill aged men, women, and children, and prisoners.
He offered a bribe for prisoners, but would demand
an accounting before paying the bounty on scalps,
which were to come only from the dead, killed in
battle. In conclusion, Burgoyne adjured the Indians
to give implicit obedience to his orders.

Moved by the forensic power and the fine, impos-
ing presence of the king's resplendent chief, an old
Indian rose to speak the promise of all the braves.
In the background lurked the interpreters, lieuten-
ants of St. Luc, smirking as they contemplated the
profits in scalp money and loot to be had in the land
of the Yankees and the hated "Bostonais."

Liquor was brought ashore from the *Lady Maria*
for the war dance, which the European officers
watched with an uneasy loathing.

In the morning the warriors had gone.

On up the lake came the armada of vessels. Each
day a brigade moved forward, landing for the night
at the campsite of the brigade that had gone ahead.
Then a storm held up the advance for three days.
After the hard rain, the black flies came to torment
the men, unable to build their smudge fires of the
wet wood. The Germans, who were accustomed to

oven-baked bread, wasted their ration of flour in futile attempts at making "fire cakes" like those of the British. Again on the lake, with a full, wide view of the armada, confidence and cheer returned. A watch boat raced north down the lake with word that General Fraser's advance corps had passed the narrows, had landed at Button Mold Bay, and were readying themselves for the assault landing at Crown Point the following day, 25 June.

The first company of light infantry went over the bows of their assault boats on schedule, deployed among the buildings and the outcroppings of rock along the shore, and looked about them. Quiet, always held suspect by alert, seasoned troops, was everywhere. It was deathly still at Crown Point. Major the Earl of Balcarres, on one knee, his New-foundland dog "Bateau" sitting, bolt upright, by his side, ordered a squad to rush the entrance to the fort. The light infantrymen raised their muskets to the alert as the squad ran forward over the bridge. All eyes were on the high ramparts. Nothing happened. Suddenly, the men were aware that one of their own was standing in the entry way, beckoning to them, and the major, his dog obediently at heel, was sauntering over the bridge.

Crown Point was deserted.

3

On the Left! At the Double! March!

Twelve miles up the lake from Crown Point, Fort Ticonderoga barred the way of the British advance. General Burgoyne's intention was to leave Lake Champlain at Ticonderoga and go to the Hudson River by way of Lake George and the long portage, the traditional route of British armies since 1755. While still in London, he had decided against the alternative way, which was via Skenesborough and the uncertain overland road from there to the Hudson by way of Wood Creek and Fort Anne. Either way, Fort Ticonderoga must be taken. It dominated the fork of the two roads to the south.

Ticonderoga was important to Burgoyne for yet another reason. Ever since the French had built the great stone fort in 1755–56, it had been the back gate to the Atlantic colonies. Its fall to Jeffrey Amherst in 1759 finally had removed the threat of an alien dagger, constantly pricking the throat of the British colonists. Americans had fought there side by side with British regulars, and Ticonderoga's formidable strength was legendary. When the fort fell to a little

29

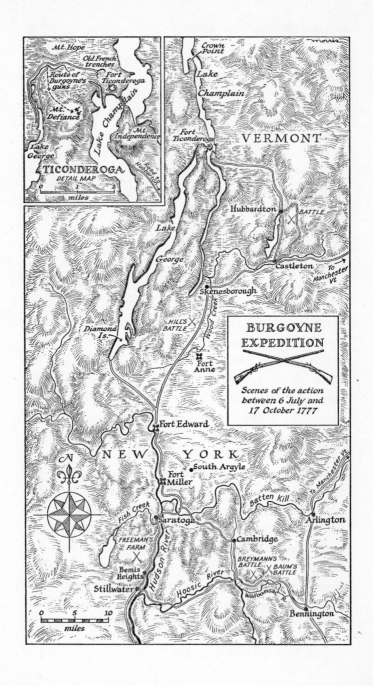

Mt. Hope

Old French trenches

Route of Burgoyne's guns

Fort Ticonderoga

Mt. Defiance

Lake Champlain

Mt. Independence

Road to Hubbardton

Lake George

TICONDEROGA

DETAIL MAP

0   1   2

miles

morris

Crown Point

Lake Champlain

VERMONT

Fort Ticonderoga

Hubbardton

BATTLE

Castleton

To Manchester Vt

Lake

George

Skenesborough

HILL'S BATTLE

Wood Creek

Diamond Is.

Fort Anne

BURGOYNE EXPEDITION

Scenes of the action between 6 July and 17 October 1777

Fort Edward

N E W   Y O R K

N

South Argyle

Fort Miller

Batten Kill

To Manchester Vt

Fish Creek

Saratoga

Arlington

FREEMAN'S FARM

Hudson River

Cambridge

BREYMANN'S BATTLE

BAUM'S BATTLE

Bemis Heights

Stillwater

Hoosic River

Walloomsac R.

Bennington

0   5   10

miles

band of Green Mountain Boys under their leader, Ethan Allen, the Americans roared with laughter at the discomfiture of the British, and took heart in the success of their revolution. Burgoyne's recapture of the place would turn the old joke back on the Yankees.

During the two years of its occupation, the American army had greatly enlarged and extended the Fort Ticonderoga defense system. The old French fort on the Ticonderoga Peninsula jutting out from the west shore of Lake Champlain, had been provided with shore batteries to bolster its defenses. A barbette now covered the portage to Lake George, and gun positions backed up the old French trench system that covered the western approach. Across the lake, American engineers had built a new fort of actual and strategic strength, which they called Mount Independence. On the lake between the two posts a bridge had been built and other obstacles placed to fix the British fleet in a killing ground of converging cannon fire. To hold this large fortress against Burgoyne, Major General Arthur St. Clair was sent by General Philip Schuyler, commander of the northern department of General Washington's army. He was a second choice. Horatio Gates, who had held Ticonderoga in 1776, had refused the command from Schuyler in a move for higher stakes in the political game of New England against New York. In the Continental Congress, Schuyler's New York star was falling, and he had been given but twenty-five hundred soldiers to hold Ticonderoga, whereas five times that number would have been none too many. Arthur St. Clair, a blue-eyed Scot, first saw his new command only the day before the royal standard was run up the mainmast of the *Thunderer*. Those officers of Burgoyne's army who had been with Wolfe on the Plains of Abraham in 1759 remembered the Yankee general against whom they were now going, as Lieutenant St. Clair of the British line. In his position of high rank and command, Arthur St. Clair thought clearly and without guile, and was courageous in his decisions. At Ticonderoga he faced his former comrades in arms without visible emotion, neither minimizing his desperate situation in the path of the British colossus nor panicking into rashness or fright.

General Burgoyne had envisaged the Ticonderoga position as representing the main American resistance to his plans. In anticipation he had assembled a siege train which, together with the guns of his battalions, numbered one hundred and twenty-eight pieces. This did not include the fleet's permament armament, much of which could be brought to bear. In spite of Ticonderoga's small garrison, Burgoyne gave St. Clair the compliment of a full-scale siege. He wanted to ensure the capture of the fort with its garrison of ten regiments, the hard core of the whole northern army of American Continentals. The American militiamen, as soldiers, were inconsiderable.

On the first day of July the British army began its advance up both sides of Lake Champlain. The guide was on the center, Riedesel and his two German brigades going up the east shore with Mount Independence as their objective; Phillips, with the English, took the west shore. In between were the ships of the Royal Navy, escorting the guns to their siege positions.

On the 2 July, Fraser's advance corps began the movement that would extend Burgoyne's right flank as far as the sawmill and the American escape route to Lake George. At nine o'clock that morning a column of smoke was seen rising from the barbette battery on Mount Hope. Further on, Fraser and Phillips could see more smoke, which they judged to come from the sawmill, the adjacent bridge, and other works.

Out ahead, the Indians were getting the scent of battle, wildly scouting the smoke and running back with exaggerated and conflicting reports as to the strength of the American force. They had also discovered some liquor. At one o'clock in the afternoon General Fraser finally ordered out his nephew, Alexander Fraser, with his company of selected rangers to determine the true state of affairs. An Irish corporal, crawling up to the American outworks in the old French-built trenches, known as the French lines, made the first contact with the rebel army. He was taking aim at a Yankee he had sighted through a sally port when he in turn was fired upon. Both soldiers missed, but their shots triggered a whole fusillade of firing from the French lines, in which the guns on the fort joined. In the confusion, the Irish corporal fell and feigned dead, Captain Fraser withdrew his

men, and the Indians fled. An American sortie took
the corporal prisoner. Fraser continued his scout and
found that no Americans remained outside the line of
trenches. Phillips ordered up his brigades, and the
Ticonderoga Peninsula was sealed off. On the extreme left, Riedesel had come up to the marshy creek
behind Mount Independence.

The plan was going well, and Burgoyne had no
need to improvise with orders. With his aide, he rode
around the positions, talking with men cheerfully at
work with pick and shovel, or with drag ropes at the
guns. His particular interest lay on his extreme right
where, beyond the creek, the steep rise of Sugar Loaf
Mountain swept upward to the almost perpendicular
drop at its eastern summit, overlooking the lake and
the two rebel forts. His artillery officer, Major Griffith
Williams, and Lieutenant William Twiss, his engineer, were sent out to determine whether a cannon
mounted on Sugar Loaf could carry into the forts;
further, could Twiss build a road by which guns
could be taken to the mountain top?

In the evening the two officers returned to headquarters, tired and hot, but elated at the prospect
from the summit. The view could only have been
improved if seen over the top of a 12-pounder; and
a road — with a stiff climb at the end — was entirely possible.

During the night, the guns were moved around
the perimeter of the mountain. British sentries in the
line cursed their passing because the noise they made
might arouse the curiosity of the Yankees, quiet in

their own positions. All during the day of the 5 July, the gunners and the engineer's detail toiled in the hot, insect-infested woods behind Mount Defiance. Gun teams snorted down the necks of brush-cutters and pawed at the slippery bark of the logs. Men took over from the teams for the last climb to the rocky summit, and made it by their sweat. By late afternoon the first gun was being assembled. Below in Fort Ticonderoga, Major Wilkinson saw the glint of sun on the brass tube of a telescope. General St. Clair was looking up at the new commander of his fort.

In the dark early hours of the 6 July, a house took fire over on Mount Independence. On being informed of this, the brigade major of the day for the Germans awakened Riedesel. For long minutes the veteran general stood in front of his tent, watching the flames of the house burning in the "Yankee" lines. Then abruptly, he ordered a boat and escort to be prepared and went in to his tent to dress. A long day had begun for the baron.

It was just getting light when Brigadier General Fraser was called to hear the report of three rebel deserters who had come into the picquet which was watching the French lines. The deserters said that the Americans had gone, some by boat to the south, the main body eastward into the hills on the road to Hubbardton and the Green Mountains. Fraser's first order was to beat the alarm, that his corps might turn out ready for immediate duty.

There were no enemy soldiers behind the French

lines. The gray stone fort was deserted. The boats
had gone from the foreshore, and the storehouses,
forges, and bakeries stood empty, their doors agape,
their interiors in shambles. Running in through the
hospital door, a British lieutenant saw but one figure
in all the gloomy ward; the man, covered with a
blanket, was dead. Outside again, the lieutenant
could look down onto the narrow passage of the lake
with its two bridges leading to Mount Independence.
Out on the pier bridge, a platoon of grenadiers was
forming into single file to cross the charred plank
spanning a gap in the bridge inexpertly made by the
retreating Americans. The lieutenant called his men
together and led them down the bank to the bridgehead, where General Fraser was marshaling his
troops.

Across the bridge, the grenadier platoon walked
boldly into the American battery covering the approach. In a shelter lay an American gun crew,
dead — or were they drunk? The grenadiers gathered
around in admiration and wonder, as the sergeant
kicked the men out of their stupor. Suddenly a gun
roared, an Indian stumbled back into the group, and
the lieutenant cursed loudly. The cannon which the
drunken Yankees had been left to man had been dis-
charged by the prowling redskin. It had been poorly
laid, in an attempt at covering the bridge, and
through the embrasure the grenadiers could see their
mates of the advance corps approaching.

Mount Independence, too, had been abandoned
by the rebels, but Riedesel was there with a group

of his green-coated riflemen. He had crossed the creek in time to see the last of the "Yankees" marching off down the track to Hubbardton. While he and General Fraser discussed the situation, and aides were sent flying to Burgoyne with the news, the soldiers of the advance corps scratched through the debris of hasty departure and argued over choice bits like so many fat red hens. The general's house — always a prime focal point for loot — had been burned. It was that which had made the blaze that General Riedesel had been awakened to see. His estimate had been a correct one: the Americans had escaped.

Permission to pursue the retreating rebel army did not reach Fraser, on Mount Independence, until the sun was well up on a day that promised to be hot. At the morning alarm he had been able to muster only half of his advance corps. There was now no way to gather up his whole force for the chase. In the confusion that took hold of the invasion army on discovering the enemy gone, Commodore Lutwidge had cut the bridges in order to let his big ships go through. No less eager to pursue than the commodore, Fraser started off with his light infantry, followed by elements of the 24th Foot and of the grenadiers. Riedesel watched them go; then he hurried away to muster a sufficient number of his Germans to follow in reserve.

Soon Fraser's column was across the flat open ground back of Mount Independence. The light infantry was moving fast, and the big grenadiers at the rear of the column were moving at a jog trot to

close up. If the men expected coolness in the shade
of the forest, they were doomed to disappointment.
The woods were still, and as hot as fur, and the
track, along which they traveled almost at a run,
was deeply rutted; insects tormented faces streaked
with rivulets of sweat. The soldiers had not eaten
since the previous day and were hungry — until
thirst claimed their whole attention. At the first hill
the pace slackened, and at one o'clock Fraser called
a halt for rest. Quiet returned to the forest as the
men slept, oblivious to the torment of insects, heedless of the stain made by forest mould on white
trousers and pipe-clayed belts.

Later in the afternoon, Riedesel caught up with
the British column. With him were the *Jägers,* a
handful of von Barner's blue-coated riflemen, and
some grenadiers — not more than eighty in all. The
Germans were as tired as the Englishmen had been.
They slumped to the ground, giving a tail of varie-
gated hue to the red and white body of the British
column snaking along the brown slash of the track.

After the two generals had conferred, Fraser
roused his own men and marched them three miles
further toward Hubbardton. The effects of the heat,
hunger, and fatigue were still evident, and the men
were in no condition to fight, not even against the
American rebels who, in all probability, were as exhausted as themselves. On a defensible ridge, Fraser
fell out his corps. As the men settled in, the officers
circulated among them warning of a 3:00 a.m. rev-
eille.

For two hours, Major Robert Grant of the 24th
Foot led the picquet of light infantrymen down the
forest path into the growing light of dawn. From a
saddle between two small hills, the road dipped into
a valley through which Grant judged that there
probably ran a good brook. They were getting into
the mountains now, and soon could expect to cut
into the north-south road from Crown Point to Hubbardton and Castleton. The road was not new to
Major Grant; he had traveled it some twenty years
earlier as a provincial officer, before he had secured
the King's Commission. Now he swung off down the
trail, the light infantrymen, as alert as rangers, close
behind him. At the bottom of the hill, the woods
ended in a clearing. Grant marched out from under
the trees. There was the brook he had expected to
find, its bank lined with American soldiers! The
Yankees were splashing water in their faces and over
their bare chests and shoulders, while in the roughly
cleared field beyond, the rest of the regiment was
preparing breakfast. Behind the major, the light infantry was pouring out of the woods and deploying
without orders. To direct their disposition, Grant
mounted a nearby stump and turning around, gave
the order to fire. At that instant, a rifle ball killed him
dead.

The Americans had been taken completely by surprise. It was Colonel Nathan Hale's New Hampshire
Continentals, who, with the invalids and the strag-
glers, comprised the rear guard. Colonel Hale attempted to organize some kind of resistance. But

more and more British debouched from the road, and
he was forced to fall back with his outnumbered
forces. The British line came steadily on, the light
infantry on the left, the 24th on the right. Hale saw
his second in command fall and his men flee into the
woods. He himself was enveloped in the advancing
line of redcoats, and was made prisoner.

Pausing only to fix bayonets, the British line advanced across the brook. Again in the forest, they
felt the sting of American musket fire, not in volley,
but individual shots from behind trees, rocks, and
bushes. Under control of their officers, the British
advanced cautiously in the line of skirmish forced on
them by the trees, catching the occasional Yankee
in his firing position and stolidly accepting their own
casualties.

General Fraser, his small headquarters group running after him, had taken over direct command. His
reconnaissance had fixed the position of the main
body of the American rear guard as up a hill in
roughly prepared works, covering the track from
Mount Independence at its juncture with the north-
south road leading to Castleton. On the southern
flank of the American position there was a steep hill
which controlled the entire battle. If the British held
this hill, the Americans' escape route to the south was
cut, and reinforcements could not get through from
St. Clair's main army, presumed to be at Castleton.
On the other hand, if the Americans held the hill, a
British assault would be caught in enfilade fire. Fraser
wanted that hill.

The task of taking it was given to Major John Acland and his grenadiers. It was hands and knees, push, pull, and scramble up the steep slope. At the top, the grenadiers barely had time to unsling their muskets to meet and drive back the Yankees, who had been sent out to seize the same objective. Red-faced and bare-headed as he wiped out the sweat-band of his grenadier's bearskin with his handker-chief, Acland sent two of his companies to his left to cover the right flank of the 24th. He could mark them by their musket fire, as they advanced in the woods on the other side of the clearing.

They appeared to be meeting with some success, and Acland was not surprised to see sixty Yankees come out into the clearing, their guns clubbed in the generally accepted token of surrender. "Stand with your arms!" was the order to the two companies of grenadiers, as they relaxed to accept the rebel prisoners. Thirty feet away the Americans stopped; each side looked the other in the eye. There was a quick motion in the Yankee line, as clubbed muskets were swung 'round and fired from the hip in a hard volley at point-blank range. The impact on the British was audible in screams, curses, and gasps, as the line staggered back. Then with a savage roar the grenadiers surged forward to carry the long bayonets to the "sniveling, sneaking, dirty, low-born rebels!" It was the charge of the wounded bear, and it carried the big grenadiers in among the dogs that had hurt them. Back on the starting line, redcoats were down, wounded and dead. When their mates returned, they could assure the casualtes that they had been avenged.

There was fire fighting all along the line, from Acland's grenadiers on the right to the Earl of Balcarres, commanding the light infantry half a mile away on the left. In the center, General Fraser could sense no gainful advance against the strong fire from the American position. All his troops were engaged. None were left with which to reach around on the American flank. Nearby was General Riedesel, stalking up and down and cursing at his troops, who had not run as fast as he to get to the sound of the firing. At the sound of a hunting horn down the track, Riedesel raced off to intercept his *Jägers* at the brook. Those English officers who had hunted in Europe recognized the clear sound of the silver-coiled horn, and identified the call as the "greeting fanfare." The music seemed to drift off to the left behind Balcarres, as the hunting call changed to the faster, more staccato "veline." Then rifle fire drew volley fire out beyond the American right, at which the whole British line moved forward as Riedesel and eighty of his Germans, *Jägers* and grenadiers, turned the American flank.

With his two colonels now casualties, his escape road to Castleton cut off, on his right riflemen that a Green Mountain boy could respect, and battle-wise regulars coming on in front, Colonel Seth Warner of the Vermont Continentals did what any experienced ranger would have done. He cut and ran straight up the mountain at his back. His men followed, a few of them dropping off to climb a tree or to stretch out along a rock in the hope of one last aimed shot. The Battle of Hubbardton was over; there was no pursuit.

All up and down the road stood tired British and German troops, counting off the scouts and picquets and guards. The remainder were sent back along their route from the brook to search out the wounded and dead. There were many of these. Fifteen officers had been hit by the considered fire of the Yankees. Balcarres had been wounded, though not seriously. As Acland came off his hilltop to report to Fraser, he limped heavily from a wound in his thigh. There were many American dead, too. On Acland's hill, a drummer boy found the body of Colonel Ebenezer Francis, who had commanded the 11th Massachusetts Continentals. Even in the untidy disarray of death in battle, his fine, well-proportioned figure was remarked upon by the grenadier officers who had gathered around. Captain Shrimpton was reading through the dead man's papers when a rifle cracked and the captain dropped, wounded, over the corpse. No one saw the hidden rifleman, and no one found him; only the sharp report of his rifle had been heard.

Soon it began to rain.

4

A Regiment of Foot

While the Hubbardton force was binding up its wounds on the slopes of the eastern mountains, another of General Burgoyne's regiments was moving through the rainstorms to the ground where it, too, would meet the American soldiers in battle. At nightfall on 7 July, two hundred soldiers of the 9th Regiment of Foot made a fortified bivouac at the mouth of the defile, where Wood Creek enters the Champlain Valley. To the south, and in front of the regiment, lay a bay like the arm of an undulating forest sea, its shores the dark mountains, its depths the bed of the Hudson River. A mile beyond the bivouac Fort Anne, held by the Yankees, was a hostile island.

In its almost one hundred years of existence the regiment had earned its nickname of "The Fighting Ninth." Raised in Gloucestershire in 1685 to put down the Monmouth Rebellion, it had moved to Ireland to help in quelling the long-continuing troubles of that pugnacious isle. While it had made up a part of the English garrison there, many Irishmen had joined the ranks of the 9th, contributing to the

fighting reputation of the regiment, both at home
and on expeditions overseas. In 1769 the regiment
had returned to Ireland after seven years' service in
tropical North America. Its ranks were depleted,
both officers and men sickly after long years in the
fever-climate of British Florida, following on the
rigors and casualties of the siege of Havana, on the
island of Cuba. By 1776, when once again the 9th
was called upon this time to go to the relief of
Quebec and to suppress yet another rebellion, it was
fighting fit. Its ranks had been filled by new recruits
from Ireland, from England, and a few men from
George III's German kingdom of Hanover. Under
the harsh tutelage of the veteran sergeants, the new-
comers had soon learned the drill and discipline
which imbued them with the spirit of the old 9th of
Foot. Lieutenant Colonel John Hill took the regiment to Canada. As was the custom in the British
army, the titular colonel, Lieutenant General Edward, Viscount Ligonier, was far too exalted a per-
sonage to concern himself with the command of a
single regiment. In John Hill, the 9th had a meticulous professional soldier with thirty years of commissioned service behind him, with little hope of
promotion, but enjoying the respect of his fellows
and the reliance of his superiors.

When, in 1777, the 9th became the senior regiment of Brigadier General Powell's Second Brigade,
it was near full strength of six hundred men. Colonel
Hill, however, had under command only some four
hundred muskets in the eight line companies. As was

the case with colonels commanding other regiments,
Hill's grenadier and light infantry companies had
been seconded into a grenadier battalion and a light
infantry battalion, both of which were under command of the advance corps. In addition, fifty of the
older soldiers were left behind as a regimental depot
and cadre in Canada.

Upon leaving St. Jean, the 9th had rowed and
sailed itself up Lake Champlain, landing at Crown
Point. The regiment had then marched up to Ticonderoga and gone into the line at the barbette battery
on Mount Hope, when, at dawn on 6 July, Burgoyne
discovered that St. Clair's army had escaped him.

Sensing the confusion of the morning, Colonel Hill
fell in the 9th and made it ready for any eventuality.
Thus it was found by a galloping staff officer, who
hurried it down to the boats. Already the great barrier bridge from Ticonderoga to Mount Independence had been breached, and the tall frigates, the
Royal George and the *Inflexible,* were tacking in the
wide lake south of the forts, waiting impatiently for
the gunboats and infantry bateaux, so it could begin
the pursuit of those Yankees who had gone by water
to Skenesborough. All during the morning and into
the afternoon, the 9th followed the big ships through
the narrow channel of the Lake Champlain marshes.
The July sun was still high as the pursuing British
came out onto South Bay, and the frigates, safely
through the confining corridor, shook out their white
sails and swanned out over the bay like hoop-skirted
ladies entering a ballroom.

A watchboat swung in close to Colonel Hill, with
orders from Burgoyne to land his troops up the bay
on the east shore. The boat then sheared off in search
of Colonel John Lind and Major Squire, of the 20th
and 21st regiments, respectively, who would be
making the landing with Hill's 9th. According to
Burgoyne's plan the three infantry regiments would
cross over the mountain on the east shore of South
Bay and block the road to Fort Anne while the gunboats would sail boldly into the Skenesborough basin,
sink the vessels to be found there, and drive the
rebels on shore and up the road, where the infantry
waited to receive them.

Viewed from the lake, the mountain that Colonel
Hill was set to cross was deceptive. Its trees, which
seemed to promise cool shade from the hot July sun,
in reality hid a dense undergrowth that held the day's
heat and sheltered a myriad of buzzing, biting insects.
The slope, which from a distance appeared so gentle,
was in fact either steep or precipitous, with rock outcroppings and ledges criss-crossed with wind-felled
trees. The landing itself was a wet one, bringing the
soldiers to the foot of the cruel mountain discom-
forted by wet feet and mud-caked legs.

In the vault of the forest, with the bulk of the
mountain intervening, John Hill did not hear the
wild cannonade of the Royal Artillery's gunboats as
they caught the Yankee fleet in the pool below the
falls at Skenesborough and took possession of the
Americans' baggage at the landing place. Above the
beating of his heart and the throbbing in his ears as

he struggled up the mountain, the middle-aged colonel *did* hear the two great explosions as the American
warships were blown up, one after the other. At these
sounds of distant action, Hill redoubled his efforts to
assault the difficult mountain. His own honor, as well
as that of the regiment, was at stake. With the Royal
Artillery already engaged, Colonel Hill, in effect, was
racing the 20th and the 21st to the expected battleground, in the age-old rivalry, keen as a bayonet, that
is the whetstone of morale.

But the pace up the mountain was slow, and long
before the three regiments had reached the western
summit, the recall gun sounded from the frigates, far
below in the bay. The rebels had gone. The honor of
the action went to the Royal Artillery.

When the 9th marched into Skenesborough at
dusk, they found a sizable frontier town. The falls of
Wood Creek turned a big sawmill. Sheds and ware-
houses lined the shore behind the shipyard, where,
in 1776, General Benedict Arnold had built the fleet
which for a year had held back the British. Three of
Arnold's vessels were now beached and abandoned
below the falls. A large, sprawling, stockaded fort
overlooked the works, and untidy barracks could be
seen by the men of the 9th as they trooped past the
wide-open gate. They passed by a tenant house re-
sembling a dwelling in a Scottish glen; then another,
built in the French Canadian manner. The latter had
a cannon-ball hole alongside the lintel. Across the
water, Major Philip Skene's big stone house could be
glimpsed on the north shore among its shade trees.

From the boatloads of baggage being unloaded at its wharf, and from the activity of staff officers and servants around the doorway, Colonel Hill judged that the manor house already had been made army headquarters.

The 9th marched through the town, taking the portage road around the falls to the launching place on Wood Creek. There the regiment halted, broke ranks, and made camp.

There were no boats on the foreshore of the stream. They had all gone south with the sick and wounded and the women of the rebel army. The healthy had gone by the road that followed the course of the creek. Colonel Hill and his adjutant strolled a few yards up the road in the cool of the late evening, but turned back where the road entered the woods.

From the 9th's fortified bivouac, a mile from Fort Anne, at the entrance to the Hudson Valley, it was ten miles back to Skenesborough and the comforting companionship of the 20th and 21st. It was also a full day's march. All during the hot, humid, shower-drenched day of 7 July, Colonel Hill's soldiers had been on the road, working like a *corvée* of French Canadian laborers. Their efforts had cleared a way through the worst of the delaying damage done to the road by the retreating Americans, so that now, as they settled down for the night, they felt secure in the knowledge that the way behind them was open for reinforcements in men and packhorse guns, should the rebels attack in the morning.

The first Yankee to appear on the morning of 8 July was a bedraggled deserter, who came sneaking in at sun-up, protesting his loyalty to King George. The man had restless eyes that looked everywhere and saw everything. Colonel Hill interviewed him and from the man's obsequious outpourings and loud volunteering to 'list for a King's soldier culled the information that at Fort Anne, Colonel Long's New Hampshire Continentals had been reinforced by Colonel Van Rensselaer's militia, bringing the garrison up to a thousand men.

With his own troops numbering a scant two hundred (the movement up the Fort Anne road was a reconnaissance in force by half of a regiment, not a general advance), Colonel Hill passed the order to his officers to hold where they stood. To advance his small force against a reinforced enemy fort would be foolhardy; to retreat back down the road would be to invite ambush and attack on an extended column in thick woods. In their present position, Hill estimated that the 9th could hold until General Burgoyne sent reinforcements to mount an attack or to extricate the regiment. All this was put into a situation report, and sent by messenger to Skenesborough.

When next the colonel had time to notice him, the Yankee deserter was nowhere to be found. Half an hour later the Americans attacked.

In front of Hill's field works, where the dense underbrush thinned out to give a distant view of Fort Anne on its eminence, the British picquets watched the Americans form up. Groups of carelessly dressed men emerged from behind the fort, drew together for a moment to cross over a foot-bridge, and then, with much shouting back and forth, spread out on both sides of the road leading to the British position. When once shaken out and away from his neighbor, the individual American appeared to grow calm with purpose, as the men formed quickly into rough lines. The military groups of platoons and companies seemed to have dissolved, and the British saw advancing toward them many single figures, each one picking his own way around, or over, or through, the brush and stumps of the partially cleared ground. The Yankees carried their muskets carelessly at the trail, or easily, high across the chest, or jauntily sloped over their shoulders. None of the muskets had bayonets. Like the spy of the early morning, the men had restless, curious eyes; every head in the advancing line seemed to be constantly turning, looking, peering, as though expecting to tread on a rattlesnake at every step. The Americans were silent now, as they met the fire from the British picquet line. The volley broke the American line, which retired, drifting back on itself as casually as it had advanced.

A second attack followed quickly on the first, but this time the officer in command of the picquet observed more obvious and familiar control, as Colonel Long's Continentals took over the initiative from Colonel Van Rensselaer's militia. Light blue uniforms predominated, bayonets caught the glint of the sun, and back at the bridge two regimental colors were being shaken out before joining the advancing lines.

Having forced a general deployment of the Yankee force, the British picquet retired into its own lines. These consisted of a hastily and ill-prepared screen of logs and brush on the west side of Wood Creek, extending a scant two hundred yards from the alders on the banks of the stream on the left to the foot of a rocky promontory on the right. Working with camp axes, knives, and their bare hands, the men of the 9th had succeeded in clearing only a few yards of brush from their front. It remained a knee-deep tangle of withering green branches across which the Yankees must charge into the face of a British volley. But the British front afforded no ground suitable for a counter attack with the bayonet. Colonel Hill was on the defensive.

Quietly, the 9th waited, its men, in rank behind the barricade, questioning in whispers the men of the picquet, who already had seen the Yankee soldiers. The officers, standing calmly and tolerantly behind their command, sprang to rigid attention as Colonel Hill came to give each of them a final report and a word of instruction. Then, as the colonel passed on, in a little procession with his adjutant and the boy drummer in a yellow coat, the military tableau melted back into the natural pose of English gentlemen oblivious to danger. Under the protecting face of a rocky ledge, the regimental surgeon waited with his assistant, Sergeant Robert Lamb, carrying his bag of instruments, dressings, and medicine. Jane Cromer, the wife of a soldier, busied herself nearby, clearing the ground of stones and sticks in order to make a place for the wounded.

The surgeon and his assistant were off at the first crack of enemy musket fire, and heard the British return volley while bending over their first casualty. They were still busy with the wounded when the Americans came on again. Then the two medical men became separated for a time, as Lamb strove to collect the severely wounded at Jane Cromer's improvised hospital, while the surgeon went off to follow the fortunes of Lieutenant Richard Westroop's company in a counter attack.

Temporarily, the whole company was lost to sight behind the green curtain of underbrush, and only cries and shouts and the sudden crack of musket fire marked its progress. At last the troops returned, elated and triumphant, shoving their prisoners before them and dragging behind them the battle flags of Long's Continentals. Lieutenant Westroop failed to return with his company; a corporal reported having seen him fall, and on turning over the body, had found the lieutenant shot through the heart. The company clamored to return for their officer, but a seventeen-year-old subaltern steadied the men down and got them back to their posts, to receive the next Yankee attack.

The captured flags were sent to Colonel Hill, who was found on the bank of Wood Creek, anxiously listening, and watching the woods on the other side of the stream. Above the undulation of sound that washed up and down his battle line in a roar of surf-like volleys, and the individual American rifle fire that crackled like a wave receding over the shingle at Brighton, Hill had detected the sound of men

calling to each other across the flat calm of Wood
Creek. He listened for confirmation of the fact that
the Yankees were turning his left flank and, by re-
crossing the stream, gaining the rear of his position.
The colonel saw the muzzle flash, felt the passage of
the ball, and heard the shocked exclamation of his
adjutant as the shot struck home. The Americans
were across Wood Creek, and the position of the
British was untenable.

Leaving his adjutant with a wounded shoulder,
Colonel Hill dashed off to organize a general withdrawal from the left, to a new position on the steep
hill to the rear and right of the 9th.

Captain William Montgomery's company, holding
the British left, were on a front which was temporarily quiet. Squad by squad, the regulars turned from
the barricade and jogged off toward the mountain.
Captain Montgomery himself lay flat on his back,
trying, by cramming a handkerchief into his mouth,
to hold back to a groan the scream in his throat.
Seated hard on the captain's abdomen was Sergeant
Lamb, pressing with strong thumbs on the big artery
in the groin, which already had pumped a stream of
red blood over Montgomery's white buckskin
breeches. The regimental surgeon was working
quickly in the wound to find and tie off the severed
end of the artery.

A hundred yards away, Colonel Van Rensselaer, of
the great colonial family of the Hudson River, was
also down in the brush, suffering from a shattered
bone in the leg. For the moment, however, he felt

little pain, and his heavy Dutch voice could be heard clearly through the woods, interpreting as retreat the silence in the British lines, and urging his New York militia to attack . . . attack . . . attack!

The surgeon had located the end of the artery, worked a loop of the ligature over it, and had drawn the knot tight. Captain Montgomery had fainted. Sergeant Lamb's work with the captain was done. He and the surgeon hurriedly consulted together, and as the first Yankee stepped cautiously out through the underbrush, Lamb rose to his feet and ran for the mountain. The surgeon was still at work on the operation in hand, when both he and his patient were taken prisoner.

British and Americans alike were now short of ammunition. Already the battle had continued for three long hours. To the north, toward Skenesborough, black clouds roiled above the mountains, and there was a distant rumble of thunder. Against this ominous continuo, the sharp sound of a rifle came like the snap of a broken fiddle-string in the heavy, still air that muted the hill and the opposed bands of soldiers.

Somewhere, distantly and vaguely, between the far-off rumble and the nearby quiet, the sound of yet another instrument was introduced. It was the long, continuing yell of an Indian war whoop, repeated and repeated, again and again. With it came a slowly rising elation among the British, pinned to their hilltop, while below them the Yankees, on hearing the eerie sound, picked up their powder horns and shot bags and slipped away. The Americans were all too familiar with the war whoop of the savages, which turned their thoughts to their women and children, alone in isolated cabins on scattered farms.

Colonel Hill was standing in the middle of the Skenesborough road when a single British officer, his uniform coat over his arm, came striding around a bend in the road. The newcomer stopped short. Then he threw back his head, gave a "Whoop! Whoop! Whoop!," and with a grin, bowed to the colonel. There were no other "Indians." On hearing the sound of gunfire, those who had started out with the British had refused to go any further, so the officer had come on alone, whooping as he came, to inform the 9th that General Phillips was coming up presently with two guns and two regiments; the rain had delayed them.

By nightfall the battleground was all but deserted. Phillips had arrived with his relief force to escort the battered and Yankee-wise 9th back to Skenesborough. The Americans had gone from Fort Anne — all five hundred of them. The deserter/spy had reported at exactly double the Yankee strength at the fort. General Philip Schuyler had ordered Colonel Long to hold at Fort Anne until the brass ordnance could be removed from the fort at the southern end of Lake George. Long's battle on 8 July had gained for Schuyler the time he needed.

Fort Anne itself had been burned. Sergeant Lamb could see the smoke still rising above the trees, as he and Jane Cromer tried to make their wounded charges comfortable before night. A deserted hut had been discovered on the western slope of the hill, and it was there that the twenty-three British wounded had been carried. Through all the following week, alone in the woods, Sergeant Lamb cared for his comrades with all the rude skill at his command, while Jane Cromer attended to their needs as best she could.

5

Major Skene's Great Stone House

Philip Skene left the *Royal George* in South Bay and went immediately to his manor house, so that, as laird of Skenesborough, he might be on the threshold to welcome the man who had restored his property to him — General John Burgoyne.

Skene had not been in residence in May 1775 when the Whig rabble had seized his house and property and taken prisoner his son and two daughters. Since that topsy-turvy day, Philip Skene himself had been jailed as a Tory, but had contrived his own release and the exchange of his son. In an act of chivalry curiously at odds with its usual behavior, the mob later had returned his daughters to him. Soon afterward, he had gone to London, where, using the same influence that in the 1760's had secured for him the large key grants of land at the Lake Champlain–Hudson River gateway, he had made his voice heard in the council shaping the scheme that was to send Burgoyne through those same grants. Major Skene had come out to Canada as political adviser to the expedition. His duty it was to advise the general

on local affairs, and to screen and organize the country people who, according to the major's firm Tory
conviction, would welcome the British soldiers as
liberators from the Whig oppression. His canny
Scotch hope was for a new colony between New
York and Canada, with himself as governor and his
own manor house at the head of Lake Champlain as
its capitol.

Two years of occupation by rebel soldiery had left
the house in no fit condition to receive an illustrious
guest, but the general's own furniture would make it
adequate, even luxurious, as headquarters for the
British officers. The last case of the general's wine
had been carried into the springhouse and the cook-
fires had been lighted in the summer kitchen when
Skene was advised of the approach of the general's
barge. The polished craft, its eight painted oarblades
dipping rhythmically into the water, headed for the
manor house dock, where Burgoyne's host waited to
welcome him. On the other side of the pool, Captain
John Carter, whose gunboats had recaptured Skenesborough, ordered a gun salute which brought soldiers
in their shirtsleeves running to the water's edge to
cheer for "Gentleman Johnny."

Between the rising of the sun and its setting on that
6th day of July 1777, General John Burgoyne had
entered in triumph Fort Ticonderoga and Skenesborough, two of those places which, on a map spread out
on a London dining-table, had seemed so very distant
and so very formidable. Burgoyne's generals, Fraser
and Riedesel, were in close pursuit of a fleeing rebel

army. On the morrow he would send a force down
the Hudson, to chivvy along the rebel rear guard,
which appeared to have abandoned at Skenesborough
all the baggage of the American army. Tonight he
would dine as the guest of his political adviser, and
would break out a few bottles of his best champagne,
already set in the spring water to cool. .

In forcing the fortress of Ticonderoga without a
siege, Burgoyne was in the position of a man who
puts his shoulder to a door he expects to find locked
and barred. Instead of entering the room, he bursts
into it, and through it. It was thus that the general
now found himself at Skenesborough, twenty miles
down a road that he had not intended to follow, with
his army asprawl over a hundred square miles of the
countryside.

While still in England, Burgoyne had seriously
considered marching to the Hudson and Fort Edward
by way of Skenesborough and Fort Anne. Finally,
however, he had decided to take the water route over
the lake, despite the prospect of another siege to
capture the fort at Lake George's southern end. The
Skenesborough-Fort Edward road was only a wagon
track at best, while the portage roads at both ends of
Lake George were well-built highways that had
sustained the travel of many armies for twenty years.

Comfortably ensconced in Major Skene's big house,
General Burgoyne was loath to return to the fort in
the road at Ticonderoga. In the drill with the bayonet
a successful lunge is never followed by a return to
the "on guard" position; instead, the point of the

bayonet continues to be presented, and the advantage is pressed by short jabs. So, off balance after his wild thrust through an empty fort at Ticonderoga, Burgoyne decided to alter his plans. After regrouping his battalions at the Skenesborough point, he would jab through to Fort Edward. At Ticonderoga, the stockpiling of matériel and transport, which had been scheduled to run concurrently with the siege, must be completed as quickly as possible in order to give weight and strength to the lunge down the Hudson River to Albany.

On 8 July, in the first move to concentrate the brigades at Skenesborough, General Riedesel brought his Germans from the eastern slopes, via the Castleton road. Marching warily along the same forest road on the following day, General Fraser reunited his Hubbardton force with the rest of his advance corps in a camp above the falls at Skene's sawmill. After extricating Colonel Hill from his victorious dilemma at Fort Anne, Phillips set the defenses at Skenesborough before giving his full attention to the reorganization of the artillery establishment.

Of the one hundred and twenty-eight cannon, only sixty-six could, or would, be maintained by the army after Lake Champlain and the fleet of naval vessels had been left behind. Thirty-eight guns would march in the field train; it was a heavy proportion, but Phillips was a "gunner." A siege train of twenty-eight pieces would go with the baggage — evidence of the respect in which, since Bunker Hill, Burgoyne held the Americans as builders of field fortifications.

Beyond Ticonderoga, where the attenuated siege

train and the heavy baggage of the army would take
the Lake George route, thereby establishing the main
supply line, an adequate supply of horses became the
key to the success of the whole expedition. Horses
were needed, with their drivers and their carts, to
haul the boats over the portage road to Lake George;
later, they would be needed for a like purpose, to
carry yet more boats from Lake George to the Hudson. A herd of horses had been driven from Canada
down the west shore of Lake Champlain, and had
reached Ticonderoga. But there were never enough
of the beasts, and army orders had been promulgated,
exhorting, threatening, and expropriating an additional supply. The Indians were offered inducements
to bring in any horses they might find in the woods,
and Mr. Hoakesly, the wagonmaster general, was
constantly on the alert to conserve the strength and
numbers of his overworked animals.

While his subordinates carried out the tactical
preparations which must be made before his army
could advance in either a jab or a lunge, Burgoyne
moved Riedesel and his whole division to Castleton,
twelve miles east of Skenesborough. This move was
intended to be interpreted by rebel spies as the beginning of a general invasion of New England by way
of the Connecticut River. With such a threat at their
backs, the New Englanders would hesitate to send
troops into New York to bolster the defenses of the
Hudson River line.

Six mean small huts comprised the village of

Castleton. The baron, well acquainted with the soldier psychology, did not consider it a good place for his Brunswickers and Hanauers. Far better for the German troops to be in the crowded lakeside town, even if it meant an occasional fight in the grog-shops with their British allies. The idleness the men would find at Castleton, deep in the terrible, unfamiliar wilderness, might well bring on the lassitude and homesickness that could shatter the brittle German discipline, based as it was on fear.

Through the passes of the Green Mountains, threatened and guarded by Riedesel, lay the town of Rockingham, surrounded by the fertile country of the Connecticut. There, so the general's intelligence sources informed him, many horses could be found, as well as stores and wagons for the taking. With this in view, Riedesel proposed to Burgoyne a foraging expedition for his idle Germans — one which would emphasize the strategic threat to New England, serve to harass the lurking forces of "Von Werner," as the baron called Warner, the Yankee colonel of Hubbardton, and, last but not least, produce mounts for the Brunswick dragoons. With horses, Prinz Ludwig's Regiment of Dragoons, Colonel Frederick Baum commanding, could be made to serve a useful purpose instead of being the butt of the army's jokes, as they waddled about in their great boots, dragging their sabers behind them. But even this appeal by a former Black Hussar to the colonel of the finest light dragoon regiment in the British army, brought no action.

Burgoyne was sympathetic but too preoccupied

with tactical problems for the move south to give any
consideration to Riedesel's plan for an eastern di-
version. Graciously, he sent some bottles of Rhine
wine to his division commander, with the suggestion
that the baroness be sent for, to share in the wine and
in the progress of the expedition to Albany.

The other ladies of the army were also invited to
join their husbands: Mrs. Major Harnage and Mrs.
Lieutenant Reynolds, and, of course, Burgoyne's re-
sponsive friend, the wife of an ambitious and acquies-
cent commissary. Even as the gentlemen waited,
Lady Harriet Acland, without benefit of order or invitation, was coming by fast canoe to nurse the fever
brought on by the deep wound in her husband's
thigh.

Major Acland's grenadiers had made a litter, on
which they had carried him all the difficult way from
Hubbardton to Skenesborough. He fared better than
those wounded with him on the hill at Hubbardton,
who had to wait in brush shelters for doctors to come
to them from Ticonderoga, and then for horse transport to carry them back to the hospital at the fort.

No one came for the wounded in the derelict hut
near Fort Anne. It was a week before Sergeant Lamb
and Jane Cromer felt that those of their patients who
had survived were well enough to undertake the
journey to Skenesborough. The men straggled
through the woods, limping, staggering, supporting
each other, suffering as much from cabin fever as
from the throbbing pain of their wounds.

No one had come near them since the battle except

for a single wounded Yankee, who had lost his way and stumbled in on the British quite by accident. He had gone away again, grateful for the care he had received and keeping the secret of the sick camp in the woods. But the Americans were never far away. All day long, and late into the summer evenings, Lamb and his wounded had heard them on the road, their presence betrayed by the sound of their tools — axes and saws and picks. At intervals, the soldiers of the 9th heard the warning shout that preceded the crashing down across the road of a great hemlock tree, or the prying loose of a boulder on the mountain, which rolled thunderingly down to Wood Creek. As one after another, the days of pain and anxiety following the long, hot nights, during which many of the wounded died, the sounds of demolition receded southward past the charred ruins of Fort Anne. When at last Sergeant Lamb broke camp, the distant chunking of the axes was a sensation rather than a sound, like an echo, confusing reality with memory.

General Philip Schuyler was fighting General Burgoyne with what he had. His plea for reinforcements had gone unanswered. Schuyler had left the men of the Mohawk Valley to meet Barry St. Leger's threat from the west, while he hurried north to give comfort, if he could not give aid, to St. Clair. Schuyler's troops were too few to alter St. Clair's decision to give up Fort Ticonderoga, and they were too late to join in the rout. Coming up to Fort Edward with Burgoyne only twenty-three miles away, Schuyler's northern army stood, seven hundred Continentals and twice

that number of militia. Long and Van Rensselaer had
held off the first British foray, while the valuable
guns were being removed from the fort on Lake
George.

Still hoping for, and expecting, reinforcements
from Congress, Schuyler now set his woods-wise
militia to the task of delaying the British. Up the
wagon track they marched in work gangs, their tools
on their shoulders. They approached as near to
Skenesborough as they dared. Then, as they fell
slowly back, they obliterated the road behind them
in a mass of flooded causeways and broken bridges.
Sergeant Lamb heard the Americans at their work;
General Burgoyne appeared to give them no heed.

In the cool of the stone manor, Burgoyne was hew-
ing at his own tall tree behind the American lines,
his tools the pen, the jingling purse, and the four men
who came furtively into the candle-lit room and were
gone before sunrise. Schuyler was under attack by
the New England faction of the Continental Congress and its army. In an attempt to bring down the
mighty Schuyler, Burgoyne was presumed to be in
contact with the New York general, whom he and
Skene hoped to bring back to loyalty in a thundering
crash that would shiver the lesser men of America.
As an Englishman, Burgoyne could not understand
the native loyalty of the Schuylers; nor could Skene,
the transplanted laird, credit it. Schuyler continued the correspondence (before witnesses) in order
to buy time, heedless of the whispering storm around
him. It was a pretty story that he and St. Clair had

sold Ticonderoga for silver bullets, fired into the fort by Burgoyne's marksmen! Many loyalties wavered, but never that of Philip Schuyler.

Almost four weeks had passed since General Burgoyne had issued his bombastic proclamation, calling the Americans back to loyalty to the Crown. A Yankee burlesque of that proclamation was brought to the British general at Skenesborough, and he could read it with genuine amusement — six hundred American men came with it. They were quickly absorbed into the man-hungry Tory regiments, led by such men as the Jessup brothers, John Peters, Daniel McAlpin, Francis Pfister, and Colonel Houston of Saratoga. Some, with experience as watermen and familiar with the rivers and their crafts, joined Hugh Monro's company of bateaumen. Most of the six hundred came without weapons; none had military training in the British army sense. Their usefulness to Burgoyne lay in their homely civilian skill as axemen, to clear the trees from the road to Fort Edward, and, as pioneers, to rebuild the bridges and drain the swamps.

With a patrol of rangers and engineers, Lieutenant Twiss made a survey of the demolitions, measuring the streams, counting the bridges and culverts to be rebuilt, and staking out long stretches where it would be necessary to build corduroy causeways. Writing on his knee, the engineer officer then made an estimate of the time, in man hours, required to repair the damage. His report on the twenty-three miles of road to Fort Edward was a formidable one, but not

discouraging. Burgoyne made his final decision. All
thought of retracing his way over the eighty miles
of road to Ticonderoga, to travel the waterway up
Lake George, could be abandoned.

The army began its march to the Hudson on 24
July. As usual, Fraser's advance corps led, if indeed it
could be called leading. More often than not, the
men stood at ease, slapping mosquitoes, while a gang
of loyalists finished a log bridge with a roadbed of
earth still wet from the marsh out of which it had
hastily been shoveled. The soldiers cursed the "colo-
nials" for the mud that slopped onto their spatter-
dashes, and grumbled (like all soldiers) when called
upon to aid "civilians" in levering a big butt log to
the side of the road. Behind the advance corps and
the laborers, as far away as Castleton, the rest of the
army filed along the road, suffering the long, incom-
prehensible delays, then shuffling on to the next
discouraging halt, a hundred yards, a quarter of a
mile, further on the road to Fort Edward.

Well mounted and debonair, Burgoyne and his
staff made the one bright spot in the long crawling
column. Young officers took hold of their men again
when they saw the colorful group beside the road,
and a spring returned to the step of the soldiers.

On the second night of the march, Burgoyne made
his headquarters at burned-out Fort Anne. The general's own wagons had come up; a Brunswick dragoon
with saber drawn walked "sentry go" at the open
flaps of the commanding officer's sleeping tent; dinner, served under a great oak tree on china, glass,

and silver from Burgoyne's own mess chest, had been good. The road from Skenesborough was open to the brigade guns, and the first of the Germans would be coming up in the morning.

Riedesel had sent a happy but hasty message to his baroness, telling her to come with the three little girls by boat across Lake George. He then gave his complete and absorbed attention to the anxious work of getting his close-ranked Germans forward, fed, and ready to fight.

The British column was unmolested, as Schuyler's Americans fell away before it. Captain Fraser's marksmen, and the Canadians and provincial rangers scouting forward to the bluffs above Fort Edward and the high ground overlooking the portage road to Lake George, glimpsed the rear guard patrols of the Continentals, following the flow of the Hudson away from the flood of Burgoyne's army, cutting a new channel southward through the forest.

The army was at mess on the evening of the 26th, when a band of Indians came into the camp, holding high on frames two raw scalps. One of these, they insisted, was that of a Yankee officer. The arrival of the savages interrupted Lieutenant William Digby, Grenadier Company, 53rd Foot, who was setting down in his journal the events of the day. David Jones, officer of Burgoyne's Loyalist troops, and a long year's journey from the home and the fiancée he had left behind in the village at Fort Edward, saw the scalps paraded to the general's tent. Jones sat up late that night, his back against a hickory tree, scrap-

ing down a new ramrod until it was far too slender
for use. In the woods nearby, the Indians danced out
their victory song.

These were the new Indians — Menominees, Win-
nebagoes Chippewas, Sacs and Foxes and wild Sioux
— fine tall men from the westernmost of the big lakes,
and from the great plains beyond. St. Luc had summoned them, and their friend Langlade had brought
them east to the White King's war. Charles de Langlade was a half-breed trader, who, in 1755, as a
French cadet, had stood in the mile-long gantlet line
through which General Braddock had led his two
British regiments during the march toward Pitts-
burgh. At the Skenesborough Indian Conference, at
which the western warriors were welcomed to Burgoyne's army and the rules of selective scalping were
explained to them, Langlade had stood beside St.
Luc. Afterward, he had affably translated from Sioux
to Chippawa to French, as the British officers bought
trinkets and toys from their new allies — things to
be shown, in days to come, to curious guests in English drawing-rooms, in quiet London squares.

It had been easy to think of Burgoyne's Indian
Conference as an entertaining masque on the lawn
of Major Skene's stone manor house, where gentle
savages were but costumed soldiers of the King. The
next day, after sleeping off the effects of the dancing
and the liquor that followed the conference, the Indians had gone away. Now, the two dripping scalps
nailed to the tree at Fort Anne served to remind the
British that their savage allies were not far away.

6

The Iroquois Wolf

At the end of the French and Indian War, the country to the north of Albany enjoyed fifteen years of peaceful penetration before the American Revolution turned it once again into a warpath of nations. Many settlers came to the region, spreading out boldly all through the valley of the Upper Hudson. Some found a livelihood along the main stream, others sought out tributary rivers to turn the millwheels for grinding the grist, brought to the mills by other settlers from their outlying farms.

Major Philip Skene, retired from the British army after the fall of French Canada, built his great stone manor house at a strategic pass through the mountains — a first step toward the realization of a shrewd Scot's dream of baronial splendor. Other pioneers were of less pretense. Even Philip Schuyler's farm at the confluence of Fish Creek and the Hudson River, with its mansion of sawed boards was, after all, only a farm.

Towns sprang up, among the first being that at the great transhipping place, Fort Edward. It was there

that the prosperous widow, Mrs. Sarah Fraser Campbell McNeil, made her home. As a Fraser of the
Frasers of Lovat, Mrs. NcNeil could look with con-
descension upon "pretty Lady Kitty" Duer, daughter
of a Scottish earl and wife of the English Captain
William Duer, who had served on the staff of Lord
Clive of India and who was now the respected justice
of the area.

During the fifteen years of peace, other towns grew
up around the mills on which the farm tracks converged. The millers, the gun-makers, the smiths, the
tanners — these worthies built their houses along new
streets and in shaded squares where stood the neat
white village church. At crossroads, innkeepers hung
out their signs, to cater to the hunger and thirst and
the fatigue of travelers in the valley, or of those who
had occasion to go as far away as Manchester or
Bennington, in Vermont, or even further, through the
Green Mountains to the towns along the Connecticut
River.

The outbreak of the revolution in 1775 startled the
communities of the upper Hudson but did not shatter them. In general, their loyalty was to the new
state of New York.

Tory Dr. James Smythe fled to Canada, whereupon
Whig Ezekiel Baldwin took over the doctor's red
house and opened it as a tavern where politicians of
"the right party" could talk.

When, in 1776, young David Jones recruited a
company of militia to help General Gates and General Arnold defend Fort Ticonderoga against the

British generals Carleton and Burgoyne, he was
hailed and wished godspeed by the patriots gathered
on the lawn outside the tavern to see him march
away. But they cursed David Jones when the news
came that he had marched his men around "Old Ti"
and straight into the British camp, where the whole
company enlisted for the King.

Actually, the people in the valley were neutral.
Their hearts were in their farms, their anxieties were
for their families, and their yearning was for the war
to pass them by. Such a community was the town of
Argyle, in Charlotte County, on the Moses Kill, six
miles east of the Hudson River.

Duncan McArthur had his farm close by Lake
Cossayuna, three or four miles north and east of the
village settlement. He had worked hard since coming
to Argyle, and had prospered. In spite of the war, he
had built·a new log house for his wife and growing
family. The house measured twenty by twenty-four
feet, and was situated so as to give a pleasant view
of the lake — a much more attractive location than
that of the old cabin, which was down in the hollow
by the brook, at the edge of the first hard acre he
had cleared. Between the cabins was a barn, to which
was attached a split-rail paddock.

On the morning of 25 July 1777, Farmer McArthur
had made arrangements to break the colt that he
had raised from a foal. Two of his neighbors had
come to help him, bringing their wives and families
with them and planning to make a day of it. The
men and boys gathered at the corral, studying the

suspicious young animal, while the women and girls
busied themselves in moving the family's possessions
from the old cabin to the new one. From the edge of
the woods at the north end of the high pasture, still
uncleared of stumps, the McArthur farm appeared
to be a community of three families. And so it seemed
to Tommo, called "Le Loup," as he watched from the
clearing.

Le Loup was a half-breed French Iroquois, who,
under the old French Canadian government, had
held the rank, or appointment, of interpreter. Unlike
Langlade, under English rule he had gone completely
Indian, with all the vengeance of an outcast making
him a savage among savages. He was the war chief,
or "captain," of the Christian Iroquois of the St.
Lawrence, which, together with his fluency in his
father's tongue, had given him the right to reply for
his Nation to Burgoyne's oration at the conference
on the Bouquet River.

With a war party of nine Iroquois, Le Loup had
left Skenesborough the day after the western tribes
had been welcomed by the British. He was bent on
loot. Up to the morning of 25 July, the party had
been without success, though — or perhaps because
— the Indians had followed the injunctions and re-
strictions set on them by Burgoyne. They had taken
one prisoner, a poor specimen, but a man capable of
being used to carry burdens until a horse could be
found, after which he might — or might not — be
scalped. Near Fort Edward, Le Loup had had a
brush with an American scouting party, and one of

his warriors had been killed. That night, at his fireless
camp, he had sworn revenge upon the first farm to lie
in their path. Next morning, the direction of the war
party had been to the east and south toward the new
settlements of the Battenkill.

The first farm to come in sight was that of Duncan
McArthur. From his hiding place, Le Loup counted
again: three roofs, three families. Too large a settlement for the nine Iroquois to attack with assurance
of easy success. In the distance, two miles to the
northwest, Le Loup saw a faint haze of smoke above
the trees, indicating another farm, another clearing,
another family. He dropped back from his lookout,
picked up his warriors and the prisoner, and headed
north and west for the Allen place.

George Kilmore, the miller at South Argyle, had
promised his son-in-law, John Allen, the loan of two
of his Negro slaves to help with harvesting the wheat
crop, and had sent them off at sun-up on Friday, 25
July. With them had gone Kilmore's youngest daughter, with a Negro girl to look after the three Allen
children while the two sisters visited together. The
party was expected to return home that same evening. When, on Sunday, they had not come back,
George Kilmore was somewhat annoyed, and dispatched another of his slaves on horseback to fetch
them home at once.

From the other side of the village, it was no more
than half a mile to the Allen farm. Soon the Negro
returned at a gallop, his yells of "Indians!" rising
above the beat of pounding hooves, as he tore

through the Sunday quiet of the shady street. Still carrying in his hand the Bible he was reading, the miller hurried to the door. He knew the message his man was bringing to him: his family and his slaves were dead.

The burial party, setting out at once, quickly reconstructed the raid. The men had come in from the fields, and all had gathered at the table for the noon meal. The two older children had been put to bed in the corner of the one-room cabin; the baby had been in the high-chair. One of the Negroes had fought hard at the front door, in a desperate effort to give the others a chance to escape through the door at the back of the cabin. The burial party knew this because of the special mutilation of the body, by which the Indians acknowledged a brave foe. His neighbors spared Kilmore other details, telling him only that the nine dead had been given decent burial.

Scouts had gone at once to the McArthur place and to the other outlying farms, afraid of what they would find. Everywhere, it was a quiet day of well-earned rest, which the scouts' arrival soon turned into the panic of preparation for immediate flight. By mid-afternoon, the roads were full of the refugees, who, as they met and talked together, recalled General Burgoyne's bombast about "giving stretch" to his Indians. The old men, Scots who remembered '45, found the massacre of the Allen family easy to comprehend, and likened Gentleman Johnny to Butcher Cumberland and all the red-coated Sassenach ilk. By nightfall, no one in all the Batten Kill was neutral.

On the Sunday that the settlers of Argyle took flight — and took sides — Captain Tommo, Le Loup, was back in the camp of Burgoyne's army. He had had his revenge at the Allen farm, which he had looted after the massacre, and had passed on, his blood lust sated for that day. In the woods he met the eight-year-old Alexander boy, who stood and gaped at the war party as it passed him on its way to Fort Edward. The fort was still in American hands, so Le Loup went around it to pick up the Fort Anne road, down which the road repair gang was working its way under the protection of Fraser's corps, which had been joined by St. Luc.

Under imminent threat of engulfment, Fort Edward was already a barren, gloomy place. It had never been of great value as a fort, dominated as it was by higher ground, and it had been allowed to go to ruin. Schuyler had abandoned the place on 12 July, when St. Clair came up to him with the regiments from Ticonderoga, and had fallen back on the Moses Kill, six miles south on the east bank of the Hudson. There he concentrated his 2200 Continentals, who were soon reinforced by Nixon's brigade of 600 Continentals and two good major generals, Benjamin Lincoln and Benedict Arnold. Schuyler had left his Albany County militia as a rear guard at Fort Edward, with orders to receive the refugees, keep contact with the enemy, and retreat only at the last moment.

By Sunday, 27 July, those of the militia who had not already deserted were restless to be off. The few

patrols they sent out soon made contact with the
enemy. When they fired on a British scout, or drew
fire from them, it was within sound of the fort. From
the pine bluffs, when the wind was out of the north,
the Yankees could hear the chunk of axes, clearing
away the trees that they themselves had felled. All
of the refugees had moved south, and the village was
uninhabited.

Only the Widow McNeil stayed behind in her
house a quarter of a mile north of the fort, on the
road by which her kinsman, General Simon Fraser,
would soon be coming. During these last days the
American patrol avoided the McNeil house, in spite
of the fact the widow's pretty granddaughter lived
there. The captain who had been sent to evacuate
the household had been driven away by the enor-
mously fat Scotswoman, whose voice in anger could
scald a hog. She could save her greetings and her
scolding for her high-and-mighty cousin!

The advance corps was not far away, and was
drawing nearer. Lieutenant David Jones of the Loyalist Volunteers, while carrying out his duties with
Fraser's staff, had prepared the way for his own
homecoming to Fort Edward. On 11 July, before
Langlade brought in the western savages, Jones had
sent a British agent with a letter to Jane McCrea, his
fiancée. His spirits had been high: he told her that
he had come safely through the Battle of Hubbardton, that he was on his way to her, and that, if her
brother was evacuating to Albany, she was to go to
Mrs. McNeil's house and wait for him there. Later,

when Burgoyne's Indians had taken the warpath —
even before he had seen the first scalps brought in —
the young lieutenant had devised a safer plan for the
reunion with his fiancée. He contrived her "capture"
by Indians whom he knew to be trustworthy. As an
escort for the young girl, Jones chose Duluth, a warrior from one of the western nations, which, uncor-
rupted by close contact with Europeans, were regarded as braver and more humane.

When she received the letter of 11 July, Jane was
placed in a dilemma which she met with all the direct
cunning of an eighteen-year-old girl very much in
love with a man whom she had not seen in a year,
who suddenly had called to her with a faith which
she herself shared. She left the house of her brother,
with whom she had lived for the past seven years,
and went to "visit" her friend Polly Hunter, Mrs. Mc-
Neil's granddaughter. If the girl was determined to
stay behind, she could not be in safer hands than
those of the formidable widow, and under the banner
of the Clan Fraser.

Jane's subterfuge did not end with her brother.
When Duluth, bearing Lieutenant Jones's message,
came to her at the McNeil house on Saturday, 26
July, she arranged to meet the Indian at noon the
following day, at an abandoned cabin not far distant.
Neither Sarah McNeil nor Polly knew of the young
girl's plan.

As it was Sunday, no particular notice was taken
of the fact that Jane was wearing her best dress.
Without drawing attention to herself, she left the

McNeil yard, crossed the road, and started to climb
the hill beyond which Duluth waited at the abandoned cabin. She did not know that she was following close behind a small American scouting party, led
by Lieutenant Van Vechten. Neither she nor the
Americans knew that, beneath the big pine trees at
the crest of the sandy hill, Le Loup, fresh from the
massacre of the Allen family, lay in ambush. As the
Yankee column bent over the top of the hill, Le
Loup and his Indians opened fire. The lieutenant was
killed at once. His men turned and fled down the hill.
Jane McCrea heard the musket fire, so close at hand;
she heard, too, the screeching war whoop of the
Iroquois as they took up the chase. She ran. At the
road, she turned out of the ruck of running soldiers
and made for the safety of the McNeil house.

The Widow McNeil, too, had heard the firing from
the ambush, and was in search of Jane. As the girl
came in, breathless, she was bustled down into the
cellar, where with Mrs. McNeil and Polly she waited.

The Indians, outdistanced by the scared Americans, returned to follow the girl whom they had seen
turn away through the trees, running like a startled
doe. Carefully circling the McNeil house, the war
party closed in. With a rush, Le Loup burst in the
door. The terrified women in the cellar could hear his
footsteps on the floor above them. In the middle of
the room he stopped and looked around for the trap-
door leading to the cellar. Then he took two steps
and lifted the door wide. The two young girls
screamed as the redoubtable widow rose to confront

the sweating, painted savage poised, tomahawk in
hand, at the top of her cellar stairs. With the excitement of a kill only a few moments before, even the
terrible ire of Mrs. McNeil could not quench the
battle fever in Le Loup. With a shove, he propelled
the big woman out of the door, the girls after her.
The eight warriors had gathered in the yard, with
two horses they had taken from the Allen farm, and
with the prisoner who had been with the war party
for so long.

Emotions, which had cooled as it appeared to the
frightened ladies that they were to lose only their
possessions, and would be taken as prisoners to the
British, flared again at the moment of departure.
Jane and Polly had been mounted on one of the
horses, but by no amount of effort could the fat Mrs.
McNeil be gotten up on to the other one. She would
have to walk, and in order that her progress might
not be impeded by her clothing, the Indians ripped
off her dress, leaving her almost naked in her shift,
and furiously voluble in her wrath. Quick to anger,
Le Loup pressed forward, menacing the indignant
woman and heaping threats and abuse upon her in
French, Iroquois, and camp English. Common sense
smothered the Scotswoman's wrath, and she turned,
a billowing white mainsail of pride, to lead the procession to the British camp and to the tent of her
kinsman, Simon Fraser.

So the war party began its return. At the top of
the hill where Lieutenant Van Vechten had died,
Jane McCrea saw Duluth. He had heard the firing

and, not finding Jane at the rendezvous, had come
in search of her. As her horse approached, Duluth,
who was talking to Le Loup, reached up to grasp the
bridle. The girl sat quietly as the two Indians talked
together in mounting anger. She was calmly confident in the arrangements that her fiancé had made
for her safety. Looking forward over the horse's
ears, she saw Mrs. McNeil's uncompromising back
rounding a bend in the trail. Polly did not look back,
as she, too, disappeared from view. Startled, Jane
had no time to cry out as she was jerked from her
horse and Le Loup's tomahawk crashed through the
side of her head.

A man named Albert Baker witnessed the whole
grisly episode from his hiding spot on a pine bluff.
With his small son he had returned to his abandoned
house to recover some tools that had been left behind. Baker saw Jane McCrea die under Le Loup's
hatchet, and saw the Indian scalp her and strip her
of her clothes. He saw the Iroquois roll the body
down the ravine that lay between the Indians and
the bluff where he was hidden. He saw Jane's body
come to rest against the trunk of a fallen tree, then
saw that it lay against another naked body, as white
as that of the girl. As the Indians hurried off after
the rest of the war party, one remained behind. As
Baker and his little son watched, Duluth slipped
down the steep hill and covered the two bodies decently with leaves. Albert Baker waited until the
Indian finally had disappeared; then he ran to the
fort, carrying his little boy all of the way.

The Albany County militia buried Jane McCrea and Lieutenant Van Vechten at sun-down, on the line of their retreat from Fort Edward. It had been a restless week-end in the valley of the Upper Hudson. Squalls of anxiety and indecision had torn at the loyalties and conscience of the people there. The smoke, which had hung over the Allen farm on Friday morning and had betrayed it, had gone. The two scalps, brought into Burgoyne's camp on Saturday, had fallen to the ground and had been trampled under the feet of the marching regiments. On Sunday, the wind that soughed through the branches above the hastily dug graves of the murdered girl and the young lieutenant, killed in action, was rising to a gale.

7

The Face of Gentleman Johnny

Wrapped in the general's caped cloak, Mrs. McNeil
let loose a torrent of fury and invective upon her
kinsman, Simon Fraser. There was no need for the
evidence: the frightful lock of long, fair hair, which,
when doubled through the tie of Le Loup's loin-
cloth, brushed his leggings below the knee.

Le Loup's was the guilt for the murder of Jane
McCrea. The Iroquois had struck with the cold,
quick blow of the rattlesnake. But the blame for the
murder of Jane McCrea, and of the Allen family, lay
with Burgoyne, who, by shaking the rattle at the
serpent's tail, had thought to control its fangs.

Accepting the responsibility of high command,
Burgoyne reacted to the crime with the whirlwind
of a general disobeyed, and with the lightning of a
gentleman whose honor has been traduced. He
ordered his Indian commander, St. Luc de la Corne,
to deliver up Le Loup to a court-martial; and he sent
an aide to beat the ranks for a soldier with experience
as a common hangman.

In angrily opening to the Iroquois chief the **door of**

traditional British justice and punishment, Burgoyne
momentarily disregarded his first duty, set down in
the hinge phrase of the soldier's creed: ". . . for the
good of the Service." That clear-eyed highlander,
Brigadier Fraser, cautioned the general to walk warily
among the Indians lest they all go home, leaving the
advance corps blind in the forest. St. Luc, an arrant
old fox, threatened the rape and pillage of civilian
Canada, should the tribes now go home because of
the hanging of their brother Tommo, called Le Loup.
The shrug which the Chevalier gave to his powerful
shoulders disclaimed any desire to restrain his wild
cubs.

Jane McCrea's murderer was pardoned, and a
third Indian Conference was called for 4 August, a
week hence. It was useless to set an earlier date, as
the war parties were still out. One by one they returned, flaunting their scalps and prisoners as they
approached, sorting the gaudy loot at their campfires
and dancing their boastful dances in anticipation of
further rich lands to plunder. When the warriors
squatted down with their mirrors in their hands to
renew the war paint, St. Luc and Langdale came
among them, admonishing them to put away their
packets of bright colors. The British general wished
to have another conference with his red allies. Following behind the two leaders came the interpreters
who directed the small war parties, and to whom was
given a share in the loot. These men from the outer
edges of civilization pictured the plunder of Albany.
Then, as black eyes flamed in eagerness, adroit words

shattered the image, mocked the military role, and left the impression upon the warriors' simple minds that the rape of such rich cities was only for the lordly English. Consequently, the Indians came to the conference in a sullen mood, and Burgoyne rose to speak with the gold braid of his epaulets heavy as bullion on his shoulders.

The conference was saved only by the savages' admiration for flowery oratory, and by John Burgoyne's ability to supply that commodity in fulsome torrents. Grunts of approval greeted each well-phrased point of his persuasive appeal, while from the leaders and the chiefs came a compromise agreement to remain with the army. Nevertheless, the western nations set off the next day for their far-off homes. Langdale went with them, while St. Luc found occasion to return to his Canadian seigniory. Of the eastern Indians, many stayed on for a while as scavengers, their scouts ringing the army just beyond the provost lines, where helpless English and German deserters fell prey to them.

Burgoyne was left with the rattles of the snake still in his hand. The lidless eyes no longer kept his watch, the venomous fangs were withdrawn, and the viper-head had turned away from the enemy. Burgoyne himself was in danger of the swelling numbness of the rattlesnake's bite.

Captain Lieutenant Alexander Fraser had "gone native" in the deceptively casual manner of his breed. For the duration of the Carleton campaign of 1776,

he had slipped out of the confining regimental coat
of the 9th Foot, to assume direction of the Indian
scouts attached to his uncle Simon Fraser's advance
corps. His companion in this irregular service was a
kindred spirit, Lieutenant Thomas Scott of the 24th.
Together, the two officers had gone into the deep
woods to find out their secret and to learn their ways
and make them their own. Their only disappointment in the free life of the forest was in the Indians
themselves. The two British officers found the savages, as soldiers, difficult to manage — difficult to the
point of positive detriment to the service. The duty
of scouting was performed by the Indians in an extremely slipshod fashion. Furthermore, both gentlemen found the manners of the Indians excessively
crude. Even among the slum-spawned and sod-grown
privates of the British line, they had been accustomed, through leadership, to strike a spark of de-
cency and the will to learn how to perform a duty,
however alien. With the Indians this appeared to
be impossible.

For the campaign of 1777, Fraser and Scott had
conceived, recruited, and organized their own "war
party" of regular British soldiers. Recruits for "Captain Fraser's Marksmen" had to be of good character,
sober, active, robust, and healthy — or so they came
to be considered. But in no army will the colonel of
a regiment give up such a man, and the original forty
recruits were more aptly described as rebels to discipline, self-sufficient outcasts, and enemies to the
"System." An officer of young Fraser's type caught

the imagination of such men. They followed him into his strange element of the wild forest, and emerged at the outer extremity of Burgoyne's army like a supple hand, capable of slapping, striking, or gentle probing.

With his Indians gone or loitering with the camp followers, General Burgoyne had need of Fraser's marksmen — and many more like them. Having fought forward of the army, matching aimed fire with American riflemen outside the walls of Ticonderoga and at the road junction at Hubbardton, the corps had dwindled in number. Now, on the Hudson, Captain Fraser was offered the pick of the British army to find replacements for his marksmen. A Swedish baron, Lieutenant Salans, joined the corps at this time, but his ranger service with his friend of the 9th Foot was to be brief. Fraser found young Philip Skene to be a likely recruit, and he, too, was invited to come with the marksmen. Captain Lieutenant Thomas Scott gave employment to young Joshua Pell, who, though a colonial, was an acceptable candidate for Scott's special section of long-range scouts and couriers.

If Burgoyne had need of eyes to look around the next bend of the river to which, at last, he had come; if he needed to see where the enemy would stand against him — he was equally in need of word from his friends, Sir William Howe and Barry St. Leger, who were converging on the predetermined rendezvous at Albany. Their approach — indeed, their imminent arrival — must be confirmed.

The face of a commanding general is a mask behind which he suppresses overconfidence and hides doubts, fears, and disappointments. Lieutenant General Burgoyne's mask was that of "Gentleman Johnny." It was an easy face to show in the open gateway at Ticonderoga, as the victorious army flowed by in the bright sunlight. At Skenesborough House, couriers in their strange disguises saw the face by candlelight in the doorway of the private office, with a swirl of talk and laughter from the dining-room beyond wreathing it like laurel; then the door was closed, shutting away the sound, and only the gaiety of the face remained as the big man, resplendent in white and scarlet, strode to his desk. Now, it was a serious face above the extended hand that gave the courier urgent dispatches for General Howe. But it was a kindly face, too, that sent the messenger over two hundred danger-filled miles to his destination.

As the fatigue party carried the traps of the general — and of his companion — into the red house on the bank of the Hudson, where headquarters had been set up not far from Fort Edward, they still saw the face of "Gentleman Johnny." Of the several couriers who had been sent to Billy Howe, only two had been heard of: both had been caught by the rebels and hanged. Word of a third courier came to General Burgoyne on 3 August, the day before the final Indian conference. He, too, had been captured, and the letter that he carried had been found in the false bottom of his canteen. His fate was not known, but a fourth courier had managed to get through the double Yankee lines — those that faced Burgoyne and those that watched Howe — and he had returned on 3 August with a letter to General Burgoyne from General Sir William Howe.

Billy Howe had written eighteen days before from his comfortable and well-appointed quarters in New York City. The somewhat indolent commander in chief of all the British forces in the Atlantic Colonies had made what was for him an instantaneous response to the announcement of Burgoyne's bloodless capture of Fort Ticonderoga. After only two nights of sleeping on the news, Howe wrote the commnader of his northern army that this was indeed "a great event."

The necessity for sending his congratulations offered Howe an opportunty to acknowledge the receipt of two earlier letters. The first of these was written from Plymouth, before Burgoyne set sail for Canada; the second was from Quebec, written on Burgoyne's arrival there in May.

Of the grand design, so painstakingly worked out with Lord George Germaine in his cabinet at the Royal threshold, there was in Howe's letter no glimmer of recognition or response. On the contrary, General Howe announced that, instead of marching north along the Hudson in concert with the northern army's descent on Albany, he was going south by sea to Chesapeake Bay and Pennsylvania! He had already declared this intention when, in early April, he had written one of his infrequent letters to Governor

General Carleton. At that time it had been assumed by Carleton, as it was by Burgoyne, that General Howe had not yet received Lord Germain's explicit orders to proceed to the north, and that, on receiving the orders, he would act accordingly. But Howe's congratulatory letter, delivered to Burgoyne on 3 August, gave no indication that any such orders from London had ever reached him in New York.

By moving the main British force from New York to Pennsylvania, Billy Howe put yet another rebel army between himself and Burgoyne. General Schuyler was on the Upper Hudson, where he faced the invasion from Canada with only a weak force, but where, according to Howe's letter, 2500 reinforcements were expected momentarily. At Peekskill, General Israel Putnam, with 4000 soldiers, was in control of the highlands. Now, General Washington's Continentals were in New Jersey, beyond which lay Philadelphia.

Sitting at his headquarters desk at Fort Edward, with his whole army in inexorable and confident motion around him, Johnny Burgoyne could see in the letter from his commander in chief but two points of faintly glimmering hope for some measure of cooperation from the south. If Washington turned north, then Howe would follow him. This offered a wry picture of Burgoyne as a terrier, holding "at bay" — the phrase was Howe's — a thundering herd of American generals led by Washington, while General Howe himself ambled up from Pennsylvania like a reluctant, almost somnambulant bear. The other possibility of assistance lay with Sir Henry Clinton, a fearless, able, and active guardsman-general, whom Howe had left in command of the New York City garrison with orders to act "as occurrence may direct." Perhaps the barking of the terrier upriver would bring the Clinton airedales racing north.

Though General Burgoyne's "Thoughts for Conducting the War from the Side of Canada," and the orders from the highest authority, which were to put those thoughts into effect, seemingly had disappeared, Burgoyne's duty remained clear and simple and forthright as that of any soldier. To be sure, he had authored the plan, yet Gentleman Johnny was only a lieutenant general, under the direction of superior officers. In Canada, General Carleton had ordered him to take his army to Albany and there to put himself under the command of General Howe.

With the objective and purpose of his journey set so clearly before him, Burgoyne had no need to look elsewhere in order to see where his duty lay. Then, too, his own ambitions and hopes were bound up in the successful completion of the march down the wilderness river which now carried his fate to its destiny. In only one field was Lieutenant General John Burgoyne free to use his own discretion: he was in full and absolute command of his own army.

Be he subaltern or general, the instinctive thoughts of an officer are with his command. No matter how far afield his inner thoughts may whirl, they soon wind back on an invisible string to wrap themselves around that strong center pole, his troops. Deep in

speculation, Burgoyne watched through his office
window as a soldier carried a basket of laundry to
the lines for the maid of the lady who rested in the
chamber above. On the road outside the Red House,
the squeak of an axle marked the passage of a cart;
grease for that axle was a matter for the attention of
Captain Money, the quartermaster. Pen in hand, the
general leaned forward to make a note in regard to
grease and wagon maintenance. The question posed
by the soldier and the laundry could wait. Perhaps it
did not yet come within the duties of a chaplain.
Both matters were the responsibility of Burgoyne, as
a commander of troops. His, too, was the responsibility for tomorrow's Indian Conference. He sent
for his adjutant general, Lieutenant Colonel Robert
Kingston, and when that officer appeared, ready to
get down to work with his chief, General Howe's
blandly casual letter was locked away in Burgoyne's
private box.

Burgoyne kept his headquarters at Fort Edward
for a little more than two weeks. They were anxious
and busy days for the general, as he moved about
among his troops, showing an ever cheerful counte-
nance. He kept Howe's letter a secret unto himself.
Perhaps there would be a second letter, with the
welcome news that Howe was approaching up the
Hudson. Meanwhile, he had sent couriers to Clinton
and expected an answer at any moment. Surely, Sir
Henry would come up the river far enough to draw
away some of the Yankee troops that faced the

British, and Burgoyne could give out such news to
his officers and his troops with a face of convincing
cheer. No word had come from Barry St. Leger
either, who now should be well started on his way to
the Mohawk River, on the western approaches to
Albany.

While the general waited, the army worked. All
the stores that had been gathered together at Skenesborough had to be carried over the Fort Anne road
to Fort Edward. It was not until 16 August that the
last bateau was hauled out of Wood Creek and
hefted up onto an oxcart, to begin its rough journey
to the Hudson. Simultaneously, a supply line was
being built up Lake George, and more and more
bateaux and gunboats traded back and forth through
that narrow corridor of blue water between the high
green mountains.

Brigadier General Henry Wilson Powell replaced
Brigadier General James Hamilton in command at
Ticonderoga. For the defense of that vital trans-
shipping point, General Powell had one weak British
regiment, the 53rd, and the Brunswick regiment,
Prinz Friedrich, under Lieutenant Colonel Christian
Julius Praetorius. In his aloof, humorless way, Powell
contrived a defense that scattered the thousand men
under his command over the four miles of forts and
roads from Mount Independence to the landing place
on Lake George. He did not forget to bring down the
big guns from Mount Defiance, and dispensed both
justice and punishment in using for the job the rebel
prisoners from Hubbardton and Fort Anne.

Troops other than Powell's were guarding the supply line. Lieutenant James Hadden saw them on his
way to reinforce Captain Jones's company of artillery, in the new single brigade of General Phillips's
right wing. Hadden's sloop stopped in at Diamond
Island, thirty miles up Lake George, with stores for
Captain Aubrey's two companies of the 47th, stationed there. The Captain showed the gunner officer
the sighting of his cannon, poured him a drink, and
envied him his place in the army's line of battle.
At Fort George, Hadden saw a busy magazine of
stores. Barrels, bales, boxes, and crates of every size
and shape were piled along the beach. Sailors, with
the help of a work gang of Loyalists, unloaded another convoy of twenty bateaux while Hadden was
waiting for a wagon on which he could throw his box
of clothing, his bed-roll, and his saddle, bridle, and
pistol holsters.

Hadden himself would walk the twelve miles of
portage road. He had no horse with him, and, with
an artilleryman's eye for transport, he could see that
the wagons were overloaded, the horses tired and
underfed, their harness patched with thongs and
broken collars padded with the coats of the drivers.
All along the hot, dusty road, Hadden saw carts
broken down and abandoned by their drivers, can-
nibalized by others who came later, until only a few
boards of the box remained, with perhaps a broken
axle-tree, its hardware carefully removed. The road
from Fort Edward to Fort George was a bottleneck,
holding Burgoyne's army to its beachhead on the

Upper Hudson until a supply of horses sufficient to
work it could be found. Already the lack of horses
had committed the movement of the army to a train
of boats down the river. Those teams which Colonel
Skene had led Burgoyne to expect the Loyalists of
the Upper Hudson Valley would supply were not
forthcoming. They had been driven off in the face of
the Indian raids.

To the east, in the Green Mountains of Vermont,
in the village of Manchester and beyond, was farm-
land rich in horses, oxen, and beef cattle. Ever since
leaving Skenesborough, General Riedesel had wanted
to take his Germans into that country, but permission had been refused. Now, as the need for
bringing supplies from Fort George mounted in
urgency with each passing day, Burgoyne recon-
sidered the plan. At last, he gave his limited consent
for the Brunswick Dragoons alone of the German
contingent to execute a raid toward Manchester for
horses and cattle. Mounted, the troopers could also
be useful as scouts, in the manner of the new-
fashioned cavalry called "hussars." For the entry into
Albany, two hundred dragoons all ajangle, the hooves
of their horses striking sparks on the cobbled streets,
would make a fine parade.

Though a "horse-soldier," Riedesel grumbled at
this new concept of his raid into Vermont. Nevertheless, he went forward to the assembly point to see his
troops off, and so it was that on the 14 August the
devoted baron was at the mouth of the Batten Kill,
eleven miles below Fort Edward, when his indomi-

table baroness and the three little girls drove up to
the door of the Red House at Fort Edward and established themselves there. A suggestion of perfume
still remained in the upstairs hall and in the big bed-
room at the front of the house. The baroness sniffed
and turned away down the hall toward the back, her
arms filled with fresh clothing for her much travel-
stained small daughters.

Only that morning, Burgoyne had moved his headquarters to the Duer House at Fort Miller. His commissary's wife had gone with him.

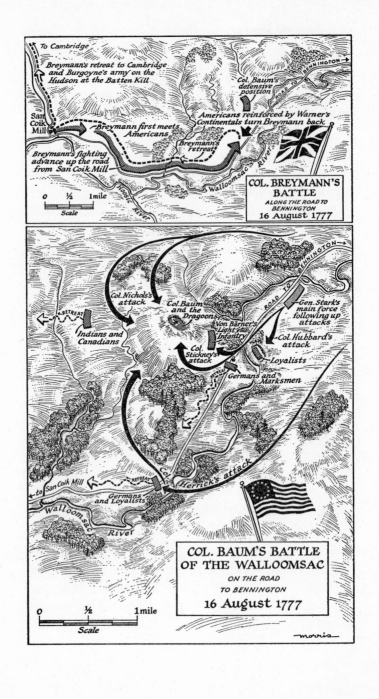

To Cambridge

Breymann's retreat to Cambridge and Burgoyne's army on the Hudson at the Batten Kill

Col. Baum's defensive position

San Coik Mill

Breymann first meets Americans

Americans reinforced by Warner's Continentals turn Breymann back

Breymann's retreat

Breymann's fighting advance up the road from San Coik Mill

Hoosic River

Walloomsac River

ROAD TO BENNINGTON

0   ½   1 mile
Scale

COL. BREYMANN'S BATTLE
ALONG THE ROAD TO BENNINGTON
16 August 1777

Col. Nichols's attack

RETREAT

Indians and Canadians

Col. Baum and the Dragoons

Von Bärner's Light Infantry

Gen. Stark's main force following up attacks

Col. Stickney's attack

Col. Hubbard's attack

Loyalists

RETREAT

Germans and Marksmen

ROAD TO BENNINGTON

to San Coik Mill

RETREAT

Germans and Loyalists

Col. Herrick's attack

Walloomsac River

COL. BAUM'S BATTLE OF THE WALLOOMSAC
ON THE ROAD TO BENNINGTON
16 August 1777

0   ½   1 mile
Scale

morris

8

The Restless Winds of August

In mid-August, northern New York State lies quietly under the hot summer sun. The frequent thunder-showers, rolling up against the warm wind, give little relief from the heat. Even the trout in the streams seek a shady bank by which to doze, and cannot be tempted to the surface even by the fall of the choicest fly. Only man, with his will to carry out his plans and schemes, forces the season and pits his sweat against the sun and rain of summer.

On 13 August 1777, Lieutenant Colonel Friederich Baum planned to march his raiding force of 700 motley troops from the mouth of the Batten Kill to Cambridge, fifteen miles away. Though the sun had scarcely risen, and the shadows of the tall elms fell far out over the waters of the Hudson, sweat gleamed on the black faces of his Negro drummers as they beat out the quick roll of the Assembly for the dragoons. One hundred and seventy officers and troopers of Prinz Ludwig of Brunswick's Dragoon Regiment lined up to the beat of the drum. The big regimental sergeant major, whose mustachios bristled up to his

ears in a challenge to his men, boomed out the number to Major Christoph von Maibon, adding a report
in detail as to the whereabouts of the other men:
sick, camp guard, Canadian depot, not on parade.
Maibon looked with distaste at the trousers of striped
ticking and the infantryman's gaiters worn by the
troopers. He held to boots for a cavalryman!

On either side of the dragoons another German
unit had fallen in. On the right, Major von Bärner,
though junior, commanded one hundred and fifty
light infantry, his own blue-coated riflemen and von
Geyso's *Jägers* in green and red, plus a few grenadiers who only the day before had joined the force.
On the left, a two-gun detachment of Hesse-Hanau
artillery was hitched and limbered, ready to move
off. Lieutenant Bock reported the gunners present.

The rest of Colonel Baum's expeditionary force
was more difficult to account for, being less regimental on parade. Captain Fraser's fifty marksmen
slouched, deliberately seeking rest wherever they
could find it. The Tories, under Colonels Francis
Pfister and John Peters, could hardly be called a military unit. They were going east with Baum to recruit
other Loyalists into their skeleton "regiments."

Major Philip Skene, still confident of the basic
loyalty of the local people, was also with the expedition. Now, in the early morning, he stood with
the headquarters group around the chunky Colonel
Baum. Skene talked easily with the immaculate
Captain de la Naudière, whose suave grace empha-
sized his catlike movement, as he excused himself to

slip away to join his Canadians. From talking with his habitants, still gathered about their campfire, de la Naudière would learn the true temper of the Indians who camped nearby.

As Baum gave the order to move out, General Burgoyne rode up to take the salute. He was gone again before the long, straggling queue of women, musicians, and officers' servants took to the Cambridge road behind the German van. The whole army was on the move; and Burgoyne would be needed everywhere. With Baum's force off to the east, Fraser's corps was to cross to the west bank of the Hudson, its place at the left bank bridgehead being taken by Breymann's reserve corps of German shock troops. Phillips was bringing forward the British regiments from Fort Edward to Fort Miller, and when the main German contingent once was in motion, Riedesel was to return to the Duer's House headquarters (on 14 August) to give General Burgoyne the latest reports on the Lake George supply line.

General Riedesel did not yet know that the destination of his dragoons had been changed. He had written the orders for the expedition into Vermont, setting down in detail the purpose of the raid and the route that Baum was to follow. The objects of the "secret expedition" were five: "To try the affection of the country; to disconcert the councils of the enemy; to mount the Riedesel's Dragoons; to compleat Peter's corps; and to obtain large supplies of cattle, horses, and carriages." The route was along three sides of a rectangle, of which the fourth side

would be marched by the main army, down the
Hudson River. Baum's first objective was Manchester,
where Seth Warner's Continentals lurked. General
Burgoyne considered it highly probable that "Mr.
Warner" would retreat before Baum's troops. At the
staff meeting Riedesel had objected to this premise
when the plan was outlined, but had fallen silent before the scornful conviction with which Burgoyne
and Phillips, the other major general of the expedition, had expressed their opinion of the "Green Mountain Boys," as Warner's regiment was called. For a
moment, the baron had expected Simon Fraser to
speak up in strong support of his doubts. But the
commander of the British advance corps, who, like
Riedesel, had faced the Continentals at Hubbardton, remained silent, his eyes turned toward the window. The baron followed the Scotsman's gaze. In
the home pasture beyond a snake-rail fence, a single
shade tree gave shelter from the sun to two of Gentleman Johnny's well-groomed chargers. The tree
was a lofty elm, its green branches arching out like
a fountain in the palace gardens at Potsdam, its
trunk of a diameter to afford ample protection to any
Yankee rifleman.

From Manchester, Baum was to march his force
to Rochester, on the Connecticut River, thence south
to Brattleboro and back to the main army, which
would be somewhere on the great road that followed
the west bank of the Hudson to Albany.

It was not until Colonel Baum was moving his
troops up to the start line at the mouth of the Batten

Kill that his objective was changed to the town of Bennington. A messenger from the Tory scout, Captain Sherwood, had come with the welcome news that a big rebel magazine, containing all the supplies that Burgoyne so urgently needed, lay in that Vermont town, guarded only by some four hundred local militia.

To the men in the close-ranged ranks of the German regulars, the new direction of their march meant fewer miles of hot and dusty track. Bennington, as they quickly found out, was only twenty-eight miles away, and by the time the evening halt was called and they had dressed ranks before dismissal, fifteen of those miles had passed under their weary feet. During the day they had heard musket fire, and on approaching Cambridge the dragoons had halted in ranks, while the *Jägers* and light infantry scouted the little settlement. Primarily, the deployment had been an exercise for von Bärner's men, intended to impress the villagers. They had prepared the way for the parade of the dragoons down the single street of the town, their arms swinging in unison, every eye looking straight ahead, their rich young voices dutifully singing the melancholy, hymn-like air to which they habitually marched. A barefooted, thin-shouldered woman ran out of a log house to snatch back her child, who had slipped away to march with the big men in blue and yellow. Otherwise the town appeared to be empty.

After supper, Pastor Melsheimer of the dragoons had knocked at the door of the parsonage behind the clapboard church. But the woman who came to the door could not understand his broken English, nor had she recognized the Cloth. The pastor had returned to the headquarters fire, where, through an interpreter, Colonel Baum was interrogating the few Yankee men that Captain Fraser and the Indians had captured during the course of the day.

From the prisoners, Baum learned that, instead of four hundred rebels guarding the horses and stores at Bennington, there were eighteen hundred! In a message sent back to Burgoyne that night, Baum passed on this new and startling bit of intelligence, and advised the general that he was proceeding warily.

Five miles to the south of Cambridge, the Owl Kill meets the Hoosic River at a right angle, where the direction of the river's flow changes from north to west. Above this confluence yet another river, the Walloomsac, comes from Bennington and the east to form a ragged but well-defined cross of waterways where it meets the Hoosic. Baum's road from Cambridge to Bennington crossed to the west bank of the Owl Kill to meet the Albany road, where, almost immediately, it passed over another bridge at a mill named, appropriately, St. Croix. From that point, the road followed the north bank of the Walloomsac to Bennington, except for one short cut across a bend. It was at St. Croix, its pronunciation corrupted by the local twang to "Sancoik," that Baum first encountered the Americans.

Two hundred Yankees crowded into the mill and

spread themselves through the surrounding bushes. They heard the Germans approaching from as far away as the first bridge, and watched agape as the head of the first column — *Jägers* in coats of green, with red facings like those of Seth Warner's Continentals — passed the Albany road and turned toward the bridge over the millrace. The Americans had little plan and less leadership, so when someone yelled "They're comin'" and fired his musket, everyone joined in with a ragged, poorly aimed volley. The Germans came steadily on, the green-coated men fanning out to right and left, occasionally dropping to one knee to fire at the mill with their short brown rifles, steadied by the red slings wrapped around their arms. The Americans could see no effect from their own fire. Instead, blue-coated soldiers in big, black cocked hats trotted, in a compact mass, up the road toward the bridge. Each man held in his right hand a gleaming, short, curved sword. A Yankee smashed one of the windows on the safe side of the mill, away from the charging light infantry, and clambered out through the broken frame. Others followed, piling out of the doors and windows, all of them bound for the safety of the Bennington road and the offer of distance that it promised. At first, the Americans ran; then, as the exhaustion of heat outbalanced their dread of the men in blue and black, they dropped into a fast walk which they kept up for the three miles to the bridge over Little White Creek.

There, the last of the retreating Americans saw Eleazer Edgerton, the carpenter of Bennington, hat-

less as usual and now coatless as well, his sleeves
rolled above his elbows, beckoning them to hurry.
With him were two other Bennington men, busily
prizing the planks of the bridge. The last man
gathered himself to leap over the gap that already
had been made. He sprang forward, stumbled, and
fell; then he picked himself up and ran on. Behind
him, Eleazer and his two friends worked feverishly
to destroy the bridge. Just as the flames caught the
pile of shivered dry planking, the first shots came
from the pursuing German light infantry. His task
completed, Edgerton ducked off into the brush. He
stopped once to shoot back, just to keep the "Hessians" away from his bonfire until it caught a good
blaze.

The hour thus bought by the carpenter of Bennington saved the Sancoik detachment, bone-tired
with the physical weariness that rides the back of
panic. The hour that it required for Baum to cross
Little White Creek with his guns and wagons dulled
the youthful eagerness of von Bärner's men. With
their keen swords sheathed, the German light troops
continued to lead the way up the narrow valley
floor of the Walloomsac. Now, the pace of the Germans had slackened to the workhorse tread of the
dismounted cavalry, as doubt and caution dragged at
the worn heels of Dragoon Lieutenant Colonel Baum.
After the habit of the alert officer, he was studying
the hills that rose steeply on his left, picking out a
defensive position, when a party of Tory scouts came

in with the news that the rebel army had come out
from Bennington and awaited him across the second
Walloomsac bridge that lay beyond. On receiving this
intelligence, Baum's doubts resolved themselves into
decision, his caution solidified into defense, and the
selection of a suitable position moved over from the
side of speculation to that of instant choice. With his
enemy scarcely a mile away, Baum sent a second
message to Burgoyne, this time asking for reinforcements.

Across the bend of the Walloomsac, Baum's enemy,
too, waited for reinforcements. As the hot, still afternoon wore on and help did not appear, the American
army, too weak to attack, retired in order to Bennington. Tomorrow they would return with their general
to drive the Germans from their hills.

Their general was the almost legendary John Stark.
His frame was tall and spare and supple, though
where his principles were concerned, his back was
hickory-stiff. His face was finely boned, and when
angered or crossed, his jaw firmed and his eyes
sparkled like a hatchet striking on the rock of his
native New Hampshire. John Stark resembled a
tomahawk, and carried himself as such during all the
years of the American Revolution.

By 1775, when he was forty-seven years old, Stark's
military reputation in his native colony was second
only to that of Robert Rogers, whose lieutenant he
had been during the glorious years of fabulous deeds
with Rogers' Rangers. Whereas Rogers had gone

away from New Hampshire at the end of the French
and Indian War, Stark had returned to espouse the
cause of his expanding New Hampshire, and to become a part of its heroic legend.

Upon hearing of the battles of Lexington and
Concord, John Stark did what might have been expected of such a man. And he did it so suddenly
that when his New Hampshire Regiment, recruited
as he rode, was added to the gathering American
army near Boston, Stark had to send home to Elizabeth, his wife, for a change of clothing.

Colonel Stark's New Hampshire Regiment fought
with gallantry on the American left at Breed's Hill,
manned the siege lines around Boston, and followed
George Washington when he led the Continental
Army to New York. Colonel Stark took his regiment
north into Canada during the spring of 1776, and
fretted through the long summer of apprehension
that followed that disastrous campaign, while Gates
prepared the defenses at Ticonderoga, and Benedict
Arnold built his fleet to hold Lake Champlain against
Guy Carleton and John Burgoyne.

As a New Englander from the back lots of New
Hampshire, Stark found service difficult on the northern frontier. He was unable to assert himself against
the smooth façade of General Philip Schuyler's aristocratic New York confidence. Nor would General
Gates, whose military career had been built up of
well-mortised British army brick, heed the old ranger
Stark when the latter expounded upon his military
credo of attack by courageous men confident in their

firearms. Stark fared better under Washington, who gave the New Hampshire colonel command of the right wing of the advance guard at the winter-night crossing of the Delaware River, and at the dawn attack up the streets of Trenton, where Howe's German troops slept off the effects of their Christmas celebration.

When the promotion list came out after the winter campaign of 1776-77, the name of John Stark was not included. It was the second time the Continental Congress had passed him over for a general's star. In anger and protest, Stark resigned his commission in the Continental Army and went home to New Hampshire. He was not the first officer to feel such a slight to his personal honor and to that of his native state at the hands of a muddling Congress of conniving delegates from thirteen jealously separate governments.

Stark did not remain long in retirement. The corn crop of 1777 was only musket high when New Hampshire called him back to arms. Within a week he had mustered twenty-five companies of rugged New Hampshire militiamen. Five days more, and Stark had his brigade on the banks of the Connecticut River. On 7 August, his men were ready for action, and Brigadier General Stark took up a position on Burgoyne's flank at Manchester, in Vermont. Beside him stood Colonel Seth Warner, who, since Hubbardton, had been left by General Schuyler to watch and threaten Burgoyne, and if he moved toward New England, to delay him.

Philip Schuyler knew that Stark had come again to the war. Schuyler needed the New Hampshire Brigade on the Hudson, and sent General Benjamin Lincoln to fetch it. Lincoln, extremely able (and exceedingly fat!), was one of the two major generals Washington had sent north to help out against the invasion from Canada. Each commanded a wing of Schuyler's army. Benedict Arnold had gone west on a flying expedition to relieve Fort Stanwix, under siege by Barry St. Leger. In command of the American right, Benjamin Lincoln had gone into western New England to bring in the militia there, for a concentration of force above Albany. On Burgoyne's move to Fort Edward, Schuyler now knew that city to be the British objective.

Perhaps it was unfortunate that Lincoln was one of the officers promoted over the head of John Stark, but the circumstances were mitigated to some extent by the fact that Lincoln was a Massachusetts general, and therefore a New Englander. When the two men met in Manchester on 7 August, Stark was adamant in his refusal to obey Lincoln's order to rally his brigade to Schuyler. Stark produced his orders from the General Court of New Hampshire in justification of his stand. Benjamin Lincoln read carefully the extraordinary orders under which Brigadier General John Stark was given discriminatory powers to act either with, or separately from, the Continental Army. It was obvious to the Massachusetts general that his fellow New Englander chose to act independently of the New Yorker, General Schuyler.

And in the face of the imminent British onslaught, there was nothing that Lincoln could do about it. Prevailed upon by persuasive Massachusetts reasoning, Stark remained in Vermont, assuming the role of a valued ally of standing equal to that of the Continental Army. Under sympathetic treatment, John Stark made one concession: he would march his brigade to Bennington, to await developments (both political and military) while guarding the stores accumulating at that place. Stark had a further reason for leaving Manchester and going on to Bennington, twenty miles away. One of his spies had told him that Burgoyne, even then, was bound for New England and was proceeding by way of Bennington. Upon receiving this information, Stark was obviously bound by the General Court to bar the road until his ally, the aristocratic Schuyler, could come from Albany with his Continentals. On 8 August, when the New Hampshire men were marching to Bennington, Burgoyne's own informer had not yet arrived with the news of the inadequately guarded stores at that town.

It was only by rumor and hearsay and misinformation that Stark and Baum came face to face in the same narrow valley of the Walloomsac on the afternoon of 14 August 1777.

9

The Hill Overlooking the Walloomsac

For the second time that afternoon, Colonel Friederich Baum found himself climbing the hill overlooking the bend and bridges of the Walloomsac
River. He was on the steep southeast face of the
hill, which was dead ground to his main defensive
position on the summit. As he plodded upward Baum
was hot and tired and feeling his long years of
service. Once more he stopped to rest, standing as
though the calves of his slim horseman's legs could
not be trusted to lever up his barrel-like body should
he sit down. He heard behind him the labored
breathing of one of his aides, the young Irishman,
on loan from Riedesel's staff.

Working around the steeply tilted land and out of
the thick scrub growth, the command party came
upon the fire positions of the fifty *Jägers,* stationed
so as to command both the dead ground and the
narrow gully of a brook, now almost dry. While the
spruce young captain pointed out his fire positions,
the old colonel sat drinking from a canteen as he
looked over the battlefield he had chosen.

Below, and three hundred yards distant, was the
first bridge over the Walloomsac; the Yankees had
not destroyed it when they had retreated, a few
hours earlier. Baum had just come from the position
there, held by fifty of his own light troops, thirty of
Captain Fraser's rangers, and one of Lieutenant
Bock's 3-pounders, guarding the bridge and set to
rake the road to Bennington. If the rebels attacked,
it was from Bennington that he expected them to
come. On an elevation above the road, just beyond
the bridge, one hundred and fifty Tories were at
work, throwing up field fortifications, and at his inspection Baum saw them make the dirt fly. The
colonel had discovered a sturdy log cabin on the far
side of the river between the Tory redoubt and the
bridge, and into this he had ordered the women who
trailed the expedition. From where he now sat among
the *Jägers,* he could see the roof of the cabin, neatly
and safely tucked away in a fold of the ground.

Three-quarters of a mile away, on the road up
which he had marched from Sancoik, Colonel Baum
had left another post. This was manned by some of
the Tories who had come from the Hudson, together
with ninety others of like mind who had joined the
expedition since it set out the previous day. The
"uniform" of the latter consisted of white paper,
pinned to their hats! The rear position was stiffened
by fifty grenadiers under Captain von Schiek, if necessary, they could lead a bayonet charge through the
Yankee rabble to greet the reinforcements, expected
to arrive the next day (15 August) by a forced march.

On the crest of the hill, to which Colonel Baum finally climbed from the canted perch of the *Jägers,* was the hard core of his defense. It was sunset when he regained his tent. Clouds were gathering, and for a moment a hot breeze stirred the leaves as it passed by. Every native officer he had talked with on his rounds had smelled rain in the air. If this came, it would be good. If the rebels attacked, the dampness would make their muskets useless, and there would be time for the reinforcements to arrive for the charge with sabers and bayonets on which Colonel Baum depended to win through to Bennington.

The hilltop position of the Brunswick Dragoons was cleared of trees, yet trees dominated it. From the steep slopes, the trees thrust up their leafy branches like curious children peering onto a table-top. To the north and northwest, the virgin timber of the American forest stopped the inroads of the clearing at a low ridge, capped by a knoll. To the northeast, at a distance of approximately a mile, a tree-covered mountain edged the horizon. Baum had placed his earth-and-log barricade to face the gap between the two features, and had caused wings to be thrown up facing east and west. The woods in front of the redoubt were patrolled by Indians, and by de la Naudière's Canadians. The second cannon was mounted in an embrasure to shoot down the hill onto the Bennington road, in support of the other gun at the first bridge. Other embrasures had been cut in the field works, to which the little 3-pounder could be moved quickly by drag-ropes. In the very center of the en-

closure, the ammunition tumbril of the Hesse-Hanau
Artillery stood ready with its supply of rolled powder
charges. A gunner was stacking canisters of grapeshot between the wheels. On his hilltop, with his
dragoons around him, Colonel Baum felt secure.

Sensitive to everything having to do with his men,
the Colonel awoke in his tent when the first drops
of rain fell. All around him he could hear the sounds
of restless movement in the camp as the troopers and
gunners sought shelter, cursing their lot as they re-
settled themselves in the wet darkness of the night.
Colonel Baum went back to sleep; it had taken years
of just such bivouacs to earn a colonel's comforts.

When his servant wakened him with a breakfast
somehow contrived, the rain was still falling. By
nine o'clock, it was the general opinion in the German camp that the drizzle would continue throughout the day. For a while, the dragoons honed their
big sabers. Then they resigned themselves to making the best of it. Baum made the rounds of his positions. Everyone and everything was wet. Only the
women in their log cabin were really dry, but he did
not tarry there to lay himself open to the interminable questions and wrangles and complaints of
the soldiers' wives.

In his headquarters on the western edge of Bennington, General Stark was little better off. His men
were as wet as the Germans were, and during the
day and into the night of 15 August, he was harassed
by ardent militia captains, eager to "smite the hireling invaders" and to "bring vengeance on the mur-

derers of sweet Jennie McCrea." No one seemed to
consider the fact that damp powder nullified the advantage of fire power, on which Stark had counted,
although the parson who commanded the Berkshire
County militia quoted a conglomeration of biblical
passages sufficient to damp the fires of hell. The rain,
however, was giving Stark a day of grace in which
to concentrate his force. Seth Warner was with him
in his headquarters, and at the prospect of battle
Warner had sent to Manchester for his regiment of
Continentals. The troops were now somewhere along
the road, plodding slowly through the mud as the
gray day wore to a close.

While Stark's reinforcements — Vermont Continentals, with two hundred Green Mountain Rangers
— were coming the twenty-two miles from Manchester, the reinforcements that Colonel Baum had
sent for had traveled only eight of the twenty-five
miles that would bring them up to the dragoons.
They had made a good start from the mouth of the
Batten Kill. Baum's messenger had arrived in the
early morning, and by nine o'clock, only an hour after
receiving Burgoyne's orders, Colonel Breymann had
his men on the road. All of Heinrich Christoph Breymann's troops were steady, trained veterans, picked
from among the five infantry regiments of Riedesel's
Brunswick and Hesse-Hanau division. Although they
were called grenadiers, and wore the high, metal-
fronted mitre traditionally associated with that name,
their forte was the attack with the bayonet, which required close ranks and rigid discipline if it were to be

pushed home. Colonel Breymann was a disciplinarian.

Again and again, Breymann halted the colunm to dress ranks, broken by the slippery road as it climbed up the hill out of the valley of the Hudson. Patiently, the grenadiers shuffled back and forth as the sergeant moved along the ranks, lining up with out-thrust chests. When all was ready, the order to march was given, and in measured succession, the blocks of companies stepped out, to squish, slide, and stumble over the muddy track — until the next halt. Up front, Colonel Breymann could twist around in his saddle and glare at the long line of five hundred gilt or silver mitre-caps, bobbing and lurching every which way in the driving rain; he was not pleased. Behind the struggling grenadiers, Lieutenant Spangenberg, heedless of dressing, tried desperately with his gunners to keep up with the slow pace of the infantry. The road was a morass of slippery wet mud that made the two 6-pounders of his battery slew behind their limbers, while the horses, their necks bent to their collars, stumbled to their knees on the upgrades, or were in danger of a broken leg as the weight of the load shoved the breechings against their croups on a downgrade. Behind the artillery, the ammunition wagons of the column, overloaded for their construction and for the strength of their animals, fared even worse than the guns. Breymann was still seven miles short of Cambridge when he called a halt for the night. In eight hours of forced march he had covered only eight miles.

At first light on 16 August, Breymann had his men up on their feet, the sergeants shouting them into line, the officers thwacking about with their gold-headed canes. Beyond Cambridge the road was better.

On his hilltop overlooking the deserted valley of the Walloomsac, Colonel Baum waited, guessing at the cause of the delay. He sent Colonel Skene back with all his horses, as extra teams for Breymann's wagons. Still he waited, watching and listening both up and down the Bennington road.

General Stark went to the door of his headquarters and walked out into the yard. It was still raining, but it was a light, misty rain. The cloud mass was lifting above the long summit ridges of the distant mountains, which appeared clear and fresh in the gray light. Here and there on the green slopes, thin wisps of blue-white mist hurried upward, as if in fear of being left behind by the rising cover of sky. To a man of the New England hills, such flecks of cloud were a sure sign of clearing weather. Stark shouted for his drummer, and had the boy beat the Officers' Call.

They came, the lean and the portly, the young and sturdy with the big red wrists of plowmen, the middle-aged, pale from the crossroads store and the Portsmouth houses of business; men as old as the general himself, in loose uniform coats of an earlier war. All were most soldierly and earnest as they searched in their minds or memory for the correct military terms in which to report their respective commands ready. As the room settled into silence,

John Stark outlined his plan of attack on Burgoyne's scattered forces. His troops would advance two embracing arms, seemingly a friendly army made up of Tories going to join Burgoyne, until at the last possible moment, or upon discovery, the attack would be made. The arms would then embrace the enemy in the hug of the black bear. Command of the two arms was given, respectively, to Colonel Nichols and Colonel Herrick. With the main force, Stark himself would be like the jaws of the bear, snapping up the Tories across the Walloomsac and the guard at the first bridge, then bringing the two arms together on the dragoons' hill and at the Germans' rear position. To Colonel Stickney went the task of rushing the first bridge, while Colonel Hubbard, to whom was attached the Berkshire County militia under its fighting parson, was to storm the Tory redoubt on the American side of the stream.

It was crowded in the room as Stark gave his orders, and moisture rose out of the damp homespun and broadcloth of the officers' coats. As the orders droned on, first one man, then another, shed his thick coat; waistcoats and stocks soon followed, until all the listeners stood in their shirtsleeves. Gone was the thin veneer of militarism, as each New England neighbor studied and questioned his role in the coming attack. When the orders group broke up and the sweating, shirt-sleeved officers streamed out into the yard, the clouds were breaking and the heavy damp heat of the room seemed to have followed them into the summer noon.

Nichols and Herrick were the first away, having the

longest distance to travel around the hills and mountains of the army's flanks. Then, for General Stark,
began the anxious moments of unfolding his army.
Until the flanking forces opened fire he could not
move his main body forward. The sun came out, and
he fretted. His horse danced under the twitching of
his hand at the reins. At last, calling to Colonel
Warner, whose Continentals were still waiting beyond Bennington town, Stark spurred westward down
the road for a closer look at the bridge. The gun
sergeant of the Hesse-Hanau 3-pounder saw the two
officers coming on at a gallop, and gave an order
while blowing up the slow match of his linstock. He
waited for the riders to stop, then he aimed his little
gun. Stark saw the puff of smoke. He did not heed
where the shot fell, but thought better of his foolhardy boldness and, with Warner, galloped back to
where his command was readying for battle.

Baum heard the opening gun of the battle as a dull
thump, far away in the blanket of humidity. It sent
him striding to the lookout from which he could see
to the American camp, far up the valley beyond the
second bridge. From the same spot, he had seen
Nichols's men, and those of Herrick, leave camp. As
one group went north and another south, he judged
that the militia was going home. Baum could not
identify the two horsemen who dashed up to his
cannon, then dashed away again. Their image would
not hold in the long, wood-encased tube of his spyglass as he rested it across the shoulder of his personal
orderly. Though heat waves danced across the big

circle of the lens, Baum could see that one of the
"Yankee" officers was a farmer: he rode all aflap. The
other crouched over his horse's neck, like an Italian
jockey, not sitting erect, like a dragoon! Shortly after
the single cannon-shot, the colonel was called to ob-
serve to his rear, where small groups of local farmers
appeared to be coming in to join the Tory regiments,
as Major Skene had so confidently anticipated. Presently, white-shirted men were seen coming down off
the ridge to the northwest of the dragoons' log barricade. As they drew nearer, Baum could see that
among them there were a few Indians, his own scouts
bringing them in to volunteer. They were, in fact,
Stockbridge Indians from Western Massachusetts,
allies of the Americans and friends of John Stark
since the days when they had comprised the Indian
Company of Robert Rogers's Rangers. This was
Nichols's right arm of Stark's "pincer," while the
"farmers" in the valley to Baum's rear were Herrick's
men, who had already crossed the Walloomsac and
were now closing in around the Germans' westernmost post, on the road to Sancoik and Cambridge.

Nichols's men opened the fire. Baum's shocked surprise was but momentary, as instinct and training
came vaulting over the wall of error. An order from
the colonel had the dragoons back under cover of the
log barricade; a second order began their return fire
by troop volley. It was impossible for the German
commander to estimate the effect of his return fire, as
all the Yankees seemed to fall down behind rocks or
trees or into folds in the uneven ground. Fire still

came from the foot of the ridge, and, as the first excitement wore off, Baum noticed that this fire was spreading to his right in an arc that covered the whole front of his log barricade. As he continued to scrutinize the uneven ground before him, his eyes began to pick out individual rebels, betrayed by a puff of smoke as they fired, or by a white arm ill-concealed behind a boulder. His officers, too, were seeing the Yankees, and were now directing their volleys at the small individual targets. More and more single figures would rise up, run for a short distance, then dive into a new and better position. The fire onto the German position continued strong. Bullets thudded into the protecting logs, ricochets whined overhead; occasionally, a dragoon would be hit, falling back with a moan or a curse. As the fire-fight settled down to a steady exchange, Baum realized that the action had become general: all of his positions were now engaged. To the east, the colonel could see the main force of the Americans marching down the road from Bennington, led by the two officers he had noticed earlier. They were following closely behind their skirmishers, already at the bridge and at the Tory earthworks across the stream.

The fight was hottest at this last position, where it was also most bitter, for it was between neighbors. There Colonel Hubbard, with the Vermont and Massachusetts men, led Stark's attack on the rail and earth entrenchments. Burgoyne's local Tories met the onslaught of the people who had driven them from their farms and homes. Many of them knew the names of the men they were shooting at, and knew their wives and children. Tories from Pittsfield took careful aim at their former parson, who — even in battle — reviled them for their convictions and exhorted them to see the error of their ways. Little quarter was given when Stark's militiamen rushed over and around the Tory redoubt, and American faced American in the fury of hate and resentment. Both victory and hopelessness bring a quick cooling to the heat of battle, when contempt and despair take over from the elation of the victor and the fright of the vanquished. A guard led away the Tory prisoners, who carried with them their own wounded.

At the first bridge over the Walloomsac, Baum's light troops, British and Germans, fared little better than did the Tories in the redoubt. Although their aimed fire held off the skirmishers, the return fire and the threat of complete encirclement drove them back. Some retired down the road, where they ran into the confusion of the rear post, now completely surrounded by Herrick's men; others climbed the hill, pushing through the *Jägers* in the dead ground to the safety of Baum's position on the summit. Alexander Fraser found himself among the latter, assisting the wounded and weeping gun sergeant up the steep slope. Under accurate rifle-fire, the Hesse-Hanau 3-pounder had been useless, all the gunners dead or wounded; yet Fraser had to lead the sergeant away from the piece, which is an artilleryman's pride and honor and love. Fraser, too, left much behind at the bridge he could no longer hold: he left his marksmen dead, and among them his friend, Baron Salans.

Stark now moved his main force to the bridge. A

German woman lay dead on the abutment. She had run from the log house, either to avoid the leering farm boys who had captured it after the Tory redoubt fell, or she had been running to join her man. The general thought of Elizabeth Stark, his "Molly," safe at home in Londonderry, New Hampshire. He crossed the Walloomsac, dismounted, and as his soldiers crossed the river he directed them into position to assault up the hill.

In the log barricade, Baum was holding back Nichols's men to the north, but was forced to spread his soldiers more and more thinly as Herrick's men drifted into the fire-fight, having by-passed and taken the grenadiers' post on the Cambridge road. Still no reinforcements appeared. He had been engaged for two hours, and his ammunition was giving out. At the ammunition tumbril, Baum had set the officers' servants and the lightly wounded to rolling cartridges for the dragoons at the breastworks. The light troops, who had come up from the bridge, helped to fill out his lines, thinned by the accurate fire of the Yankees, and he saw green-coated *Jägers* from the slope firing shoulder-to-shoulder with his big, blue-uniformed troopers. All his positions had fallen except for the hill-top barricade, but he felt secure if only his ammunition held out until reinforcements arrived. To the north, Baum saw a white-shirted Yankee run toward the barricade, then drop from sight. From the corner of his eye he saw another rebel move forward. Were they preparing to rush him? Baum strode across for a better look through the gun embrasure.

He had drawn his long sword and was unhooking the
scabbard to hand it to his orderly, when the ammunition tumbril blew up. Propelled by the blast, Baum
pitched forward. Everyone in the barricade was
shocked and stunned. All firing ceased as the soldiers
stared in dazed wonderment at this new havoc that
had been added to the havoc of battle. It was then
that the American attack came.

They came down over the top of the logs and
around the corners of the open wings of the barricade. They came charging up out of the gullies in
the rear. They shouted and yelled, and some were
screaming the name of Jennie McCrea. The Germans
fought hard for their lives, swinging their muskets
against those of the Yankees. Some of the troopers
had out their sabers and stood at bay, fending off the
jabs of the rifle-barrels. Stones were hurled, while
men grappled together in straining silence. Overwhelmed, those Germans who could, fled down the
hill into the trees. Again on his feet, Baum gathered
about him a group of dragoons, and in some kind of
order they began to cut their way through a ring of
Yankees. They were making good progress toward
the west summit when a musket ball took the colonel
through the body. He sagged, dropped to his knees,
tried to rise, and fell heavily. All resistance ended
with the fall of Colonel Friederich Baum.

General Stark did not get to Baum's hill until the
battle was over, nor was he able to organize an immediate pursuit. When asked which way the survivors had gone, each officer pointed in a different

direction. Few had got away at all. Almost all of
Baum's Germans — dragoons, *Jägers,* light infantry,
and gunners — were dead, wounded, or dazed prisoners of war, seated under guard in their log barricade.
Most of those seen going away had disappeared into
the woods that stretched north a hundred miles to
Canada and the St. Lawrence. Stark knew that they
would wander there, lost, until they died or were
found, gibbering from their discovery of the forest's
immensity. As if in support of Stark's surmise, the
small sound made by a single shot drifted in from
the direction of the mountain. Somewhere over there,
Burgoyne's Indians were scavenging the far outer
edge of the battle.

From the prisoners, Stark learned of the looked-for
reinforcements, not yet arrived; nor was there any
sign of their approach. With his own troops scattered
and playing amid the spoils of war, he realized that
he must act at once to prevent a surprise attack
against himself. Quickly gathering a force together,
he set out in the direction of the Sancoik mill. Before
mounting, however, he sent for Warner's fresh regiment; his own men, he saw as they marched past,
were all but spent after their exertions during the op-
pressive heat of the long afternoon. Though a sparely
built man, Stark himself had sweated through his
blue uniform coat until it was black across the shoulders.

10

The Road Beside the Walloomsac

For the grenadiers of Colonel Breymann's reserve force, the march through the heat of the afternoon was agony. At the frequent halts to dress ranks, when the men straightened their high-fronted hats, the metal plates of their caps were almost too hot to touch. Sweat streamed down their faces and ran into the tight stocks at their throats. But under the harsh eye of their colonel they kept together, and only a few of the really sick dared to fall out. These now staggered on, holding onto the tailgates of the carts that brought up the rear, behind Lieutenant Spangenberg's two 6-pounders.

It took all of the morning of 16 August to cover the seven miles to Cambridge. Beyond that village, Breymann's force moved faster. At two o'clock in the afternoon they were met on the road by the draft horses which Baum had sent to them by Philip Skene. That officer had remained at the Sancoik bridges with with a handful of reliable men, to protect the bridges against possible malicious destruction. Skene asked Breymann to send a proper bridge guard on ahead, and, while the fresh horses were being hitched to the guns, tumbrils, and wagons, Major Ferdinand von Bärner led out the eighty men of his light infantry detachment. Free of the ponderous shock troops, von Bärner's quick young soldiers swung off up the road to the Sancoik mill.

At half-past four, Colonel Breymann's horse clumped over the planking of the mill bridge. Behind him, singing their dismal marching hymns, the tall, erect grenadiers were making the left turn into the Bennington road. Breymann found Skene and von Bärner on the shady side of the mill, interviewing the first escapees from Baum's battle on the Walloomsac. The men brought conflicting estimates and impressions of the battle and its outcome. A Tory said that Baum was completely cut off and was fighting for his life. A sallow British officer, who had been with the Indians, said that things were not so bad—though of course the Indians had fled. Two German officers who had been cut off from their men when Herrick infiltrated Baum's rear position concurred with the calm opinion held by the British gentleman in forest garb. As the officers talked and the column of grenadiers trudged by, a single dragoon mounted on a spent horse rode in from the east. His tale of the fighting on Baum's hill was one of woe and disaster. But as the man was only a trooper without the credentials of a courier, his word was ignored, and he himself, under suspicion of cowardice and desertion, was turned over to the provost guard at the rear of the column.

A mile up the road toward Bennington, Major Skene, now riding with Colonel Breymann at the head of the reinforcing column, appeared to have cause for his optimism. Halfway across a large field, where a rail fence snaked down from the woods, lolled a group of some twenty-odd farmers, waiting for the column to come abreast. Skene could see, pinned in each of their hats, the white paper patch of the Loyalist. Stepping his horse carefully through the muddy ditch, Major Skene gave the animal its head and a touch of the spur as it came up onto the harder ground of the field. The horse plunged ahead to go at a gallop, but was checked by Skene into a more dignified canter. Two men in stained rifle-shirts had risen up from behind the rail fence, and to the Tory leader's surprise, were aiming their rifles at him! Skene pulled hard on the reins and felt the horse sink back on its haunches, as its front feet lifted from the ground. With a sickening sensation, the Major felt his mount continue to rise under him. He was aware of the two shots, as the horse screamed and tossed its head high. The reins went loose in his hands and Skene half slid, half jumped from the saddle in time to throw himself free, as the stricken beast came crashing over and down.

On the road, von Bärner's light infantry already was in extended order to the flank and was firing on the Yankees, all of whom were now behind the rail fence. Breymann was shouting orders in harsh German, and as Skene gathered his legs under him to jump up and run for it, he could see — and as an old soldier, approve — the complicated evolution which was bringing the lead company of grenadiers into line to the front.

Safely behind the blue and white ranks of von Rhetz's grenadiers, Major Skene was scraping the mud from his clothes when Spangenberg's guns went forward on the right of the road. The Tory looked up, and over the broad shoulders of the Germans he saw that a company of rebels had deployed, with more of their fellows coming down the road behind them. The volley fired by von Rhetz's company was a foolish one; at their distance it could only waste ammunition. But as the thick, acrid powder smoke cleared slowly away in the heavy air, Skene noticed that the grenadiers had their ramrods out to reload for yet another volley. Only cannon-fire could break up the enemy formation now. Spangenberg already had unlimbered his first gun, and the crew was loading from the trail-box magazine. The other 6-pounder wheeled smartly in front of it to bring it around into alignment, gun-wheel to gun-wheel, muzzle to the enemy. A crackle of rifle and musket fire flitted up and down the rail fence where the rebels disguised as Tories first had been. Now, near where Skene's horse lay, there were other still figures. They were light infantry dead, left behind as their skirmish line went forward. But when von Bärner and his men reached the fence, the Yankees had gone.

Spangenberg's guns were now in action, and at long last the grenadiers of the von Rhetz regiment had stopped their futile volley firing and were moving forward with bayonets fixed and presented to the fore. The rebel fire had all but ceased; the rebels were now streaming back along the road by which

they had come. Skene had to step out of the road as
the next company of grenadiers came up in column.
His left hip, which had landed on the hilt of his
sword, was very painful. At the rear of the now moving column, he would get another mount; but first he
had to retrieve his saddle and bridle, and his pistols.
Skene limped out onto the field. Some of the light
infantry, now returning from their successful charge,
would help him move the dead horse.

On up the road to Bennington, Colonel Breymann
marched his men. The singing was louder now, and
the massed feet of the companies came down together on a firmer beat. On the left of the grenadiers,
the hunting horns of the light infantry sounded a confusion of attacks and recalls. Sections were sent off
at the double to drive back the Yankee riflemen, who
had dogged the column from the edge of the forest.
At the rear of the German line of march, the ammunition carts and the supply wagons fell behind the
advance, as they halted to tend the wounded and
salvage the dead, passed by in the forward press of
the German advance.

Twice, Breymann had deployed his lead company
and unlimbered his guns. Twice, the grenadiers had
followed up a thundering series of volleys with a
bayonet charge that left them, gasping for breath,
on the ground where the rebels had feigned a stand.
Fatigue and discouragement overcame Breymann's
trained regulars at the end of the long hot day. Tem-
pers blew on the gray ash of exhaustion, which flared
into jostling in the reforming ranks, loud words, and

the too quick flaying of the officers' canes. Weariness was there, too, in the closely packed mass of men, as more and more heads turned to look at the wounded and the dead beside the road. Discouragement floated up to the surface of tired spirits, ready to plunge over into panic or to soar to the sublime achievement of heroic endeavor.

John Stark's mixed force of militiamen from New Hampshire, Vermont, and Massachusetts was as fatigued as Breymann's regulars. The men tried to stand in the open and meet the oncoming grenadiers with a blast of aimed fire, but they grew wary as they saw the cannon unlimber and prepare to load. There was an omnipotence in the unity of the crashing volley-fire, causing the militiamen to duck their heads, though reason should have told them that the range was out. At last, when the line moved forward, with the low afternoon sun glinting on the ice-blue bayonets, the men of the Yankee militia scattered like lumbermen from the fall of a tree.

Twice, Stark brought the fleeing militia back into line, and twice they ran away. Not until they fell back into Colonel Warner's Continentals, coming up with the 3-pounder captured at the Walloomsac bridge, did the militia steady down and prepare to hold their line. They ranged themselves from the marshy ground by the river bank on the left, up to the road where Stark himself was loading and aiming the little 3-pounder, and on toward the open right flank, short of the woods. Behind the militia, the three hundred and fifty Continentals waited in reserve.

A quiet calm had settled, too, over all of Colonel Breymann's men, as they recognized the fast approaching climax of the day's battle. The company commanders, short of ammunition, were holding back on the volley fire, while several of the light infantry had slung their useless rifles and drawn their short curved swords.

Lieutenant Spangenberg was having trouble bringing up his guns. As the river side of the road now appeared to be marshy and soft, he had attempted to gallop the guns through the field on the left of the column. But in doing so his teams had come under fire from the rebel riflemen at the edge of the wood. The near leader of his number-one gun had been brought down in a tangled mass of horses and harness and riders. The gunners were now hauling that gun forward with drag-ropes. An off horse on the number-two gun had been wounded and was becoming unmanageable. Major Skene, who had joined Spangenberg, was reaching from his saddle for the head of the frightened beast, when, for the second time that day, his horse was shot from under him and he went down. Spangenberg himself rode in to gain control of the team, and somehow the gun was got forward into position. Undaunted, Skene had cut a gun-horse free from the number-one limber and was mounted again. The lieutenant sent him back to find the ammuntion cart and bring it up along the road. For the guns, now without teams, this was their last stand; they would need ammunition.

Before the guns could be brought into action, von Bärner had led his light infantry across the field in a flanking movement, intended to envelop the Yankees' short right wing. Warner and Stark, standing beside the American gun, saw them move out and guessed at their intention. No order was necessary between the militia general and the Continental regimental colonel; the New Hampshire and the Congress troops were now working in concert. With a swing of his arm, Warner set his Green Mountain Boys in motion. At a slow, steady jog-trot, they followed Seth Warner behind the ragged lines of the New Hampshire men, who turned to grin as their neighbors passed by. They met von Bärner's men behind the American right, and the seventy-odd German light infantry fell back under the pressure of Warner's three hundred and fifty fresh troops, themselves natural light infantrymen or rangers.

Outnumbered and outflanked, Colonel Breymann's resolve weakened as the Yankees, encouraged by Warner's fresh troops, opened a telling fire at long range. No counter-charge came from Baum. From the number of rebels harassing him, the Brunswick colonel reluctantly assumed that the troops he had been sent to reinforce had already been defeated. The single dragoon (now with the provost guard) must have been right. But not only Baum was "in great danger"; equally in danger were Breymann and his grenadiers.

Colonel Breymann gave the order to retreat. No light infantry remained to cover the grenadiers, as they fell back in their ordered blocks of companies. Von Bärner had reported to Breymann the loss of his fine corps against Warner's men. As he reported that all of his officers were casualties, he pressed his linen handkerchief against the deep wound in his chest. Spangenberg, too, was dead, and was thus spared the sight of his guns, unattended and abandoned in the gap between the retreating and the advancing armies.

For two miles, Colonel Breymann kept his grenadiers in order. Then, as the bridges of Sancoik drew near and darkness fell, the discipline by which his life was lived suddenly snapped. Somehow in the gloom the grenadiers of von Rhetz and the grenadiers of the Regiment von Specht, both of which had suffered heavy casualties, became intermixed. Shouts and orders flew about. In the other companies, a bleary-eyed officer cried "Attack!" and tried to form up his men, while a second officer, shaking off a film of torpor, shouted "Halt!" Rifle shots from the Americans, who were dogging the German retreat, poured into the confusion. A ball took Breymann in the leg. Sudden panic seized the whole corps of grenadiers. In an instant, they collapsed into a frightened mass of fleeing men. Carried along in their midst was the limping Lieutenant Colonel Heinrich Christoph von Breymann. He was badly hurt.

A few Americans followed the grenadiers over the mill bridge. But it was too dark for aimed shots, and they had used up most of their powder and ball. Then, too, the mill stream looked cool and inviting as they passed over the bridge. The day had been as hot and close as any they could remember.

11

At Headquarters

Following the Battle of Bennington (as John Stark's victory over the German mercenaries came to be known) a midsummer torpor settled over all the armies on the upper Hudson: British, American, and Sovereign New Hampshire. Victory and defeat alike seemed to be accepted philosophically by all the opposed commanders. Energy was addled, ambition brooded, and hope rested on distant eventualities.

For the cosy Baroness Riedesel, the period of military inertia that began in mid-August 1777 was a very happy time. Her family was reunited. Fourteen months earlier, she had left her home in Wolfenbüttel to follow her husband to North America. The infant Caroline had now grown into a sturdy little girl, able to walk across the lawn if she held tightly to the scabbard of her father's sword. Friederika was a shy three-year-old, while Augusta, at six, was a regal young lady who accepted as her due the homage of generals and of privates. At Fort Edward, where the baroness had made a home for her husband and her little daughters in the Red House headquarters, Gen-

eral Riedesel's duties were such as to bring him home
almost every night. Being a soldier's wife and the
daughter of a soldier, the baroness did not mind too
much the fact that all five members of her family had
to share a single small room at headquarters. She
tucked them all in somehow, and even kept an eye
on her two maids, who slept on pallets in the hall.
The general's four aides were in the house, too, and
bluff old General Phillips, who had been an easy
capture for the young and pretty baroness, was a
frequent visitor to the Red House, which served also
as commissary headquarters for the army.

Friederika Riedesel particularly enjoyed the evenings. Then, she would preside at dinner, served
under the trees beside the river; or when it rained, as
it did so often during that wet, humid summer, she
would have her faithful servant, Rockel, set up the
tables in the barn. Each night there was some new
guest, usually an officer on his way either to or from
General Burgoyne's headquarters at Fort Miller,
where the wife of an absent commissary acted as
hostess for Gentleman Johnny. After dinner the
baroness withdrew, as was proper for a lady. In her
small room, while her children slept, she mended
their clothes and hummed little gay songs to herself,
to the distant accompaniment of the men's conversa-
tion as they drank a convivial bottle under the trees
or played at cards around the big staff table in the
room below.

Baroness Riedesel was very happy. Soon enough
would come the day when the big calash which had

been made for her in Canada would be rolled out, the
horses hitched to it, and with the girls stowed safely
behind, she would climb up onto the box with the
good Rockel to follow the army once again.

Beyond the outposts of General Burgoyne's army,
twenty-six miles away at the mouth of the Mohawk
River, General Philip Schuyler was closing down his
headquarters in preparation for turning over the
command of the northern army to his appointed successor, General Horatio Gates. Into one set of boxes
Schuyler's personal staff filed the documents that told
the history of their general's two-year stewardship of
the northern frontier. On these papers would be
based Philip Schuyler's defense in the court-martial
proceedings ordered by the Congress to investigate
the fall of Ticonderoga and Burgoyne's advance to
the Hudson. In a second set of files were all the per-
manent records of the army; these would facilitate
the rapid and efficient turnover of command.

In the course of that summer of 1777, General
Schuyler's staff had packed up a succession of headquarters. The first had been at Fort Edward, where
Schuyler had stopped on learning that his lieutenant,
General Arthur St. Clair, had saved his inadequate
force by giving up the untenable forts at Ticonderoga. For this retreat, which he had taken to avoid a
stand which he knew to be hopeless, St. Clair, together with Schuyler, was to face a court-martial. It
was at Fort Edward that Schuyler set his axemen to
the destruction of the Skenesborough road, impeding

Burgoyne's march to the Hudson. There, too, John Nixon's brigade of Continentals had arrived to reinforce the northern army. Headquarters were at Fort Miller when the rear guard fell back from Fort Edward, bringing the story of Jane McCrea's murder, and the local militia began to rally as tales spread of the savagery of Burgoyne's Indians. Schuyler's staff had unpacked and packed again the headquarters boxes at Saratoga, where Philip Schuyler sadly left in the path of the British army his own lovely country house beside the river. The staff had been busy at Stillwater, where headquarters next was established.

On 8 August, the first messenger had arrived from the west, bringing word that Colonel Barry St. Leger was before Fort Stanwix, the gate to the Mohawk River valley on Albany's western approach. St. Leger's force was the now-exposed right claw of General Burgoyne's army, swooping out of the north. The next messenger told the tale of Nicholas Herkimer's drawn battle at Oriskany, on the road to Stanwix. Though gallantly fought, that encounter left the besieged garrison of Americans without help; it also put the whole Mohawk Valley in peril of an internecine war, should the Iroquois and the local Tories of St. Leger's army win through to their former homeland. In the big staff-room at Stillwater, General Schuyler had been forced to veto the contrary wish of a hostile council of his officers in order to send Major General Benedict Arnold, with Ebenezer Learned's brigade, to the relief of Fort Stanwix. Despite accusations by the New England faction that Schuyler was

deliberately, even treacherously, weakening his army
before Burgoyne's main threat on the Hudson, Arnold
dashed off eagerly to the promise of battle in the
west. Staff work was heavy on the right flank of the
American army, where Major General Benjamin
Lincoln, a New Englander like Arnold and Schuyler's loyal lieutenant, was trying to argue with John
Stark over the employment of the New Hampshire
militia and the right to command those troops.

It was a stormy headquarters that had been set up
at Stillwater, with squalls blowing from the north and
west and east to ruffle the papers on the trestle desks.
Unknown to the northern army, the terrible swift
lightning of the Continental Congress, sitting in
Philadelphia, had already been loosed, and finally
would strike down that army's dedicated general,
Philip Schuyler.

As the clerks and aides closed down his last headquarters, Schuyler, in his Albany mansion, awaited
his successor. General Gates did not arrive there until
19 August, a fortnight after receiving from Congress
his appointment to the command of the northern
army.

The only way to attain high rank in the British
army of the eighteenth century was through noble
birth, the Guards, or the influence of a patron (in
breeches or in petticoats) who was close to the
sovereign. Major Horatio Gates could count on none
of these endowments, so his career as a soldier had,
from its beginning, a well-defined ceiling. Through

bravery and ability, while still in his thirties Gates had reached the rank of major. Further than that he could not go, in a British army that was to make use of his rare capacity for efficient staff organization to bolster the careers of more highly placed men, until in time he was put out to graze on the sparse meadows of retirement. His ambition whetted by his successes in North America during the French and Indian War, Gates sold his commission in the army, tried for a worthy civil post, and once again was snubbed for his presumption. Finally, in 1772, he came out to Virginia, where he bought "Travellers Rest" and set himself up as a gentleman — albeit a colonial one.

By chance, and a snob's eye for a true aristocrat, Squire Gates happened to be calling upon George Washington at the time the latter was offered the command of the American army. Washington, who had soldiered with Gates, recognized in his guest an accomplished staff officer who would make a good adjutant general for the new army. The appointment carried the rank of brigadier general.

Gates spent the year of the siege of Boston at General Washington's headquarters, where his job with the personnel and the personalities of the Continental Army brought him into close contact with the New England leaders. With them, he developed an affinity nurtured by a common suspicion that the landed gentry sought to become a native American aristocracy.

In May 1776 Horatio Gates was promoted to major

general and sent to command the American army
then in Canada. When he sought to join his new command he found it had been driven out of Canada, a
disorganized, beaten rabble, seeking refuge in the
military territory of the northern department, commanded by the patroon Philip Schuyler. In the face
of this desperate situation, Gates and Schuyler divided the authority on the menaced northern frontier. In supreme command, Schuyler remained at
rear headquarters in Albany, maintaining liaison with
General Washington and with the Congress. Gates
commanded the troops from Ticonderoga, where he
rebuilt the morale of the shattered army, and with
the violently energetic Brigadier General Benedict
Arnold (whom Gates flattered himself he could control) had staved off a British invasion of New York
during the campaign season of 1776.

At Ticonderoga, Gates had had a taste of the
independent high command of which he had
dreamed. The true division of command on the
northern lake actually lay between Schuyler's instinctive leadership, which Gates resented, and Arnold's
driving energy, of which Gates was jealous. Gates's
contribution to the campaign had been that of a staff
officer, brilliant in matters of organization, painstak-
ing in detail, yet lacking that spark which inspires
devotion.

Horatio Gates spent the winter of 1776–77 advancing his own ambitions by ingratiating himself with
the strong New England faction of the Continental
Congress, whose military candidate he became. It

was the jealously guarded prerogative of the Congress
to make or break general officers of the Continental
Army, without reference to or recommendation from
the commander in chief. The machinations of this
system caused John Stark to resign his colonelcy on
being left off a new list of ten brigadier generals, and
resulted in Benedict Arnold's being passed over for
promotion to major general.

In 1777 the New Englanders aimed to bring down
the artistocratic New Yorker, Major General Philip
Schuyler. The attack burst into flame when St. Clair
let Ticonderoga fall to Burgoyne without a fight. It
took no cognizance of the saving of the Continental
core of Schuyler's inadequate little army. At each receding step before Burgoyne, the accusations against
Schuyler flared up anew, until they licked about the
ominous word "treason." So virulent grew the charges,
and so calumnious the rumors, that the Congress
ordered the court-martial of both Schuyler and his
lieutenant, Arthur St. Clair. By 4 August, the oily
fat worm of gossip had consumed the high reputation
of Philip Schuyler, and Horatio Gates was named to
replace him.

Two weeks later, Gates rode up to the door of the
Schuyler mansion in Albany. Accompanying him was
his aide and deputy adjutant general, Major James
Wilkinson, a soft, small young man with the fibrous
character of a clinging vine.

Neither Gates nor Wilkinson tarried long in the
correctly courteous atmosphere of Schuyler's house.
On his way upriver, Horatio Gates had no time or in-

clination to rest with the ebbing tide. The ship of his ambition lay with the army at the junction of the Mohawk and the Hudson rivers. There the vessel that Schuyler had rebuilt out of the shivered timbers of St. Clair's regiments lay anchored against the swirling flood of Burgoyne's advance.

Far away to the south, in the wide mouth of Chesapeake Bay, a British warship carried in its after-cabin another headquarters group, one which was to play a large part in the events shaping up on the Hudson River. General Sir William Howe sat down to dine with his brother, Admiral the Lord Howe. In the roadstead, awaiting the brothers' pleasure, lay a vast armada of transports with their naval escorts. Sir William Howe was on his way to invest and capture the rebel capital in Philadelphia. It was here, in the broad sea bay, that a fast dispatch boat bearing orders from England found Sir William. It was on that same day that Colonel Baum and Colonel Breymann met the Yankees on the Walloomsac.

The orders, which the General read and passed across the table to the Admiral, were fourteen weeks old. In them, Lord George Germaine, writing from London, requested Howe to co-operate with General Burgoyne's northern army. No urgency was indicated in the cabinet minister's letter. It was merely the expression, on the part of a gentleman, of a wish that, when a second gentleman's plans were quite concluded, he should go to the assistance of a third.

There were other letters from London in the newly

Lieutenant General John Burgoyne

Major General Baron von Riedesel   Brigadier General Simon Fraser

Burgoyne's Indian Conference on the Bouquet River

German Cartoon of
an American Soldier

An American Soldier
of the Continental Line

Mrs. John Nicholas Brown Collection

Burgoyne's Surrender at Saratoga, 17 October 1777

British Officer with
Light Infantry Cap

Cartoon of a
Hessian Grenadier

Mrs. John Nicholas Brown Collection

Major General Horatio Gates

Major General Benedict Arnold

arrived packet, letters that the brothers could share as they lingered over their port in the Admiral's spacious cabin. There had been a third brother, George, who was also a soldier. He was now dead, killed by a Frenchman's bullet in 1758, at that same Fort Ticonderoga which Johnny Burgoyne had recently captured from the Yankees.

The shoreline outside the cabin windows was obscured by the heat haze. When a wind rose to carry the British fleet further up into Chesapeake Bay, the two brothers would part, the General to try Washington and gain Philadelphia, the Admiral to patrol the North American coast and the West Indies.

Sir Henry Clinton was more consciously concerned with Burgoyne's descent of the Hudson River to Albany than was Sir William Howe, the commander of all British troops in North America. Clinton was in New York City with an army of four thousand regulars. Howe had left him there to hold the city and the port. In an offhand and casual way that deceptively shifted responsibility, Howe had also instructed him to aid in Burgoyne's invasion. But Henry Clinton's army was too small for him to send a part of it up the Hudson, where an American army barred the highland. He must await the reinforcements which were known to have left England in June.

So General Clinton waited, too, in his pleasant, well-appointed headquarters in New York. Through the hot month of August he waited for the troopships making the slow passage from England to New York. He waited for messengers making the dangerous journey through the rebel lines that separated him from his friend John Burgoyne. Still far out to sea the troop ships butted the North Atlantic trade winds, making slow progress. The messengers would never come; they hung from the limbs of trees with the ripening apples, the placard "Spy" pinned on their chests below the taut rope that bit deep into their necks.

The occasional courier who *did* get through gave Clinton little cause for alarm on behalf of the army to the north. Burgoyne wrote of his hope to reach Albany by 22 August. Neither British general had yet been convinced that the rebels would fight, though both had been at Bunker Hill. On 10 August Clinton had written to Burgoyne that he believed the rebellion would soon be over.

August had gone by and September was half over when a haggard messenger got through from Burgoyne to Clinton with the alarming news that the northern army was still forty miles above Albany at a place called Saratoga. Concern splashed the cool façade of Sir Henry Clinton's studied Guardsman's calm. He looked down the harbor, where for so long he had expected to see the troopships coming through the Narrows.

It was more than a week before they finally came. Clinton did not wait for the new troops to disembark and find their land legs after the three months' passage. He gathered up three thousand infantrymen and headed up the Hudson, to divert the Yankees and to assist General Burgoyne. At last, in a clear revelation of the events of an indolent summer, Clinton was making "a desperate attempt on a desperate occasion."

12

"Q" and "A"

Captain de la Naudière, immaculate except for a day's stubble awoke General Burgoyne at the Duer House headquarters as soon as word came of the defeat of Baum and of Breymann's desperate situation. Aides, their stocks hastily tied and their eyes heavy with sleep, galloped down the river road from Fort Miller to rout out the 47th of Foot, bivouacked at the mouth of the Batten Kill and therefore in closest proximity to the retreating Brunswickers. Burgoyne himself arrived in time to lead out the six companies of Wolfe's own 47th to the aid and succor of the mauled grenadiers.

Colonel Breymann met Burgoyne with punctilious correctness: a doffing of his hat and a short bow from the saddle. At the movement, a sharp stab of pain ran up the German's injured leg, but the flush in his heavy face was not that of fever. It came, rather, from the inner hurt of smoldering self-anger, of truculent self-defense, of patched-up pride, and of unexpended fury. With an inherent courtesy, Burgoyne acknowledged the greeting with a low bow, in a mark of respect which gave no hint of mockery or censure

toward the colonel of his beaten troops. Turning to
Nicholas Sutherland, the colonel of the 47th, General
Burgoyne requested him to have his regiment line
the road.

So it was that Breymann's grenadiers marched back
into the perimeter of the invasion army's camp, between the correctly respectful files of their British
comrades-at-arms. The grenadiers sang in their ranks.
In front of them Burgoyne and Breymann rode in
silence. In the rear of the German column the
wounded dragged along under the awed stare of the
stiff ranks of the 47th, who had not yet met the
Yankee rifleman. Behind the retiring army, the rutted,
muddy, pitted road wound away through the forest
to Cambridge, to the Sancoik mill, where the streams
marked a ragged cross at the edge of the Hudson
Valley, and on up the Walloomsac River into the
green hills around Bennington.

Of Baum's seven hundred and fifty men, only a
scattered handful returned to the camp of Burgoyne's
army. These were the frightened, haggard men who
had found their way through the dense woods, avoid-
ing alike the Yankee rangers and Stockbridge Indians,
and their own scalping, scavenging Indian bands.
The four guns of the Hesse-Hanau Artillery orna-
mented the tavern green at Bennington, where bound
Tory prisoners cringed under the scorn of former
neighbors, and blond German boys tended minor
wounds, turning dull, expressionless eyes to the
curious Vermonters who came to stare at the hireling
mercenaries.

Of Burgoyne's Canadian Indians, only those with scalps and loot to turn into cash returned to the Hudson. As they packed up their traps, they told the officers, who came to remind them of their promises and to urge them to stay, that the sun which once rose so bright was now obscured by dark and gloomy clouds threatening a deluge. Blaming the weather, in this obvious parable, the last of the Indian warriors who had danced on the banks of the Bouquet River now left the British army.

As the Bennington force retreated, Fraser's advance corps — already on the west bank of the Hudson — fell back. They had crossed on a bridge of rafts, and were only waiting for word from Bennington that Baum had captured the magazine of stores and the Yankee horse lines before they moved on down the Hudson to the commanding heights at Stillwater. Without the stores the advance corps could not go on, and after the torrential rains of 15 August swept away their bridge, Fraser found himself isolated and vulnerable on the western shore of the river. Lieutenant John Schank of the Royal Navy ferried them back to the east bank in a fleet scratched together from any available bateaux and scows.

While across the river, Thomas Anburey, a gentleman-volunteer accompanying the advance guard, was given the opportunity that he had sought when he volunteered to follow the army. There had occurred a vacancy in the complement of officers of the 24th Foot, which Anburey was invited to fill. He accepted the invitation with alacrity, and a brother officer lent him a hank of red-dyed horsehair to sew into his cap, and a silver epaulet for his shoulder. Once again in the old bivouac on the Batten Kill, Anburey found time to write another letter to his friend in England. The new bit of braid was ever present in the corner of his eye, as he bent over the tablet on his knee, writing of his hope of becoming the captain of a company by the end of autumn. His was the eternal optimism of the soldier: he was immortal in a dead man's shoes; death could not come to him.

Yet the end of the campaign had come for many officers and men. Of the German contingent alone, twenty-six officers were casualties of the Bennington expedition: all the dragoons, nine officers of von Bärner's light infantry and *Jäger* corps, and many cavalrymen had fallen, dead or wounded, to the long brown rifles of the "Yankees." In the days following Breymann's return, the camp was filled with men convalescing from their wounds. Colonel Breymann hobbled about, using his gold-headed cane as a staff rather than a rod, while his men, chastened after their panic, pointed out to each other the five crudely patched rents in his campaign coat, where bullets had passed him close by. Lieutenant Hannemann, his neck swathed in linen bandages, hoped that by lying very still he would recover in time to go on with the expedition. But when Captain von Geyso, who came in every day to have a flesh wound dressed, ordered him back to Canada, Hannemann could neither voice a protest nor shake his head in refusal.

For the wounded, bound for Canada, the road was

long and painful. Lieutenant Hannemann found the
jolting of the Canadian cart, returning empty, too
painful to endure, so he got out and walked. He did
not try to keep up, trusting his luggage to the driver
and only hoping to find it intact at the boat landing
on Lake George. From the point of the army on the
Batten Kill to Fort Edward, the wounded *Jäger*
walked through the British wing of General Burgoyne's army. He met work parties of the 9th, the
20th, and the 21st patching and repairing the road.
The soldiers looked at him blankly, without compassion, as though he were an alien instead of an ally.
He found German friends around Burgoyne's headquarters at the Duer House, where he rested, catching a glimpse of cool white summer dresses beside
the tea table in the shade of the tall elms.

At Fort Edward, Lieutenant Hannemann stopped
at the hospital to get a clean dressing for his neck. On
the island and on the bank of the Hudson, the army
was building up its main stock-pile, which it would
carry forward on the march to Albany. The quartermasters stood, their legs apart, checking and counting
barrels of flour and pork as squads of sweating soldiers rolled them down planks at the open tailgates
of the carts. Everyone was working hard and cheerfully at tasks which they knew to have urgent importance. Bateaux lined the river bank, while on the
shore caulkers with their wedges and mauls tamped
the long strings of greasy brown tun into the open
seams, readying still more boats for the river road.
John Schank, his white shirt open at the throat, stood
knee deep in the muddy brown water, helping a

squad of sailors launch a strange-looking pontoon. In the lee of the island, a raft of similar pontoons was anchored and moored. When completed, with timbers across their gunwales and planks spiked on top of the timbers, each pair of pontoons would make a segment of a floating bridge which would keep pace with the army and would link the two shores of the Hudson. Over Schank's bridge, the army could march across the Mohawk River, the last natural obstacle before they reached Albany.

Beyond Fort Edward, the road to Lake George was maintained and guarded by the troops of Riedesel's division. This was the critical stretch of Burgoyne's supply road. Since the western and Canadian Indians had gone home, the people who lived on farms along the poor road that followed the west bank of the Hudson had grown bold. Impromptu bands of "cowboys" under self-appointed ensigns and captains attacked any scout or foraging party from Burgoyne's army when they ventured across the river. Every British wagon-train that passed between Fort Edward and Lake George was in danger of being waylaid by a determined force of these Charlotte County rangers. To protect the convoys, Brigadier General Johan Friederich von Specht kept his headquarters at the Jones farm. There, where the road began its climb out of the Hudson Valley and entered a mountain defile, the wagonmasters would be joined by a strong escort of German infantry which would conduct them through the vulnerable pass, to the landing place at the head of Lake George.

The boat trip down the Lake George leg of Burgoyne's supply route gave Lieutenant Hannemann and the other wounded men from the Battle of Bennington a last awed look at the terrible deep woods of North America. High, steep mountains squeezed in on the narrow blue ribbon of water. The boat convoys stayed in the middle of the lake, shunning the inhospitable and seemingly deserted shores of stark, gray rock and thick underbrush that clogged the forests blanketing the mountain slopes.

Not until Ticonderoga did the road to Canada emerge from the woods. At that point European civilization began again for those who, since early in July, had been in the wild lands between the old fort and the crude way-stations on the road to Albany. To the weary men from the fighting point of the army the big vessels of the Royal Navy, anchored in the basin below the forts, gave promise of a swift passage to the city streets of Montreal.

During the last two weeks of August 1777 and in the first days of September the British post at Ticonderoga underwent a change in its character and purpose. After the battle fought on the Hubbardton road, a steady trickle of sick and wounded had found the way back to Ticonderoga, to its hospitals and the boats that would take them to Canada. The western Indians had paddled their big canoes silently under the high cliff at the tip of the Ticonderoga peninsula. Warily, the garrison had watched as the Canadian tribes paused at the landing place on their journey north. After the battle at Bennington, men of the Prinz Friederich regiment had tenderly lifted the stretcher cases who had survived the trip and had laid them on the decks of the Canada-bound vessels. Then, in late August, came Indian refugees — women and children from the Mohawk villages west of Albany, driven from their ancient homeland by the rebels after their tribal brothers, under Joseph Brandt, had fought with St. Leger's forces at the Battle of Oriskany. Burgoyne employed the refugee men as much-needed scouts; the others he sent on the long, weary trial to a new home in Canada.

About 1 September the last of the reinforcements for General Burgoyne's army left Fort Ticonderoga on their way south. These were culls from the regimental rear parties which had been left at Montreal. Men who in June had been thought too old or too feeble to march with the proud battalions now, in September, appeared able and fit to the man-hungry colonels of wan and slim battalions, anxious to keep their place in Burgoyne's line of battle.

Not many days after the final draft of reinforcements went through to the army on the upper Hudson, the last shipment of supplies from Canada was unloaded at the wharves at Ticonderoga. With the expediting of this final cargo, Fort Ticonderoga and its garrison reverted to a purely military role. Stevedores went back to being soldiers, cargo checkers again became drill sergeants, and officers moved out from the cool shade of the quarters to reappraise defense positions and to lay out new fields of fire. On down the supply line, the last cart was packed, the last bateau loaded, and one by one the transhipping points were closed down. When a sweating carter at Fort Edward rolled the last barrel of flour to the tailgate of his wagon, and remarked to the two privates who reached to ease the barrel down that this was "the one we've been looking for," Burgoyne's army was completely and finally cut off from its Canadian base.

General Burgoyne had cast himself adrift. He now floated in a hostile sea, with no friendly relieving feature on a nearby horizon toward which to steer. Between his army and Canada there remained only the sprawling complex of forts at Ticonderoga and a small post on Diamond Island, stepping-stones along the long way he had come. On their tight island, the two companies of the 47th invited a neutralizing raid by "cowboys" from the west bank of the Hudson. Even the great fortifications at Ticonderoga were vulnerable to Yankee attack. There, Brigadier General Henry Watson Powell, humorless but confidently tenacious, had been left with two weak regiments. With his main strength across Lake Champlain on Mount Independence, Powell kept watch on the slopes to the eastward, where Warner's Continentals and Stark's New Hampshire men threatened to scythe around Burgoyne.

Burgoyne knew that, between himself and Albany, the American army, now under a defensive General Horatio Gates, was digging in across his way. Of what was taking place beyond and behind the rebel lines he knew nothing at all. The long-expected word that Sir Henry Clinton was marching up the Hudson to the aid of the northern army failed to come. Couriers, sent out to meet the general coming from New York, turned back, unable to find a way through or around Gates's army. No spies came to the camp above the Batten Kill with rumor or gossip on which to base either hope or despair. Burgoyne drifted in a silent sea, with no echoing answer to his cries for help.

One messenger *did* get through to the Duer House at Fort Miller. He was an Indian from St. Leger's force, besieging Fort Stanwix, but the dateline of the letter that he handed to the general read "Oswego, 27th August," and Johnny Burgoyne needed to read no further to know that Barry St. Leger had fallen back.

Neither bluff nor threats had been able to bring about the capitulation of Fort Stanwix. St. Leger had run regular siege approaches to within a hundred and fifty yards of the fort. With a mine ready to be laid under the northwest bastion, St. Leger's Iroquois, surly and dissatisfied since the Battle of Oriskany, had mutinied. Two hundred Indians had deserted in a body, but those that remained had demanded that the siege be raised, while rumors spread that the invincible Benedict Arnold was coming with an army that could be numbered only with the leaves in the trees. As St. Leger deliberated with his British and Tory officers, the Indians ran amok. They pillaged the tents of the officers and menaced the soldiers. The council of war broke up with the officers hurrying

to rejoin their units, which already were running
away, as much to escape their own Indian "allies"
as from fear of the supposed approach of Arnold.

From Oswego, on Lake Ontario, St. Leger wrote
that he was hastening with his troops, to put them
under Burgoyne's command. But the general on the
upper Hudson knew that it was four hundred weary
miles to Oswego, and that long before Barry St. Leger
and his seven hundred regulars and Tories could
come up to him he must either be in Albany or
climbing back up his severed supply line into safe
and secure winter quarters.

John Burgoyne never seriously considered a retreat. As a soldier, his orders were as clear to him,
and as enduring, as a fife tune: he was to force his
way to Albany, where he was to put himself under
command of General Howe.

After the failure to capture stores and horse-trans-
port at Bennington, Burgoyne was four weeks in
building up the twenty-five days' supplies which he
deemed necessary to carry the army to Albany. At
last, on 11 September, all was in readiness. Wagons
were packed, boats were loaded, and Schank's floating bridge was anchored across the Hudson. Von
Specht's brigade had rolled its blankets and moved
to Fort Edward. Baroness Riedesel still had the last
of the children's clothes hanging on the line; when
the order came to move out, her maid would quickly
gather them up, and the children would have clean
clothes all the way to Albany. The commissary's wife,
in her gray traveling dress, sat by the fire in the de-

serted Duer House headquarters. Gentleman Johnny had gone to his field headquarters on the Batten Kill, leaving her with her baggage wagons and his own. She would dine alone, unless a staff officer should come back on some errand and join her.

13

Reconnaissance

During the afternoon of 11 September, the rain, which had been threatening, began to fall. The preparatory order to move out was cancelled. The six thousand men of General Burgoyne's army went into bivouac along the ten miles of road that lay on the east bank of the Hudson from the Batten Kill to Fort Edward.

The following day, the army woke to a steady drizzle. Stiff and cold, the men (and the women) cursed the land in which they found themselves, cursed their lot as soldiers, and cursed the enemy that stood in their way to the comfortable billets awaiting them in Albany.

John Schank spent the day pacing the planks of his floating bridge as though it were a quarterdeck. While his crew of sailors bailed out the pontoons, the land-locked naval officer kept a close watch on the taut anchor cables that held his odd-looking command firmly in place across the current. He had lost one makeshift bridge to the torrential summer rains of August. Now every drop of rain splashing on the flat waters of the Hudson River seemed to threaten, for a second time, the engineering feat that Schank had accomplished. The present structure was so contrived that, should the flood rise on the river above, Schank could quickly disconnect the segments and float them out of harm's way until the spate of water had passed. But the rains of September differed from the August deluge. They were cold and silent, penetrating and harsh, and they lay on the land like the snows which they presaged.

The rain stopped during the night, and before the guard corporal woke the drummers whose din began the army's day of march, the sentries had seen the stars come out all over the sky. The road dried quickly in the warm sun, and before noon the first contingent moved out onto the bridge. Most of the men in the army saw their general that day. Gentleman Johnny Burgoyne stood on the high bank on the west side of the Hudson, his constant aide, Sir Francis Carr Clarke, beside him, taking the salute of the colonels as they came up, all grinning, onto the new and hopeful side of the river. As the companies streamed by, they cheered Burgoyne, who waved the plumed and crested cap which, like them, he was wearing, and called back the watchword of the day: "Britons never retreat!"

General Phillips rode up and dismounted to watch Captain Thomas Jones bring his brigade guns off the bridge. Each gun and limber-team in turn trotted out on to the planking. As they reached the far shore the drivers lifted their teams into a rattling gallop and, with whips flaying, brought their limbers and guns up the steep cut to the top of the bank, mud flying, harness chains ajingle. On the road, the wild-eyed horses were reined into a steady trot to close up with the red-coated infantry, and to clear the bridgehead for the next gun to cross over the Hudson.

Baron Riedesel kept his German contingent on the east shore for two more days. Two miles down the west shore, the British had come to Saratoga, and to a rich bounty which they paused to gather. At Philip Schuyler's country seat the harvest was full. Fields of ripened wheat quilted the wide folds of the highlands around the house, and eight-foot stalks of maize, like rustic soldiery, ranked row upon row along the side of the road to Albany. In the deserted farm sheds, the racked scythes, flails, sickles, and husking knives awaited the harvesters. At the mill on Fish Creek the stones were in place, lacking only the miller's hand on the gear-lever, and that of his assistant to open the hopper-gate.

On 14 September, soldier-farmers worked throughout the long day to reap Philip Schuyler's harvest. Threshers and winnowers toiled on the threshing-floor. While the sergeant-miller filled sacks with bread flour, huskers shucked ears of maize for the poor hungry horses of the army's train.

The newly commissioned officer of the 24th Foot found the picquet guard that night a vantage point for reflection. In the course of a single day Lieutenant Anburey had witnessed the pillaging of a rich and prosperous estate. From his place in the first surge of a victorious advancing army he could view philosophically the devastation "attendant on war." But Anburey, the young gentleman from London, during that day of harvest had ignored, or had not seen, that quarter of the plantation where the wheat lay scorched by fire. The night now hid the blackened acre where, with the torch of resistance in her own hand, Kitty Schuyler had tried to burn her home and the yield of her husband's land.

On the morning of 15 September, the close ranks of the German contingent crossed to the west bank of the Hudson. After them came the gun park in reserve, guarded by the 47th Foot. Baron Riedesel did not see his baroness that day, though he was told that her big calash had come safely across the river with the baggage wagons before the floating bridge was broken into its component parts. It would be floated downstream with the store bateaux and would keep pace with the army.

At Saratoga the German general took his division's station along the river road, on the left of the British. Smartly, he deployed a regiment to his right, to make contact with the left of Hamilton's British division. On the rising land further to the right, Fraser's corps had the responsibility of the army's open flank, resting in the woods. While he made secure his own position in the battle line, Riedesel learned that Burgoyne himself, with General Phillips and General Fraser, had taken forward two thousand men and four cannon on a reconnaissance of the roads and clearings that lay ahead toward the enemy.

Johnny Burgoyne was out all day, and evening found him two miles in front of the main position. The woods were quiet, the cabins deserted. Almost gaily, Burgoyne called up Captain Thomas Jones and ordered him to fire the evening gun for the army then and there, to give the illusion of its being well forward of where, in fact, it was. Captain Jones stood quietly behind the unlimbered piece. He was a veteran of Benedict Arnold's night attack on Quebec. When the gun was reported ready, Jones nodded his consent to fire. The report was still echoing through the woods, and the gunners were still stamping out the little fires, started among the dry autumn leaves by the muzzle blast, when Jones gave the order to limber up and follow back to camp.

Another officer who had been at Quebec in the swirling snow of New Year's, 1776, heard Burgoyne's evening gun. He was Daniel Morgan, the rifleman leader, whom George Washington had sent north with his corps in August to bolster the northern army of the Americans. On the evening of 15 September Morgan was commanding an escort of his riflemen back to the American lines. They had been out all day with Horatio Gates, who — like Burgoyne — was making a personal reconnaissance toward the enemy.

In taking over from Philip Schuyler the command of the northern department, General Gates took onto his own sloping shoulders the full responsibility for stopping Burgoyne's march to Albany. In his head,

behind the wizened, bespectacled face of an old
grandfather, must be found the plan to halt the British invasion from Canada before it made a junction
with Sir Henry Clinton's forces. To this enormous
challenge to the new nation and to his own reputation, Gates brought a supreme self-confidence in his
own ability. He was sure of his method: the painstak-
ing staff system he had learned and mastered as an
ambitious British officer. He had proved the efficacy
of this method in 1776, when on this same northern
frontier in the short space of a summer he had halted
an American retreat at Ticonderoga, rebuilt a beaten
army into a proud force, created an American fleet
on Lake Champlain, and had erected a strong defensive position out of the old French fort at Ticonderoga, while extending the fortress system across the
lake to Mount Independence.

Gates's strategic plan for the campaign of 1776 had
proved out. By forcing a naval race on the British,
he had left no time for General Carleton and General
Burgoyne to try the defenses at Ticonderoga. But for
Horatio Gates himself this successful campaign had
been a disappointment. He had been forced to share
credit for the victory with Philip Schuyler, nominal
commander of the northern department of the army.
Even the accolade of fame had eluded General Gates,
snatched from him by his erratic brigadier Benedict
Arnold. In directing disobedience of Gates's orders,
Arnold had fought a dazzling naval battle to climax
the summer campaign. In this battle the American
fleet had been defeated and — for the purpose of any

subsequent campaign — had been destroyed, but it
was Arnold's strange genius that he emerged as the
hero of the battle and the undoubted victor on Lake
Champlain.

In 1777 General Gates had to repeat the campaign
of the previous year, but with a difference which to
some degree compensated for the short space of time
remaining to him in which to accomplish his ends.
By 19 August 1777, when Gates took up his position
of command behind the headquarters desk, the American army already had been rebuilt. No one was more
aware of this than Gates's adjutant general, James
Wilkinson. In two years of war Wilkinson had ingrati-
ated himself into the favor of three successive generals — Brigadier General Arnold, Major General St.
Clair, and the army commander, General Gates —
with such success that he now stood before Horatio
Gates's desk, at twenty years of age, an adjutant general and a lieutenant colonel. It was as aide-de-camp
to Arthur St. Clair that the young officer had endured
the night escape under Burgoyne's guns on Sugar
Loaf. From his position close to the general, Wilkinson knew that, of the two thousand Continentals at Fort Ticonderoga on 5 July, many had been
casualties at the Battle of Hubbardton. He himself
had been a casualty of the attrition that accompanies
a retreat, but had turned up again on the strength
of the newly reconstituted northern department, in a
position to ride with an ascending star. The muster
rolls which, Wilkinson, as adjutant general, showed
to Horatio Gates at the end of the third week of

August put the strength of the American northern army at six thousand men — Continentals and effective militia.

Only four thousand, however, faced Burgoyne along Schuyler's last defensive line at the mouth of the Mohawk River. Benedict Arnold, now a major general, was with Learned's brigade, successfully turning back St. Leger's threat on Albany from the west. He would not return with his men until the first week in September. Benjamin Lincoln was to the east, where, since the Battle of Bennington, he had been organizing a strike at Burgoyne's rear, and trying to persuade John Stark to join Gates's army — or, failing that, to move in closer onto Burgoyne's flank. Stark would do neither, preferring, as was his right, to sit out the expiring short-term enlistment of his brigade on its victorious battleground. Later, if the spirit moved him, Stark would take his own opportunity to strike a blow at Burgoyne.

On the way, but not yet arrived on the Mohawk River, was Colonel Daniel Morgan's hardy regiment of Continental riflemen. Gates knew Morgan from Washington's winter camp in New Jersey, and from the early days of the Revolution when, as Washington's adjutant general, he had assigned the riflemen to Benedict Arnold's force against Quebec. Gates now had to fumble in his memory for a picture of a nineteen-year-old wagoner named Morgan, who had shared with him the disaster of Braddock's defeat. In the mess gossip of the old war there had been the incredible story of the provincial who, quite

justly, received five hundred lashes for daring to
strike back at a British officer who was chastising
him. The provincial had been the same Daniel Morgan whom Gates now eagerly awaited to round out
his northern army. Morgan was a broad-shouldered,
deep-chested man, who carried the welts and stripes
of his flogging under the hunting shirt he habitually
wore as uniform. His face was scarred by an Indian
arrow which had penetrated into his mouth, to leave
its mark on Morgan's naturally slurred, soft Virginia
speech. To carry his orders to his scattered regiment,
Morgan used a wild turkey call which became the
pride and spirit of his regiment of rifle-armed marksmen.

Morgan's arrival on the Mohawk with but three
hundred and thirty-one of his men was a disappointment to Gates. The remaining one hundred and sixty-
nine of the expected five hundred were sick. To
bolster the riflemen, whom Gates proposed to keep
under his own direct command as an advance corps,
Major Henry Dearborn, with two hundred picked
light infantrymen, went under Colonel Morgan's
command. Like Morgan, Dearborn had made the
overland march to Quebec, so when Arnold returned
from Stanwix he found in Horatio Gates's army two
aggressive troop commanders waiting to greet him.

With six thousand reliable troops, Gates was an
even match for Burgoyne's regulars. But in the valley
of the upper Hudson there was no fort such as Ticonderoga on which Gates could build his defense and
thus gain the advantage. From his scouts and civilian

spies he knew that Burgoyne's supplies were limited, and that the cold mornings of a northern September would force his British opponent to move on to his objective of Albany, if only for use of that city as winter quarters. Gates, who was a patient, calculating officer, saw his advantage and success in field works, at which the Americans were adept, and against which the British must wear themselves away.

With Schuyler's northern department General Gates had inherited a serious-minded Polish military engineer of proven competence, Thaddeus Kosciusko. Before the American army had fallen back to the Mohawk River, Kosciusko had run his lines and driven the stakes for a defense at Stillwater. On 8 September, Gates's army set itself to the eleven-mile march to Stillwater. With their muskets, the men carried shovels and picks. Their step was light and gay as — at long last — they advanced against the brutal "macaroni," Burgoyne of the bloody hatchet. They cheered the elderly General Gates as he rode along the line of march, and shouted their approval to the bearded rifleman of Dan Morgan's corps, standing under a pine tree and exhibiting to all who passed the scalp of an Indian that he had taken only the day before.

At Stillwater the Americans grounded their arms and stood about with their tools in their hands, waiting to be told where to begin their digging. But Gates had gone on ahead with his Polish engineer, his staff, and his escort, in search of another place to build his fortifications. At Stillwater the river bank

was so wide and gently sloping, and the cleared fields
so extensive, as to favor Burgoyne's strong complement of well-served cannon, and to invite the terrible omnipotence of a disciplined bayonet charge
by trained European troops. On 12 September, the
American army moved three miles closer to the
enemy, onto the ground which they would fortify,
and where they would make their stand.

On a narrow strip of flat land between the river
and the hills rolling up to the western forest, a man
named Bemis had built a tavern at the juncture of
two roads. The main road followed closely along the
west bank of the river, pressed there by a parallel
series of high, moundlike hills, cut through by a
maze of deep gullies. A road on the left climbed
steeply from the river to John Neilson's farm on
Bemis Heights. Half a mile before coming to the
Neilson house, the road forked again, the western
track ambling off through the woods, the north road
passing the farmer's house and barn and skirting the
high land between the gorges, to Freeman's farm. A
complex of cart tracks cut through the gullies and ran
over the hills from Freeman's farm to the Hudson
River. North of the farm there was a wide depression,
known as the Great Ravine. A road, coming up from
the river bank, lay along the north edge of the Great
Ravine and joined the Neilson-Freeman road half a
mile beyond the latter farm.

Horatio Gates had come to his battlefield. Planning
carefully, Gates projected the course of the defensive
battle he expected to force on General Burgoyne.

Field works of earth, faced with logs, would be thrown up in depth across the narrow river plain where it defiled at Bemis's tavern. Other field works would rise on the eastern slopes of Bemis Heights, enfilading the river road which, being the only good road from the north, must inevitably be the center line of Burgoyne's advance with his baggage train and gun park. American cannon placed in the works could deny the river to the British boats. Standing on the heights with his engineer, Gates traced out additional fortifications, following the contour of the land away from the river to Neilson's big barn. This barn he fortified, before turning the lines once again to form a three-sided box facing north, with its strength dominating the river plain.

From the high ground at Fort Neilson, Gates looked down across open ground to the ravine-cut woods and hills — cruel country through which to advance. Again, Gates's British-trained eye wandered off toward the river road, where he had set Nixon's, Glover's, and Paterson's brigades to digging. Here, behind their field works, Gates felt confident that his Continentals could hold the main advance of European regulars. On either side of Fort Neilson (as the barn was now referred to), Brigadier Generals Learned and Poor, whose men formed the division under Arnold, dug in to guard against the approach of a flanking column coming in from the scattered clearings around the Freeman farm.

As General Gates had anchored his right on the Hudson, so his left was firmly tied to the barrier of

the impenetrable woods, fit only to be a playground
for wolves and bears and catamounts, and for Gates's
own wild riflemen. Into this dark region Gates found
himself led on 15 September. There was much work
yet to be done on the lines, and at headquarters his
desk was piled high with letters and papers requiring his attention. As he rode along the trail
beyond Freeman's farm, with Morgan padding on
moccasined feet beside his stirrup, the crafty American general had many things to think about and
many decisions to make. All along the line of field
works the engineers needed his prodding; a mass of
reports and orders awaited his signature. The militia,
goaded by Lincoln and stirred by the murder of
Jane McCrea, were beginning to come in, eager to
fight but without supplies or any plan of action.
Then, there was the correspondence with the haughty
Sir John Burgoyne, and this Gates relished. Burgoyne
had written to him, under a flag of truce, complain-
ing of the treatment of Tory prisoners after the Battle
of Bennington. Gates had replied to "The Famous
Lieutenant General, the Fine Gentleman . . . the
Soldier and the Scholar," with a taunt for every scalp
taken by an Indian in the pay of the British, and a
sneer for the murderer of Jane McCrea. Perhaps,
while he was in the woods with Dan Morgan, another letter would have arrived from Burgoyne.

As the afternoon wore on, Gates, too long away
from his headquarters, gave the order to turn back.
Morgan spluttered into his turkey call, and the scouts
came in and silently fell into line behind their colonel.

Then, over the tree-tops to the north, came the hollow boom of Burgoyne's evening gun. The two officers, who had been together in the woods at Braddock's defeat, stopped to listen. In the stillness that followed, they quickly made their way back to the fortified American camp — Gates to his tent, Morgan to detail the night's offensive patrols.

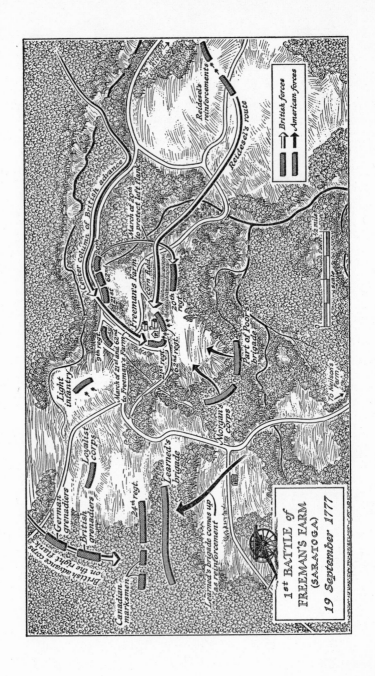

1st BATTLE of
FREEMAN'S FARM
(SARATOGA)
19 September 1777

British forces
American forces

14

To the Sound of the Guns

For six days Burgoyne's army crawled southward down the west bank of the Hudson. Moving, as it did, in a tight little enclave, it was confident. The main body of the troops did not feel the presence of the enemy. The army lived and moved as much unto itself as did the porcupine it met along the road, which, when prodded with a musket, lashed out and then, with quills raised and head down, moved on in the direction it had been going.

The army was indignant and affronted, therefore, rather than apprehensive when an unarmed party digging potatoes from an abandoned patch was ambushed by Yankees, who killed or wounded thirteen men.

The whole army knew by morning, and talked all day, of the fire that destroyed the Aclands' tent, on the campground of the advance corps. Everyone sympathized with the gentle Lady Harriet over her loss, and the officers expressed their admiration for the gallant major, who, not knowing that his pregnant wife had managed to escape, rushed back into the burning marquee to rescue her. The soldiers congratulated the Aclands' servant for having pulled the major out by the ankles, offered him a pipe of tobacco, and joked with him about his not having been sure *whose* ankle he had grasped! Though clothing of any kind was scarce, and the officers had brought no warm clothes with them below Skenesborough, somehow the Aclands were outfitted, and the major, his head and hands swathed in wet bandages to soothe his burns, marched out with the grenadiers on 17 September.

Headquarters was made that night at Sword's house, two miles north of Bemis's tavern, and remained there all the following day, while the supply train came down by road and river, bringing the hospital with it. Burgoyne found it necessary to keep with the army the sick and wounded and the convalescent. To leave them in the comfortable houses and barns at Saratoga was to give them over to pillage and reprisal at the hands of the irregular Yankee "cowboys," whom Captain Fraser and the fifty Iroquois Indians now with the expedition reported as prowling and scavenging close behind the army. To leave a hospital behind meant leaving behind surgeons and mates to tend the patients, and Burgoyne could not spare this skilled personnel.

Heavy casualties could be expected when the British army butted through the American defense line which, Burgoyne's intelligence informed him, was building at Stillwater, three miles beyond the defile at Bemis's tavern. The Yankees, harassing the British front and flank in the woods, already had been iden-

tified as Morgan's men, and there were those in Burgoyne's army who regretted that prisoner-of-war
Morgan had scorned the colonelcy offered to him in
Quebec by General Carleton. Others of Burgoyne's
officers corps had known Gates before he turned his
coat from red to blue. Burgoyne himself had seen
Arnold through his spyglasses from the deck of His
Majesty's schooner, the *Lady Maria*. On 13 October
1776, the Yankee general-commodore had appeared
as a wild, whooping figure under a red-and-white
gridiron flag, laying the long stern-gun of his galley,
the *Congress*, on any British ship that drew too near.
Burgoyne expected to meet Benedict Arnold again
in the autumn of 1777.

At dawn on 19 September, Burgoyne's artillery
prepared to move out with the army on its day's
march toward an enemy still indistinct. A thick, pale
thin mist of autumn hung over the river bank, making
strange shapes of the gun teams. Drivers were poking
about in the boxes of the troop carts and in ammunition boxes, in search of hidden ears of corn with
which to coax a little more snatch and haul out of
their tired animals during the day's work that lay
ahead. Men and horses, both blanketed against the
cold of the night that persisted into the new day,
moved slowly in the heavy mist. Not until the sun
rose high enough to burn away the mist, and, like a
bold picquet, drive off the scouting cold of the approaching winter, would the army march off toward
Albany.

At his tent in the army headquarters area, Major

Griffith Williams, commander of Artillery, awaited
the arrival of his breakfast and of his gunner captains. One by one, the latter emerged from the mist,
slouching or moving briskly according to each individual's mood of the morning: Pausch, the German, in his big cloak, all military; Thomas Jones,
glancing impatiently at Pausch, whom he could not
understand and of whom, as befitted a Welshman,
he was suspicious; Ellis Walker, who had taken the
12-pounder up Mount Defiance; and finally, John
Carter, who had commanded the gunboats on the
dash up to Skenesborough, and who was now in command of the gun park which followed the regiments.

Of these captains, each of the first three commanded the guns attached to a column of Burgoyne's
advance. Pausch was going with Riedesel's German
wing of the army, following the river road. Walker
had under command six Royal Artillery guns and
two of the Hesse-Hanau gunners. He marched with
Fraser's corps, to which had been attached Breymann's grenadiers. His would be the longest march,
following the road westward along the north side of
the Great Ravine to Freeman's farm, to protect the
right flank. Captain Jones was in support of Brigadier
Hamilton's British brigade, which would follow after
Fraser but would turn off by a track which led more
directly through the Great Ravine to Freeman's farm,
and the road to Neilson's barn on Bemis Heights.

Before the artillery orders group broke up, General Phillips, a gunner all his life, joined these
kindred souls. Since August, as second in command

of the expedition, he had taken direct command of all supplies, and in that capacity he would follow Riedesel along the river road on the march of 19 September. From that position, he could best judge the moment to call up Captain Carter's reserve of guns when, as was expected, the German wing met the main line of rebel resistance and their strongest fortifications on the flat river plain. General Burgoyne himself would command the center, with which he intended to turn the Yankee left.

The sun showed as an orange disc through the mist before the captains returned to their batteries of guns, and Major Williams's servant dared to announce the morning meal. It was ten o'clock before the three columns of the British army moved out. Pausch, riding with his lead section of guns, had a fair view across the Hudson and the flat plain beyond. Riedesel's column had halted while the leading regiment of infantry patched a section of the road that led through the swamp to a bridge, also in need of repair. As the Hessian captain looked across the river, a flash of sunlight showed on the crest of a tree-covered mountain humped up into the sky. The flash showed again. It was the glint of sunlight on polished metal — a basin, perhaps, or even a mirror — as though a Yankee militiaman were shaving. When once more the German column was halted, to repair another bridge destroyed by the retreating Americans, again the flash of light could be seen on the distant mountain. Pausch and Riedesel knew it now for what it was: heliograph signals from Ameri-

can scouts to the American commander somewhere
up ahead. From the urgency of the flashing, the
rebels could not be far away.

The bridges having been repaired, the German
division had come to a long stretch of straight road
and was stepping out smartly to the music of the
bands. Shortly after one o'clock the German column
halted again, and the jangle of harness and the
rumble of wheels on the bridge planking was stilled.
Pausch could hear the sound of distant musket fire,
inland away from the river, where he judged that
Fraser's column, with Colonel Breymann, would be
turning into the road parallel to the one he himself
was following. Almost at once, one of the baron's
aides appeared, requesting that two cannon be sent
forward.

Pausch himself took the two leading guns, each
with its ammunition tumbrils and carts of tools, and
pressed forward. The infantry fell away to the sides
of the road to let him pass. Near the head of the
column, Riedesel's aide led Pausch into a narrow
side road and up a small hill onto a flat table-land,
where he found Riedesel looking toward the west.
The sound of firing was crisp.

An aide quickly appraised Captain Pausch as to
the disposition General Riedesel had made of his
division. Two German battalions were deployed along
the original line of march, with two companies of
Rhetz's regiment pushed a little forward, to occupy
a small hill dominating the river road. In moving up
onto the plateau and calling for two guns, not only

had the baron rounded out the German position but had placed himself in readiness, if called upon, to go to the aid of the British. As Pausch could see, Riedesel's relief force was made up of the general's own regiment, together with the two remaining companies of Rhetz. The men were sitting on the grass, not at ease in the companionable relaxation of a halt on the march, but very calmly, their muskets in their hands, waiting. These men had been in North America for two campaigns without coming face to face with the enemy.

Now the firing in the west seemed to be drawing nearer. The tableau of officers, gathered around their general yet apart from him, heard the volley fire that marked the change of position of the British line to its rear, while the Yankee fire, loose and indiscriminate surged up into a frenzy. The cannon, too, fell silent as the German officers looked to each other for confirmation as to the implication of a British retreat.

General Riedesel turned quickly to his commanders, gave them the order to advance, and without further delay, set out along the track across the plateau toward the sound of musketry. The infantry scrambled to their feet. Pausch found his artillery train restless and eager, the horses sidling and tossing their heads before the drivers could get them to lunge into their collars.

Across the plateau, where the road dipped down into a ravine, Riedesel halted his column. While the infantry deployed into a defensive position, Pausch sighted his guns, ordering his gunners out to throw

down a rail fence which offered cover for the "Yankee" riflemen. Patrols of three and four men each
were sent out to locate the enemy, and when Pausch
rode up to report his guns in position, he found
Riedesel instructing his aide, Captain Geismar, to
ride to Burgoyne with word that he, Riedesel, was in
position and ready to assist. Quietly, Pausch ordered
his wagonmaster, who was well mounted, to follow
Geismar and to find the best possible traverse of the
gully for the guns and carts of the train.

So General Riedesel's relief force waited out the
afternoon, while the noise of battle thundered less
than a mile in the distance.

Beyond the spot where Captain Pausch marked
the course of battle by the sound of Captain Jones's
6-pounders, and on the other side of the gunsmoke
that trailed lazily above the tree-tops, Captain
Walker's brigade of guns was silent. There was no
field of fire in the thick woods, where General Fraser
had put his corps into a defensive position on a
height of land half a mile to the west and north
of the embattled British center. Fraser had taken up
his position soon after hearing the first fire. The
height appeared to him as the key to the right wing
of the whole advance; from it he could also counter-
attack into the flank of the Americans attempting to
turn the British center. Already, at the very first fire,
Fraser had sent a reinforcement of two companies
of the 24th to assist the center.

Lieutenant Thomas Anburey found himself at the

rear of his company, jogging down the forest road toward the sound of musket fire. With his left hand he held his sword scabbard free of the ground. In front of him were the backs of his men, their muskets held high at the port; the empty bayonet scabbards, bullet pouches, and barrel-like water bottles bobbed in unison at their hips. Close behind him, the lead team of Lieutenant Dunbar's gun pressed closer. Anburey half turned as he ran, shouting at the driver to keep his distance. The driver's arm was raised, as was Dunbar's, in a signal to halt. As the lieutenant ran into his own rear rank, he heard rifle fire to the front, answered by a volley from the leading company of the 24th. The commander of Anburey's own company already had given the order to form on the right. Now the company was advancing in a scythe-like sweep to the right. A brown figure seemed to flit, sparrow-like, between two bushes. Anburey thought it one of the Mohawks, then realized that what he had seen was a Yankee rifleman. Some of the men were firing their muskets at the brown people they saw moving away. Officers and sergeants were cursing the nervousness of their men. Anburey saw his first man killed in action, and with all the incomprehension of a soldier at his first battle, he thought it odd that his friend, Lieutenant John Don, should leap so high in the air, then fall in a heap to the ground.

Bursting through a screen of red-gold leaves, Lieutenant Anburey came upon a strange sight. On the ground sat a Yankee rifleman, calmly paying out paper money from a black leather wallet to a soldier

Anburey recognized as General Fraser's batman. Both men were smiling. On seeing the lieutenant the Yankee stopped for a moment to explain that the batman not only had saved him from capture by the Indians but had managed to retrieve his wallet, containing (among other things) his commission. Politely, the American introduced himself as Captain Van Swearingham of Morgan's Riflemen — and a prisoner, of course, of the lieutenant of the 24th.

Quiet had come over that part of the battleground on which Anburey and his prisoner stood. Dunbar came sauntering up and joined them. When Anburey's servant found them he had the lieutenant's flask, from which, as they talked, each of the three officers drank in turn. While Van Swearingham was promising the two Englishmen much more "business" before the day was over, heavy firing again broke out in front of the picquet of the advance corps. Dunbar ran off to rejoin his gun, and Anburey, too, hurried to where his men waited in rank. The Yankee captain watched them go; then, with his escort, he set out for the rear. If he was recaptured, as he might well be, for the woods were saturated with Morgan's men, he would get back his long brown rifle with its carved patch-box cover that he loved so well. The British soldier carried it in his left hand, behind the point of balance, and Van Swearingham feared that he would ram the lips of the muzzle into the rough forest floor.

It was Major Gordon Forbes of the 9th Foot, who, with the picquet of Burgoyne's center column of the

British army, early that afternoon made the first contact with Colonel Morgan's Riflemen. The four regiments of British regulars, with Jones's brigade of
guns, had entered the gully during the morning,
crossed the millstream on a bridge which they found
to be intact, then climbed up to high ground. There,
with advance sentries out, the regiment had waited
for an hour, to give Fraser time to march the wide
circle around, and to come on to the right flank of
the army.

About one o'clock, Burgoyne ordered the three-
minute guns fired as a signal to Riedesel and Fraser,
and so began the advance. Coming out of the woods,
Major Forbes deployed his hundred men for the advance on the Freeman farmhouse. Immediately he
came under aimed rifle fire from his objective. He
ignored this, as his men were behaving well and advancing steadily and without undue haste. They
cleared the farmhouse in a rush. Then, as they were
being fired upon from a railfence over to the west,
they changed direction and continued their charge,
which carried the fence line. Forbes followed the fleeing riflemen into the woods, where, among the pines,
the American resistance stiffened. Rifles seemed to
crack from every direction, and the major felt himself stung by a ball. The men began looking around
to see how their friends were faring, and Major
Forbes knew that soon they would begin to huddle.
He saw one man standing free, aiming his musket
toward the tree-tops. He opened his mouth to shout
at the man, to bring him to his senses, but saw — just
in time — a puff of smoke high in a maple tree.

Though he could not see the enemy he realized there were riflemen in the trees as well as on the ground. Reluctantly, the major gave the order to retire. He was hit again before he regained the open pasture land, where a regiment (probably the 20th) was forming into line. To his horror, he saw the men of the front rank leveling to fire. He ran toward them, shouting, but too late to stop the first ragged volley, which added yet more wounded to the casualty list of his already sorely tried picquet.

Mounted on his horse directing the deployment, Colonel Robert Kingston saw the nervous regiment fire into the returning picquet. He ordered a gun to be fired. Its booming roar shook the men into control, and the sergeants and two young officers steadied down to their work of getting the lines dressed, preparatory to advancing across the wide home pasture of Freeman's farm.

15

Action Front!

Gone were the farmer's bullocks, which had plowed the upper fields. Gone was the team of horses, which had cropped short the summer grass along the rail fence. The log barns behind Freeman's farmhouse were empty of stock. Where the ground fell away to the east at the far side of the farmyard, the edge of a cornfield spreading up out of the gully marked the brow of the hilltop clearing. The row of tall stacks seemed to be watching the lines of red-coated infantry, spreading, weed-like, over the northern end of the home meadow.

Quickly, the long line of Englishmen formed up, as more and more files of companies marched out of the woods. There was a moment when a little band of *Jägers* in their green coats ran out between the companies to dash for the protection of a ditch, where their short-rifled pieces could answer the desultory fire of Yankee riflemen. But for the odd rifle shot, all was quiet at Freeman's farm until the drums began to beat.

Fifty gaily coated drummers stood behind their

regiments; at the ready, slim backs arched stiffly,
young eyes wide. At an order, a hundred drumsticks
fell to rattling out the insistent beat of the long roll,
then fell silent. All up and down the three regimental
fronts, colonels and captains shouted the traditional
orders and ran to take their places in the line of
British infantry before the drums began to beat
again. With the one first step of fate, the whole long
line advanced to the slow, measured tap to which
the tramping men could set down their feet with
decision.

Close behind the infantry, forty-eight gunners took
up the slack on drag-ropes, and as the heavy trails
cleared the ground, the gun sergeants, leaning on the
muzzles as counter-weights, gave the order to march.
Four guns moved out after the infantry, two in the
gap between the 9th and the 21st, and two more to
the left, where the 20th and Anstruther's 62nd continued the line. Further back, four ammunition tumbrils followed, their drivers leading the plodding
dray horses.

General John Burgoyne sat easily in his saddle,
Colonel Kingston at his elbow. A horse, stirred by the
drumbeats, danced out of the group of staff officers
and division couriers standing near the general. The
rider, a French-speaking Brunswick officer from the
German wing, pulled his beast around and slipped
back into the group. Gentleman Johnny edged his
mount into a walk as the long red line of infantry
passed the little farmhouse. The line crossed the
ditch where the *Jägers* lay. The gun crews of each

two-gun battery combined efforts to worry their pieces across the ditch, then hurried to catch up with the drums, bobbing on the thighs of the drummers as they strode behind the companies. The Yankees were firing from the woods, and here and there a red-coated figure fell heavily to the grass. Lieutenant Hadden ran ahead and dragged a wounded private from the path of an oncoming gun.

At the two log barns, the British line halted. In the face of the rebel fire, they could not go on without support. Volley fire by platoon skipped up and down from the British ranks. It drove the Americans back from the edge of the wood, while the guns were being wheeled into place. With the help of Lieutenant Reid, Captain Jones set up his piece in the space between the 9th and the 21st, with his field of fire to the left, in front of the latter regiment. Lieutenant Hadden stationed his two pieces to cover the wood and to shoot into the cornfield. To his right six companies of the 62nd faced the wood; to his left two companies angled back, facing the gully.

For two long hours Hadden fired his guns. Sometimes his canister shot tore through the tall stand of corn, cutting the stalks through which the enemy tried to infiltrate around the 62nd. Sometimes Lieutenant Hadden fired round shot and canister into the woods, and the balls ricocheted off the tree trunks into the branches above. The canister was meant for the Yankee regiments forming up under the trees, preparing for a charge.

From the point where he commanded the battle

Burgoyne saw four rebel attacks form up, start off, then turn back before the volleys of his line of regulars. Unlike the Yankees who had begun the battle, these were uniformed Continentals. Most of the rifle fire was to Burgoyne's right, where Fraser, too, was holding his ground. Now the familiar crack of the long American rifle came seldom from in front of the 62nd and the 21st. When it was heard, it usually meant that a British officer was hit, or that another gunner had fallen away from his gun. As the smoke drifted off enough to afford a clear view, the Yankee marksmen tried for General Burgoyne. When, at extreme range, they toppled a big officer from his handsome mount in front of the staff group, the Yankees cheered the supposed fall of the scalp-buying British general. But the young dandy who stopped Burgoyne's bullet was Captain Charles Green, aide to General Phillips.

On hearing the sound of the firing, Phillips, who had been riding with Baron Riedesel's wing, had ridden hard to the sound of the guns. With the eye and mind of a veteran gunner, he had paused on his way to Burgoyne to order the 20th (which he found waiting in the gully) to protect the flank of the 62nd by occupying the woods and the cornfield. He also took time to send a man galloping on horseback to Major Williams with the request that four guns from the park be dispatched at once. Captain Green had been sent on ahead, to appraise General Burgoyne of what he had done and to tell his general he was coming. As the gunner general put his foaming

charger to the hill out of the gully, he met his handsome aide, borne on a litter by four officers' servants.
The captain was but one of a long line of wounded,
drifting down off the higher land like autumn leaves
shaken from a tree-top by a gust of wind. All sought
shelter in the gully, where the doctors worked by
the bank of a little stream, and chaplains moved
among the men. There a host of wagoners, smiths,
armorers, wheelwrights, servants, and busy noncom-
batants looked anxiously to where Squire Freeman
once had farmed.

The gale of battle beat most furiously on the
corner where Hadden's guns stood with the ranks of
the desperately fighting 62nd. The gunner lieutenant
was now working as a gun number. With but four
men to load the guns, he himself was laying and
firing each of his two guns in succession. Eighteen of
his artillerymen were dead or gone back wounded;
one of his three men had been hit, and even as
Hadden looked at him to appraise his strength, the
man slipped down beside a gunwheel, tried again
to rise, then sank back, exhausted.

His guns unmanned and helpless, Hadden ran
back to where Brigadier Hamilton stood encourag-
ing Colonel Anstruther, to beg for some infantrymen to pass ammunition and keep the guns firing.
He reached politely for his cap; as he prepared to
doff it to the general, a rifleman's bullet snatched it
from his hand. He left it unheeded on the ground, as
he pleaded with the senior officer for men for the
guns — his guns! But Anstruther and Hamilton were

organizing a charge, and they needed every bayonet.
Blinded with the rage of frustration, Hadden turned
and ran stumbling to the barn where Burgoyne, dismounted now, had moved up to take even closer
control of his battle. General Phillips was there, and
Captain Jones, too, and to them he repeated his plea
for gunners. With the consent of Phillips, Jones
promised men from the two other guns of the brigade, and immediately ran off to fetch them. Content
for the moment, Hadden stopped to look around him.
The 9th Foot, who had not been heavily engaged,
were flying back across the ditch to take up a reserve
position at the farmhouse. The 21st was standing
firm. One of Hadden's gunners was sprawled on the
ground in the lee of the log barn; he was one of the
men Hadden had left wounded; now he lay dead.
Exposed in the open space between the two barns,
seemingly unconcerned by the danger, Gentleman
Johnny was in earnest consultation with Captain
Willoe of Riedesel's staff, whom the general held
tightly by the arm, as if holding back the younger
man. When the German ran quickly to his horse,
mounted, and gave the beast spur into a bounding
gallop, Hadden returned to his guns.

He arrived as the 62nd, shouting hoarsely in
the throat-stinging smoke of battle, launched their
charge. Alone with his guns, Lieutenant Hadden
watched them go. The men and officers were hurrying toward the woods, where smoke puffs blossomed
at the roots of the tall trees. Behind the line of soldiers stumbled the little drummer-boys in their buff

coats, the big drums flapping as the boys tried to
hurry. Hadden laughed at the ragged beat the running boys were fumbling out of their jouncing drums.
It seemed funny that the regiment marched steadily
on, oblivious to the step the drums were striving so
manfully to give them.

At the forest edge, the attack of the 62nd wavered.
Like shy suitors at a lady's door, the regiment hesi-
tated to enter. From further back in the hollowness
of the woods American musket fire, controlled and
telling, rumbled out an invitation to the infantry to
come on. Instead, the 62nd fell back, firing volleys
as they went. Red-coated dead now dotted the field
in front of Hadden's two 6-pounders. Captain Jones
shouted in his ear, and Hadden, the spell of awe
broken, turned to his guns with new determination.
He had seen infantry, cloaked only in tradition, discipline, and honor, walk up to naked death.

While Anstruther and his officers strove to reform
the battle line, the guns fired and loaded and fired
again. The rebel fire along the whole front turned on
the two guns, still unsupported by the disorganized
62nd. One by one, the new gunners dropped. Captain Jones was down, clutching at his abdomen, his
face tight with pain. Lieutenant Reid's right arm
dangled helplessly from a stained blue sleeve. Hadden sent him to the rear, carrying as best he could
the linstock from the now silent number-two gun.
It was time to bring off the guns, but, before this
could be effected, the 62nd gave way. Alone, bleed-
ing from a slight wound, Hadden could stand no

longer. Carrying his captain, somehow he reached
the nearer of the two barns. The building was
crowded with the badly wounded, lying on the wet
straw. The barn smelled of cattle. As Hadden gently
laid Captain Jones down with the others, his eyes
were brought to the level of one of the chinks between the loosely laid-up logs. In the bright sunlight
of the pasture, a hundred yards away an American
infantry regiment was lining up. All the men seemed
to be big in size, moving with assurance under competent officers. This, then, was the Continental line,
and Thomas Hadden, of the Royal Artillery, was
caught in a stinking cow barn between that line and
the British regulars!

With the arrival of General Poor's brigade in the
woods in front of Burgoyne's British infantry, Morgan shifted his riflemen to the American left, to en-
gage Fraser's advance corps in their strong hill position. They found good shooting into the 24th Foot,
and Colonel Morgan was content to pin his enemy
down until Benedict Arnold could bring up Ebenezer
Learned's brigade.

No one had attacked General Riedesel. The stocky
German general paced the road, awaiting the call
that surely must come from Burgoyne. Willoe was
with the general, and Riedesel had also sent Geismar;
neither had yet returned with the expected summons.
He heard the firing as the 62nd made their charge.
Standing still to listen, he heard the regiment come
back and the guns, so long silent, come alive, and

then he recognized the subtle change as British cannon fire slowed down, while the rebel fire increased. When the guns fell silent again, Riedesel, for the second time that afternoon, flung out the order to follow, and without waiting mounted and rode down into the gully.

At the bottom, where the road skirted a marshy part of the mill stream, Riedesel met the returning Geismar and Willoe. While the three were talking, two of Rhetz's companies came singing down the road. Riedesel waved them on, pointing with his gold-headed stick to the slope ahead. His own regiment followed, as loud of voice as the Rhetz, and even louder of drum. Ernst Ludwig von Spaeth was commanding, and the general needed only a word in passing to convey to von Spaeth his intent to bolster up the British left. Sure of his gunner, Riedesel left Captain Pausch to deploy his own guns.

Ziglamm, the wagonmaster, had found a way up to the height of land for Pausch's battery. It would be a hard haul around the edge of the swamp and up through an edge of the cornfield. But Ziglamm had gathered together some extra men to join the gunners at the drag-ropes. The officers, too, heaved on the spokes of the wheels, as the two cannon rolled on through the corn stalks, and the big yellow pumpkins were crushed under the iron-shod wheels. Behind the guns, an odd assortment of men came out of the gully, loaded down with shells and ball and powder. Pausch had scrambled on ahead to where he had a clear view. Out in the field stood the two deserted

guns of Hadden's battery, their brass muzzles stained
black with much firing. Pausch saw the Continentals
formed up at the edge of the wood, and ran back to
urge his own guns on. With a rush, they burst out
through the last row of corn, and under their gun
captains' orders wheeled and dropped their trail.
While the gun crews loaded, the blue-coated Brunswick infantry began to arrive on the field, to left and
to right. Perhaps it was stunned surprise, or perhaps
it was the blue coats of the Germans, but the Yankee
regiment seemed to hesitate for a moment. It was the
crucial instant when mattrosses rammed home the
charge, gun captains applied the linstock, and the
guns let loose their swarms of stinging grapeshot out
of a roar and rush of smoke. The Continental line
was only a pistol shot away. As the Hesse-Hanau
gunners reloaded, Riedesel's regiment opened with
volley fire. Far across the meadow Pausch saw a
house under a big shade tree; drums were beating
and a British regiment was advancing to the attack.
General Phillips was leading the charge.

The field was obscured in the smoke. With the
going down of the sun, unnoticed, the light wind had
dropped into stillness. Without a field of fire, Captain Pausch silenced the guns. The musket fire was
slowing down. A single volley burst out on the left,
after which came silence. The smoke of battle was
dispersing. All over the meadow, the men in British
red and German blue stood calmly in their ranks,
facing an empty wood.

Slowly and painfully, the gunners of the Hesse-

Hanau Artillery dragged their cannon forward, out of
the German line. All eyes turned dully, incuriously,
on the struggling group of men. Sixty yards in front
of the whole army, the guns came to a halt. The gun
crews took up their stations as though they were on
parade. Pausch's orders were crisp and clear, as the
gunners executed the drill of loading. At the captain's
command, the two guns roared in unison. No one
counted the parting shots fired into the woods after
the retreating rebels. They were a salute to a brave
day, an evening gun of rememberance. In fifteen
minutes it was dark.

16

Muffled Drums

Harness chains rattled and limber wheels jounced bumpily over the ditch. Lieutenant Hadden, still hatless, heard the familiar sound as he stood alone in the darkness, beside his silent guns. When he reached a caressing hand to the nearest piece, the metal was cold to his touch. It was as though he had touched the faces of the dead gunners — beside the wheels, at the trail, or out by the muzzle where the grass was black with scorch. The limbers came out of the night to Hadden's low call, and in silence dragged away the two brass cannon, leaving the crumpled dead alone without the symbols of their life and of their death.

Lanterns were blinking all over Freeman's fields as Lieutenant Hadden marched off his guns. The dim yellow lights dotted out the lines of infantry, where sergeants called the roll of companies and detailed the first watches of the night. A surviving officer was hard put to find a friend to share a nip from his flask, so accurate had been the Yankee rifle fire.

Colonel Anstruther of the hard-fought 62nd was

the last senior officer to join the others at the farmhouse headquarters. He brought with him an appall-
ing list of one hundred and forty-six casualties, and
an additional twenty-nine who were prisoners of the
rebels; some of his companies had been reduced to
ten tired men. General Fraser, though not heavily
engaged, glumly reported fifty casualties in his own
24th alone. His grenadiers and light infantry were
sorely tired after their day exposed to the unseen
rifles of Morgan's men. At General Burgoyne's conference that night, no officer was present to report
the brigade artillery casualties. Lieutenant Hadden,
the last gunner — officer or man — had gone down
the line to have his own wound dressed.

While the unit commanders talked over the day,
it grew quiet on the heights above the Hudson,
where the British army lay on its arms, on the fields
that it had held. Tired men slept in their ranks.
Sentries and picquets, more nervous than alert, felt
the cold beneath the belt straps crossing their backs.
Those near the gully heard the creak of wagons taking the wounded back to hospital, and listened for
other carts coming up, carts that might bring them
food. In the woods, dry-mouthed sentries, crouching
down among tall trees, heard in the darkness the
coughs and moans of yet undiscovered wounded,
grew drowsy, and again became alert when the corporal, bringing up the relief, cautiously called out the
password.

Neither those who watched nor those who slept
knew that, at the council of war that night, they had

been given one more whole day to live. Burgoyne
had been persuaded to postpone until 21 September
the continuation of his advance on the rebels. The
battle at Freeman's farm was over.

Down on the river flats, where the rear echelon
of General Burgoyne's army was gathered, the long
afternoon had not yet ended. There, where the
women waited and the surgeons worked, the battle
did not end until the last patient had been cared for
and the fate of the last man was known.

At the first sound of distant gunfire, the five ladies
of Burgoyne's armies drew together. Quite naturally,
they gathered in the big downstairs room of the
Smith house, the quarters to which little Baroness
Riedesel had laid claim by bringing in her children's
trunks and setting down her own open dressing case
on the deep cedar doorsill. Rockel, the butler, had
brought tea to the ladies, after which he had gone
to be near the major, leaving his mistress in the care
of the two frightened maids.

Of the four ladies who waited courageously, Lady
Harriet Acland had the least chance of escaping the
dreaded news. Out there amid the terrifying noise
was not only her husband but her brother as well.
It took a long time for the news to trickle back with
the wounded. Mrs. Harnage was the first of the ladies
to learn her fate. They carried the major in and laid
him down beside his wife, who covered with her lace
handkerchief the angry bluish hole in her husband's
abdomen before she managed a smile for him. Soon

the house had become a hospital, and all the ladies went to work. Friederika Riedesel was rummaging in her trunk in search of her own linen for an ensign with a shattered leg, when she saw a man standing in the doorway, looking full at her. But before she had time either to fall into despair or to let loose her relief, the man's eyes carried hers across the room to where Mrs. Lieutenant Reynell sat, silently weeping. The man nodded his head. When the lieutenant was brought in, Baroness Riedesel was holding the girl tightly in her arms. There was no hope for Thomas Reynell: his arm was off before they brought him into the hospital. It was morning before he died, leaving his young wife and three little children on the banks of the Hudson River, in the North American wilderness.

Not until dawn of 20 September did the soldiers on the high ground receive their rations. At the same time the men of the line regiments, British and German, went down into the gully to fill their empty water bottles. The food refreshed spirits as well as bodies, and the fresh water washed away the tiredness in their bones. Now they were fit for the work to be done that day. With the carts bringing the food there also came shovels. Groups of men were told off to dig wide, oblong trenches for graves. Other groups spread out over the fields and into the woods, to gather in the dead for burial, while ashen-faced chaplains waited, book in hand.

Thomas Anburey prided himself that the two graves

dug by his detachment were deep, their sides square, the soil well piled. Into the larger of the pits he saw the bodies of the men laid neatly side by side, in ranks, as they had lived and as they died. Into the smaller grave, Anburey placed the three ensigns he had found lying all together where the British line ran closest to the woods. None of the three was older than the drummer boy now beating out the dead march on a muffled drum. Though he was short of camp gear, Lieutenant Anburey avoided the sale that evening, at which the effects of the dead officers were sold.

It was late when the courier from New York got through the lines and found his way, unnoticed, to General Burgoyne's headquarters at the Freeman house. The message he brought was written small. It was pulled from its hiding place crumpled and stained, but under a glass, by the light of a single candle, the letters were clear, the words bold, and Burgoyne read them with soaring hope. Sir Henry Clinton would soon be out, his destination the highlands of the Hudson!

Clinton had given Gentleman Johnny, always a heavy gambler, a high trump card for his tight little game with that more cautious player, Horatio Gates. With the Guards General in New York holding cards, Burgoyne could now lean back in his chair to review his hand and, possibly, revise his play. In the first exchange of tricks, on 19 September, the British had won the field by keeping possession of it. But at Free-

man's farm, Burgoyne had suffered irreplaceable
losses in officers, gunners, and soldiers, without either
sweeping the rebels out of the road to Albany or
winning any distance toward that city. The renewal
of the attack on the American left, scheduled to go
in on the morning of 21 September, was calculated
to break through the American defenses. But a battle
is always a chancy thing, and, like cards, soldiers
once played are dead. With Clinton coming up the
Hudson at Gates's back, Burgoyne could afford to
wait for a better moment to lead his strength at the
American general's field works.

It was not until shortly before daybreak that Burgoyne cancelled the attack and ordered his troops to
dig in. By mid-morning of 21 September, Gentleman
Johnny, the gambler, had reverted to General Burgoyne, the writer, penning a letter to Sir Henry in
which he urged all haste, as supplies could last only
until 12 October at the latest. By that date the northern army must either be in Albany or, admitting defeat, at Ticonderoga.

For Horatio Gates, 19 September had not been a
happy day. Things had not gone according to his
plan; the direction of the battle had been snatched
out of his hands; and by nightfall he was in danger
of losing the glory of the day to Benedict Arnold, the
hero of Valcour Island.

In the morning, when the sun-signals had been
flashed to him from the east shore of the Hudson,
General Gates had ordered his army to man the field

works. Three brigades of Continentals faced the river road, with their general peering over their shoulders, looking for the British main attack to fall. Benedict Arnold's two brigades, Continentals with militia, manned the still uncompleted salient of breastworks on the heights, near the Neilson house and barn.

About noon, the reluctant Gates had been persuaded to order out Morgan's corps. They were to make contact with the British right wing in the woods and along the road to Freeman's farm. Advancing in small groups on a wide front, Morgan met and beat in the picquet of Burgoyne's center column. It was at this point that Horatio Gates lost control of his battle. Joyous at seeing the redcoats run, the riflemen forgot their long-range tactical advantage and pursued too closely. They ran onto the oncoming British bayonets and were scattered in confusion.

Benedict Arnold, ever volatile, never patient, had moved forward of his division's position to follow the progress of Dan Morgan's reconnaissance from one of the small works, built as a listening post well forward of Gates's main line of defense. Even the rough barricade of logs and earth cramped the aggressive spirit of the stocky major general, to whom a fort was the starting point for an attack, not a place in which to cower. Arnold, awkward from an old leg wound, had climbed up to the top of the parapet when the first fire of the riflemen broke out. There he was standing when he heard the frenzied gobble of Dan Morgan's turkey call, urging his scattered men to rally. It was a cry for help, too, like that of a good hound dog

who has brought the red stag to bay. Arnold hark-
ened, and, with the weird sound of the wild turkey
beating in his ears, exploded into action. Racing back
to his division, he grabbed the first two regiments he
came upon and sent them running down the road to
Freeman's farm. They were the New Hampshire
Continentals, men of Joseph Cilley's and Alexander
Scammel's regiments. Hale's men followed, then the
New Yorkers. Most of Poor's brigade, too, was in the
firing line in the woods at the south end of Freeman's
home pasture. Morgan had disengaged, to slide over
to the American left and face the British right,
"treed" on its high ground. Galloping up, Arnold saw
his troops engaging the British line across the open
fields. Seeing the gap between the British center and
Fraser's corps in the woods, he dashed away in search
of General Learned's brigade, to exploit the situation.

It was then that Arnold ran afoul of Gates. Every
action that Arnold had taken that afternoon had been
without the American commander in chief's orders,
and contrary to his intention. Arnold had abandoned
the American army's main line of defense at a time
when Gates had expected the main British attack
down the slot he had prepared for it. To exploit an
opportunity which had not been carefully considered, the swarthy division commander had opened
a general engagement with Burgoyne, at great risk to
his command. It had been difficult for Gates to re-
store order among the excited officers and men of
Arnold's division, who were yelping at the British
stag in Freeman's fields. Wilkinson had restrained

Arnold from returning yet again to the fight, with the
result that the regimental commanders lost the co-
hesive leadership they needed, and fell back.

So ended the battle and the day for Gates and for
Arnold. In his quarters, the latter was composing a
letter requesting that he be sent at once to serve
under General Washington. Gates, his army again
under control, was in his tent working over plans
and forms and lists, while his adjutant general saw to
it that the battle of 19 September 1777 was accounted
a victory for General Gates, with no credit whatever
accruing to the disobedient major general.

Benedict Arnold did not leave the northern department for three weeks. The senior officers of the
army persuaded him to stay on. With neither duty
nor command, since Gates had taken his division
from him, Arnold remained in his quarters, taking
an occasional drink with the two aides he had inherited from Philip Schuyler, mocking "Granny"
Gates from afar, and — for the moment — keeping
within the limits of sarcasm the fury mounting within
him. On the fine days of the northern autumn, he
moved his chair to the doorstep. He was sitting there,
idly watching the soldiers at their digging, when
the first great flock of Canada geese flew by. It is
the sound of their honking which first lifts one's eye
to their flight. It is an insistent, urgently plaintive cry,
quite unlike the clipped, quick, assured call of the
wild turkey gobbler ordering his hens to follow him.
Yet it is the call of the strong-willed leader, carrying
the wide-spreading wedge of his followers behind
him down the broad lanes of the upper air.

Horatio Gates busied himself in his headquarters tent. Field works must be perfected and extended to make strong the left flank which the enemy had attempted to turn. Then, too, the militiamen, fully aroused at last, were coming in by the hundreds, each newly arrived unit requiring much staff work before it was assimilated into the northern army. But Gates as well came to stand at the flap of his tent, to watch for a time the flight of the wild geese. As the approaching cold of winter drove the big birds south, so the coming pangs of hunger would send Burgoyne's regiments marching up to the American lines.

On 3 October, in a routine order that reflected the state of his commissary, General Burgoyne put his whole army on half ration. The men took the order well.

The troops had worked hard since the day after the battle, when they had buried their dead. The field of corn at the Freeman farm had been harvested as fodder for the horse lines. Lieutenant Schank had moved his pontoon bridge downstream. Again in position, it reached from the base camp to the east shore of the Hudson, where a bridgehead redoubt was thrown up. But the bridge reached only to a blind shore, for beyond the redoubt the American militia roamed the woods in menacing strength.

The main work of Burgoyne's army, however, was in erecting a strong, safe, fortified line in which to await the coming of Clinton. The works extended in a long, jagged line across the high ground where Riedesel had waited with his reinforcements. This

part of the British works dominated the river road
and, from positions on the forward slope, watched
the crossings of Mill Creek. To the west of the long
redoubt, behind which Burgoyne established his
headquarters, a dotted line of small positions extended the fortified line through the gully to the high
ground where stood the Freeman farm. On the old
battlefield, the British engineers had traced out a
great redoubt in the shape of a broken sling swivel.
Within its earth and log walls stood the Freeman
house, serving as headquarters. This, the pivotal position of the whole line, was named Balcarres redoubt,
in honor of the twenty-four-year-old Scottish earl,
whose reckless bravery in leading the light infantry
was exceeded only by his daring at the nightly card
games with his general. Twelve hundred yards to
the north, the Germans, under General Breymann,
built their redoubt on the edge of the Great Ravine,
which was an impenetrable tangle of scrub-brush. It
faced north over newly cleared fields, across which a
road wound its way to yet more distant clearings.
Between the Balcarres redoubt and the open rear of
Breymann's redoubt stood two log cabins in which
the last remnant of Burgoyne's Canadians camped
and cooked their thick soups. Here lived the eleven-
year-old Monin, whose father, "le capitaine," had
fallen to a Yankee rifleman out where the woods were
thickest, and where only the strongest British patrols
dared go. The boy, with his dog Bellona, hunted
rabbits in the fields and waited to be taken home to
Canada by the friends of his dead father.

Baroness Riedesel, too, was to have a house in which to live with her children as soon as Major Williams's men could complete it. There, she would be near enough to her husband's headquarters to watch over the preparation of his meals and to give dinner parties at which she and her husband could entertain the other generals. Her house was close to the rear echelon of the army, where the gun park stood beside the river, near the hospital. The boats of the supply fleet lined the banks of the river, the stores they had carried stacked under oilcloth coverings, and all the followers of the army and the soldiers passing on details could see the dwindling piles. It was on the river bank, where the women and the idlers gathered, that hopeful rumors on which to feed the army were bred.

Like clean white linen spread on the grass to dry, the news was plain for all to see. Clinton was coming, of course. General Burgoyne had received a secret messenger who brought the welcome news. Three officer-couriers, heavily disguised, had gone out to tell Sir Henry that the army from Canada was ready to attack when he did, but that he must hurry. Twice they had gone out, on the nights of 22 and 23 September, while the British guns thundered to draw in the Yankee patrols, enabling the messengers to slip through. The army knew that Captain Scott had gone to Clinton on 27 September, followed the next night by Captain Alexander Campbell. A wild, romantic tale was circulating that one of the officers carried his message in the hollow shell of a bullet made of silver.

For several days the men standing to in the early morning asked each other for the true news from the north. Some said that Skenesborough was in American hands, others that Ticonderoga had fallen to the Americans. It was not until the evening alert on 2 October that the men in the lines and at the redoubts, listening for the evening guns in the rebel lines echoing their own, learned what had really happened at Ticonderoga. General Burgoyne received word from Brigadier Powell that he had been attacked by a force sent out from Vermont by General Lincoln. For four days he had been molested by fifteen hundred rebels but, recognizing the action as a raid in force, he had fended them off by remaining inside his forts at Ticonderoga and on Mount Independence. At last they had gone away, but not before taking the fortifications on Sugar Loaf, from which, fortunately, the big guns had already been removed. The Yankees had also taken the posts all along the portage road and all the boats they found at the foot of Lake George. Colonel John Brown, the boldest of the American officers, had gone up Lake George in the captured gunboats, tarrying only long enough to menace the forewarned garrison on Diamond Island before taking off eastward through the woods.

Twenty Canadian Indians brought this news from Ticonderoga. But their coming was of little interest or encouragement to the British enclave on the Hudson. All trust in their savage allies had gone out of Burgoyne's army, who had been betrayed by wanton murder and disgraced by caviling cowardice. In the

great fortified camp, twenty Indians were but twenty
additional mouths to feed. There was no work for
them to do. The woods around the army were American woods, into which even Captain Fraser's marksmen scarcely dared to venture. By day and by night
the Yankees patrolled the fringes of the British camp,
while wolves howled in the distance. In the center
of the ring Burgoyne's army waited, isolated and
alone, yet confident that when the right time came
their general would lead them out to smash through
the encircling rebels and clasp hands with Sir Henry
Clinton's men. The army knew that Clinton could
not be far away, else Gentleman Johnny would not
wait.

At midnight, when 5 October passed over into the
next day, a rocket was fired from the lines near army
headquarters. It soared high into the dark sky,
launching a final rumor: the old soldiers knew, and
quickly told the young ones, that a night rocket was
fired only when a friendly force was near. Though no
answering rocket lit the sky beyond the rebel lines, at
headquarters they must be expecting the approach of
Sir Henry Clinton. As the rocket arched upward,
those nearby saw Gentleman Johnny, standing at the
open door of his quarters. Several officers were with
him, and the light from the room beyond caught the
gleam of satin as the commissary's wife turned to go
back to the warm fire burning on the hearth.

17

General Fraser Eats Breakfast

General Fraser rode his handsome gray down into the gully behind the Balcarres redoubt. Since first he had passed that way, the leaves of the swamp maple growing by the bridge had turned scarlet, as scarlet as the general's coat. Sumac at the edge of the swamp was the crimson of his sash, while on the skyline toward which he rode the drooping branches of an old oak tree were the color of the tarnished gold epaulets at his shoulders. Breasting the hill at a snorting, plunging gallop, the general of the advance guard reined his horse back into the dignity of a controlled walk and soothed it with an approving pat. He was in behind the long, wavy line of field works and among the rows of tents, where, in passing, soldiers acknowledged his rank and showed their esteem for him. At the edge of the headquarters compound an orderly ran out to take the bridle reins. The Brunswick dragoon sentries took their pose of rocklike attention. In the bright, warm sunlight of the fine October Sunday, General Fraser paused for a barely perceptible instant before crossing over the threshold into the room where Time demanded a grave decision.

It was the second time that week-end that Lieutenant General John Burgoyne had called in to headquarters his three division commanders: Major General Phillips of the British line, Major General Riedesel, and Acting Brigadier General Fraser of the elite advance corps. On Saturday, 4 October, the four men had met in a council of war to consider Burgoyne's bold plan to cut loose from his heavy guns, his full hospital, his dwindling supply column, and the women of his army, in a wide arching dive into the forest that would bring the fighting troops out behind Gates's army and make them the vanguard of Sir Henry Clinton's expected advance. At Sunday's meeting Burgoyne's generals rejected the rash plan, as too risky for those left behind and too problematical as to the anticipated merger with Clinton's forces. The fallow silence that followed the veto was broken by Riedesel, the disenchanted German whose nationality had excluded him from Burgoyne's proud boast, at the crossing of the Hudson, that "Britons never retreat!" The baron, whose initiative had saved the day at Freeman's farm, proposed that the whole army retire to the old position on the Batten Kill, there to nurture itself at the dangling end of the Ticonderoga supply line until Clinton's arrival was more imminent. Simon Fraser, the Highland Scot, concurred in the opinion of the comrade-in-arms who had turned the Yankee right flank for him on the Hubbardton road. With a motion of his hand, Phillips abstained. As a major in the Royal Artillery, Phillips had witnessed the total casualties at Jones's guns on 19 September, when forty-eight irreplaceable gun numbers were lost to Burgoyne's army. And as a major general in the British Army, the old gunner knew the solitary responsibility of high command, where one's guideposts through the fog of war are months old instructions issued by people in a remote place, informed of circumstances no longer existent. Phillips could only sympathize and obey.

The instructions to Lieutenant General John Burgoyne were clear: he was to take his army to Albany and there place himself under command of General Sir William Howe. In the light of these orders, Burgoyne would only accept as a responsible opinion, put forward by two brave and reliable officers, the advice of Riedesel and Fraser to retreat. His duty and inclination lay in the opposite direction. At the council of war Burgoyne was forced to effect a compromise between his own natural instinct and the unacceptable (to him) caution of his subordinates.

Ultimately a solution to the problem was found. It was agreed that on Tuesday, 7 October, all four generals would make a reconnaissance in force of the American left. If it was then deemed feasible, a general attack would be ordered for the following day. If the American position was found to be unassailable, after waiting out the week, Burgoyne would retire on the Saturday to the old Batten Kill position.

The command decision came hard to General John Burgoyne. He even sought to avoid it by asking for

orders from Sir Henry Clinton. But he received no
reply and, with his fate hanging on the disembodied
instructions from London, he prepared to make his
reconnaissance. He ordered rum for the whole army:
one barrel for the auxiliaries, three for the British
line, four for the Germans, and four for the advance
guard who would be going out in the morning. On
Monday morning the carts dropped the rum off at
the various positions. There were many willing hands
to ease the barrels to the ground and roll them up
onto the racks, where spigots were driven into the
bung-holes. Popularity was natural to Gentleman
Johnny Burgoyne.

Duty calls to the common soldier very early in the
morning. A sentry, eager for companionship, wakens
the drummers and the cooks as early as he dares. At
the first sound of drums, the corporals poke and pull
their squads into wakefulness before the sergeants
can find them remiss in their first duty of the day.
Two subalterns, sharing a tent, lie awake on their
cots as they listen to the noises of the rousing camp,
and luxuriate until the servant whom they share
brings water for their ablutions, and what fare can be
managed from an army starving on half-rations.
Majors and colonels of many years' service find that
the chill of a northern New York knows where old
wounds and old injuries twinge and ache the most.
The morning mist from the Hudson River gets into
the back of their throats and sends them, snuffling
and coughing, into their field trunks, where they keep
their private stock of bone-warming liquor. Majors

and colonels are meticulous as to their dress, and
take a long time at their morning toilet — extra time
for the leisurely ablutions of the captains of companies.

Generals are exalted persons. Lieutenant General
John Burgoyne was the most exalted of all the army
that camped on the banks of the Hudson, six miles
below Stillwater. In all the northern frontier of the
war, the only man equal to General Burgoyne in
importance was Major General Horatio Gates of the
Continental Army, whose picquets faced the British
at musket-shot distance, and whose main defense
works were only a mile from the Balcarres redoubt.
Gates's headquarters tent was pitched at a road juncture, half a mile behind his front lines. The general
was early at his desk on the morning of 7 October,
with a full day's work before him. Since the British
sortie on 19 September and the nearly mutinous
brushfire fight that had contained it, Gates's army
had almost doubled in number. The militia had
turned out, its ire thoroughly aroused by the murder
and pillage by Burgoyne's Indians, and reassured in
its patriotism by Stark's victory at Bennington, Herkimer's and Arnold's turning back of St. Leger, and
General Lincoln's exhortation to the Continentals to
stand at the pass above Stillwater. To Gates, the militia presented a delicate problem in staff work. Theoretically, the men came supplied — often ludicrously
so — in their own interpretation of what constituted
a uniform and other martial equipment. Soon after its
arrival, a company, hungry after its march from a
hamlet in a distant valley, would be demanding food.

All the militia seemed to be prodigious eaters, and their powder horns were as empty as their stomachs and the flabby shot pouches hanging at their belts.

With the influx of ardent militiamen, the Americans' resources, already low in ordnance supplies, were sorely taxed. But the nicest staff problem for the former British brigade major was the brigading and deploying of this mass of citizen-soldiers. Gates put the Massachusetts units, some thirteen hundred men, under command of the militia general, John Fellows, with an assignment to proceed up the Hudson by the east shore, cross over again, and lie on Burgoyne's rear at Saratoga. Two Connecticut State Regiments were veterans of Poor's brigade. Even the problem of Stark and his New Hampshire men had been solved. The old rock-visaged ranger, with his eight hundred men, had been persuaded to leave the fair fringe of New England for the deserted fort and buildings at Fort Edward, through which Barry St. Leger must come with reinforcements for Burgoyne — if, indeed, he came at all. Searching the empty place, Stark found, decently interred in the fort cemetery, the boats with which St. Leger was to have crossed the Hudson. These were destroyed before the New Hampshire army, still shy, still suspicious, edged a little closer to the place and hour of destiny. John Stark did not know it, as he prowled the upper Hudson in the bright October sun, but the general's commission which he so truculently regarded as his due, lay — already signed — on a Congressional desk in distant Philadelphia.

Less bright on his shoulders were Benedict Arnold's

stars of rank. Gates had neutralized Arnold, who, for
the three weeks following his disobedience of 19
September, was virtually under house arrest. But
General Gates could never quite forget him. Arnold
represented the old Schuyler faction. He was the
fiery comet of the battlefield that all soldiers look to
in their own fear of death or cowardice. Schuyler
himself had been dealt with, and Gates no longer
feared him. The former general was a not-infrequent
visitor to the American camp. He had even given the
army lumber for the bridge Fellows's brigade had
used to cross to the east bank of the Hudson. But
Gates had not felt sufficiently secure to dismiss
Arnold, or even to grant his request for transfer out
of the northern department. So he was left to wither
and fall in inactivity, until a gale could be stirred up
finally to blow him away.

Meanwhile, Brigadier General Abram Ten Broeck's
New York State militia was kept away from him.
These Yorkers were Schuyler men and were inher-
ently suspicious of the New England faction, in the
army or the government. They were men whose
homes had been pillaged by Burgoyne's army, or
were imminently threatened by that army's advance
and the Tory rule it would bring. It was they who
were impatient for revenge, and who sought a bold
leader such as Benedict Arnold, now disgraced but
famed in many battles. While his defensive plans
matured, Gates kept the New York militia in the rear
or scattered in the woods, where they could stalk the
unwary British patrols and foraging parties, far re-

moved from the orderly procedure of the American staff tents.

Horatio Gates knew that Sir Henry Clinton was moving on the highlands of the Hudson. The Yankee general was in close correspondence with Israel Putnam, the American commander there. Each report that Clinton was still below the highlands meant another day that Gates could count on for Burgoyne to eat himself toward the decision being forced upon him.

So, Horatio Gates worked on through the morning of 7 October, toward the time that he would be called to dine.

General Burgoyne ate a leisurely breakfast on the morning of 7 October. He was still at table when the contingent of two hundred soldiers, selected from the several German regiments, marched past his dining-room window, on their way to the forming-up point for the reconnaissance in force. With them, and raising a cloud of dust from the dry road, Captain Pausch clattered by with two 6-pounders. The four ammunition wagons following the guns made quite a cavalcade. Later, Burgoyne was disposing of some staff details at his writing-table when Major Griffith Williams rode up, turned out of the road, and, still in his saddle, watched while his battery of guns went by. For the reconnaissance Williams had selected his two best 12-pounders — the same guns with which he had defied the great wilderness fortress at Ticonderoga. Major Williams had decided to accompany

his beloved 12's, not only to watch them but because
he hoped to place them on a hill nearby and from
there to pour a few shots in the rebel field fort. For
his anticipated shoot, Williams had ordered out his
two 8-inch howitzers, which were to drop shells in
among the rebels as they cowered behind their works.
He watched as the gun teams dragged the howitzers
past: squat brass tubes, their big mouths thrust up as
though drinking from the sky. They were very different from the long shining barrels of the 12-pounders,
crouching in their carriages like vicious panthers
readying to spring. Before the last tumbril passed,
Major Williams dismounted and joined the headquarters group of officers waiting to ride out with
their general.

There was a festive atmosphere as the men waited
in the yard, a little removed from where the grooms
held the horses, which were fully caparisoned for
battle with the bulky pistol-holders at the pommels
and cloaks rolled behind the cantles. Many of the
headquarters staff were riding out that day, among
them the two bright luminaries of General Burgoyne's
intimate family of aides: Sir Francis Carr Clarke,
whose lieutenancy in the 3rd Foot Guards was
equivalent to a captaincy in any other regiment, and
Lord Petersham, his slim boots drawn over cavalryman's shanks. Captain John Money, the quartermaster general, stood talking with Captain Thomas
Blomfield. The latter specialized in water-borne artillery, and, since Charles Green had been shot, was
acting as aide-de-camp to General Phillips.

Standing by the headquarters door and sliding the focusing piece in and out of his battered old brass telescope, General Phillips waited for Burgoyne to come out and begin the reconnaissance. Riedesel walked back and forth, stopping occasionally to talk with Phillips as though the council of war still continued. The commander of all the Brunswick and Hessian troops of Burgoyne's army had breakfasted with his wife, as usual. The meal had been a hasty one, as he had been summoned when the parade of German troops was formed up. The Baroness had hurried him, too, for she had a menu to contrive and a table to set in her new house. She was giving a dinner-party that afternoon after the men returned. The work of finding suitable food in the near-starvation camp, the decoration of the room and table, and the supervision of the cooking would keep her busy and occupy her mind while the men were out.

Simon Fraser, who was to be one of Friederika Riedesel's guests of the evening, was not among the group waiting on Burgoyne at headquarters. He was at the Balcarres redoubt, supervising the assembly of the troops for the reconnaissance. He had eaten a substantial English breakfast in preparation for the busy day that lay ahead of him.

Lieutenant Anburey, who was commanding the quarter guard of the day, had gone out toward the American lines and had returned to report them all quiet. He brought back to Fraser the extraordinary report that, in a thicket, he had discovered the bodies of three Yankees, one of them being that of a young woman apparently killed while she was bringing an apron full of paper cartridges out to the men. General Fraser was returning from a last word with his nephew, who was taking out the marksmen, the Tories, and a few painted Indians for a wide scout to westward, when the German contingent from the main camp came marching up. Lieutenant Colonel von Spaeth halted his troops on the low ground between the two redoubts. Drums sounded in the curve of the Breymann redoubt, and soon the three hundred grenadiers designated for von Spaeth's command marched down to fall into the column, now five hundred strong. Lieutenant du Fais of the Hesse-Hanau Artillery followed them to talk with Captain Pausch. Then du Fais climbed up the hill again to where his two guns were, and would remain, with Colonel Breymann and the two hundred grenadiers left to hold the redoubt.

Major Acland had his grenadiers out in good time, in the cleared space in front of the Balcarres redoubt. The Earl of Balcarres marched his quick-stepping light infantry across their front to gain their starting line on the extreme right of the British advance, with the grenadiers to their left. Close behind the light infantry followed the 24th Foot. John Acland waved to his brother-in-law, Stephen Strangways, as he marched past at the head of his company.

General Fraser was up on his fine gray when General Burgoyne rode out of the gully, the other generals and the large staff group behind him. Burgoyne waited at the Balcarres redoubt only long enough for the orders to move out to be sent to the three columns. It was almost one o'clock by Lieutenant Digby's watch when the grenadiers began their advance.

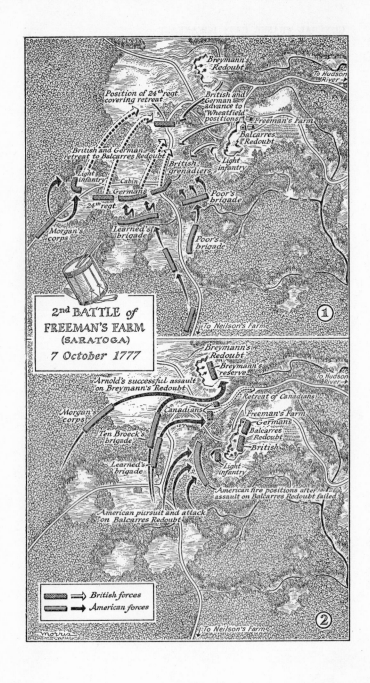

Breymann's
Redoubt

To Hudson
River →

Position of 24th regt.
covering retreat

British and
German
advance to
"Wheatfield"
positions

Freeman's Farm

Balcarres
Redoubt

British and German
retreat to Balcarres Redoubt

Light
infantry

British grenadiers

Light
infantry

Poor's
brigade

Morgan's
corps

Cabin

Germans

24th regt.

Learned's
brigade

Poor's
brigade

2nd BATTLE of
FREEMAN'S FARM
(SARATOGA)
7 October 1777

To Neilson's Farm

①

Breymann's
Redoubt

Breymann's
reserve

To Hudson
River →

Arnold's successful assault
on Breymann's Redoubt

Retreat of Canadians

Canadians

Freeman's Farm

Germans

Morgan's
corps

Ten Broeck's
brigade

Balcarres
Redoubt

British

Learned's
brigade

Light
infantry

American fire positions after
assault on Balcarres Redoubt failed

American pursuit and attack
on Balcarres Redoubt

⇒ British forces
→ American forces

morris

To Neilson's Farm

②

18

No Dinner for the General

Marching beside Captain Wight, Lieutenant William
Digby of the 53rd crossed the cleared ground in good
order with his company. On reaching the edge of the
woods, parade order was broken and the captain, the
lieutenant, and the sergeant each led a single file of
grenadiers in a twisting trail through the trees and
the undergrowth of brush. Soon they came to the
road between Neilson's and Freeman's farms, across
which a large fenced-in field of wheat sloped from
high ground into a ravine across its southern border.
Major Acland was waiting in the road when the company of grenadiers of the 53rd Regiment came out.
He showed Captain Wight where he wished the company to form a line, extending the grenadier front
from its left, in the woods, into the standing wheat.
To the west, the Germans were coming onto the field
and spreading out thinly to join up with the 24th
Foot and light infantry, making a line of men a thousand yards in length. From where Digby was he could
not see the guns, but he could hear the shouts of
the drivers as they turned the teams off the road to

the selected positions, the 12-pounders unlimbering behind the grenadiers. Orders came from the rear for the men to sit down and, though they had marched only half a mile from the redoubt, the soldiers quickly took advantage of the opportunity and sprawled themselves out in the yellow wheat. Captain Wight walked over to where Digby sat, cross-legged, behind his company, and invited the lieutenant to stroll about with him. Wight led him a short way down the line where they could see a small abandoned log cabin set at the edge of the woods beside a rail fence that defined the wheatfield. On the roof of the cabin, like a bunch of brightly dyed feathers on a dilapidated old brown beaver hat, perched three British generals and a stiff-backed German colleague — a delight to all common soldiers and junior officers to behold. General Phillips was on his stomach, steadying his long glass on the ridge-pole; a mounted staff officer (Petersham, by the look of him) was standing in his stirrups beside the cabin, stretching to pass a spyglass up to Gentleman Johnny himself.

While the generals studied the terrain to the south, a long line of foragers, leading their pack animals, filed up the road. They spread quickly out through the field to harvest the good grain, which would put energy back into the worn horses. From the roof, the generals could see a small portion of Gates's lines across the rough, broken country, cut by ravines and gullies, thick with woods, and checkered only sparingly with rough clearings. One of the latter reached over the top of a small wooded hill that rose out of a ravine beyond the brook at the southern extremity of the wheatfield. The generals were still on their rooftop when a gun team came up over the crest of the hill and into the clearing. It was followed by another, to its left, then two more. As one, the generals immediately swung their telescopes to take into focus this new development on their front. Phillips's centered on a young officer in blue and red standing with his back to the British, an arm raised as a marker to the gun crew, dragging a gun with difficulty around the stumps and through the brush of the rough clearing. Phillips was straining for a good look at the gun itself in an attempt to judge its exact size — it was small — when musket fire broke out at the southern end of the wheatfield. The foragers were now running back to the safety of the infantry line, which along its whole length was rising to its feet. They were calling to him from below when General Phillips snapped his telescope shut, slipped down the back of the cedar-shingled roof, and dropped to the ground.

The gunner officer the British generals had watched as he expertly positioned his piece was Lieutenant Ebenezer Mattoon of the Continental Artillery. The range was long for real effect with his small caliber guns, but the target was clear as he opened fire on the long line of enemy infantry. He saw that his shells were falling short of their target, and he was at the breech of his number-one gun, attempting to coax a little more elevation out of it, when the heavy British

round shot struck down the hill in front of him and
went screaming over his head in a wild, terrifying
ricochet. The ball from Major Williams's second
12-pounder rumbled through the air, high over the
hill where Mattoon had placed his battery on the forward slope, and his limbers and ammunition wagons
out of sight behind the crest. Lieutenant Mattoon
had already spotted the other British guns, set up in
batteries of pairs behind Burgoyne's line. Now he saw
that they were coming into action against him in
counter-battery fire. The Continental gunner called
up his limbers and abandoned his position before the
full force of the enemy cannonade could fall on it.
Safely in the shelter of the woods, the American battery came into the forming-up area of General
Learned's brigade, where Mattoon found Lieutenant
McLane and the rest of the guns of Captain Furni-
val's company. He joined them in a march that
skirted to the west of his hilltop clearing and was
aimed for the edge of the woods at the bottom of
the ravine, facing the blue-coated Germans in the
center of the British line.

Learned's brigade had been the last to march out
from the American position on Bemis Heights. When
the Yankee picquets reported that the British were
preparing to come out, General Lincoln had gone
forward to estimate the situation. Benedict Arnold
rode with him to the lookout point. Together, they
had then ridden to Gates's headquarters tent, and
Gates had interrupted his work to come out and receive Lincoln's report; Arnold he snubbed. On Gen-

eral Lincoln's recommendation, Horatio Gates ordered Morgan's corps out at once, to make a wide
march to the west, then to the north, to fall on the
British right and "begin the game." Drums were
beating the call to arms for Poor's Continentals to
attack Burgoyne's left. As he led out his guns up the
road to the Freeman farm, Mattoon caught a glimpse
of the last of Morgan's riflemen disappearing into
the woods. He was to support the skirmish line, sent
to hold the enemy's center until Learned's brigade
could be assembled for the main attack. He saw
Arnold, looking like the cocked hammer of a dueling
pistol. He was riding aimlessly about on his big
chestnut horse with the flowing black mane. Mattoon
did not see Gates go back into his tent to resume
his interrupted work.

Although it had been intended that Dan Morgan
was to "begin the game," he had a long route around,
over rough country, and Poor's brigade made the
first contact with Acland's grenadiers, on Burgoyne's
extreme left. Probing about through the woods on
the east side of the road, Poor's men encountered
the extension of the grenadiers' line. A fire-fight
began, with the Yankees aiming at individual men in
red, while the solid ranks of grenadiers, broken by
the gray tree trunks, poured volleys among the figures
they dimly saw, down the hill from them, among the
thicker undergrowth near the water course. Another
regiment of Poor's brigade, Joseph Cilley's 1st New
Hampshire Continentals, entered the action, and the
fight with the grenadiers was carried out into the

road and into the wheatfield beyond. Now the whole
line of grenadiers was firing by company volley and
was accepting heavy casualties. But Acland, standing
between two of the companies, noted a hesitance in
the advance of Cilley's men. He took this as an opportunity to charge, and gave the order to fix bayonets. Bayonet sockets clicked home over the hot
muzzles of the muskets, and as the officers, with
drawn swords, took their places out in front, the ranks
of British grenadiers straightened and seemed to
grow taller as they readied for the charge. Cilley's
men halted where they stood. But it was less in awe
of the threatened bayonet attack by Europe's most
famous infantry, than in wonder that men would
stand so, in the open, such easy targets to the muzzles
of the Continental line. Quickly, the New Hampshire
men brought their weapons to their shoulders, their
eyes running down the long gun barrels to the front
sights, comfortably fitting the V-sights near the
breech. Beyond, at flat range, they could see ruddy
faces under bearskin caps, white over-belts crossing
over stained and worn lapels. Some saw the crimson
sashes slashing across the white coats of officers as
they pressed on the triggers of their muskets. All
Time was compressed into the interminable minute
of sighting. Then the muskets began to fire, and the
slowest marksman noted that the man on either side
of him was reloading, and hurried his shot before the
smoke drifted in front of him so that he could not see
if he had made a hit. Colonel Cilley was shouting as
his men fired, and other firing was coming from the
woods on his right.

Major Acland went down during the long fusilade of the New Hampshiremen. Although fat Captain Simpson was a good target, he had not been hit. A man of great strength, he was able to pick up his major and carry him on his back, out of the trodden wheat. The whole line of British grenadiers was giving way before the Continentals, who, as they fired, moved forward out of their own smoke to fire again. At the edge of the woods the remaining British officers checked the men, but no amount of effort could get them to move out to renew the fight, nor were there enough of Burgoyne's elite grenadiers left to mount a bayonet charge. Acland's command had ceased to exist, and the survivors could but watch as Cilley's men veered slightly to the west to overrun Major Williams and his two 12-pounders. They saw the big rebel colonel climb up onto one of the pieces, and — but for the noise of the battle over the spur of ground where the Germans were fighting — they could have heard the Yankee officer yelling and whooping and cheering, as more and more of Poor's brigade emerged from the woods.

The battle had gone no better for the British on their right. Morgan's riflemen had quickly driven in Captain Alexander Fraser's marksmen. With the same wild abandon they had shown on 19 September, Morgan's rangers hurled themselves at Balcarres's light infantry. Showing perfect discipline under firm, clear orders, the British light infantry shifted their front to meet the attack from the west. Balcarres marked the extent of Morgan's attack by the now-familiar call of the wild turkey. Somewhere behind his own shifting line, a bugler mocked the call with a "Tally Ho!" on his curled French horn. The attack of Dearborn's light infantry fell unexpectedly on Balcarres's new left flank. Henry Dearborn's men came in hard and strong. Caught, the earl withdrew his whole command to the rail fence, and, from its protection, reorganized his firing line, which held Morgan and Dearborn at the edge of the woods.

General Burgoyne's messenger at last found Balcarres and gave him the general's orders to disengage and return to the redoubt. By ones and twos, the light infantrymen fired; then they retired in good order, trailing their muskets as they stepped lightly down the forest track.

The messenger, sent to the left flank with the same message, and then to the Germans in the center, was Sir Francis Carr Clarke. Setting off at a fast canter, he rode through the wheat, passing behind the gun line, as both Pausch's battery and the howitzers were in action. Smoke obscured the gentle rise over which Major Acland had formed up his grenadiers, and where the afternoon's action had begun. One of Major Williams's 12-pounders that had been silent for a time now fired. With the sound of the gun as a reference point, Sir Francis gave his horse its head, and at a pounding gallop, plunged into the smoke with his vital message. Too late, he realized that he had ridden onto the ground taken from Acland by Poor's brigade. The Guards officer had no time to cry out "Surrender!" before a musket shot at close range took him in the body, jerked him out of the saddle, and slammed him on the ground. Rough hands pulled him, still dazed and wondering, to his feet, and with a strange soldier helping him on either side, he dimly sensed that he was running and stumbling down a hill. Somewhere in the confusion of his mind, Sir Francis Carr Clarke knew that he had been wounded, and that he was running in the wrong direction.

Unaware that Acland's left wing had been driven in and that Williams's guns had been turned on the beaten grenadiers, in ignorance of Burgoyne's new order to retire, which the light infantry and the 24th Foot on the right flank were already following, the five hundred men of the German contingent stood where they had been placed. Some protection from the fire of the rebel skirmishers was afforded them by the rail fence behind which they stood, and through which their own *Jägers* were returning the enemy fire. At the left of their line, Captain Pausch was keeping up a steady fire along the edge of the woods. He was taking casualties among his gun crews, so when Lieutenant William Smith, bloody and excited, rushed up to him, demanding ten gunners to return the 12-pounders to action, Pausch refused. He was brusque with the wounded young officer, who seemed to have forgotten that the three to one rate of fire of a 6-pounder made it that much more valuable in the type of open fight that was developing.

The Americans had now brought up their own guns. The big puffs of white smoke rolling out from

under the trees betrayed their position. They were
Mattoon's and McKay's light batteries, firing canister
at a telling range. Under the close support of their
guns and disregarding Pausch's fire, Learned's regiments of Massachusetts Continentals were forming
up for a charge. Slowly, they advanced across the
bed of the dry brook and on up the gentle slope toward the waiting Germans. Gunsmoke rolled over
the field between the advancing and the stationary
lines of soldiers. When the smoke lifted, the rebels
had halted and in places were giving ground. In-
stantly, Colonel von Spaeth was up over the fence,
shouting for a counter-attack. Driven by their officers,
the men came out. But, though the officers kicked
and shouted and beat the men with swords, the German line would not take ranks. Instead, it wadded
itself into a milling mass of stubborn and frightened
men — terrified to go on toward the enemy, and
frightened to go back, where their own snarling officers menaced them with brutal authority. In the
quick moment of indecision, German discipline fal-
tered and the invincible hand of confidence fell upon
the shoulders of Learned's Continentals. It sent the
Americans running for the rail fence, and before the
onslaught of the hoarsely shouting Massachusetts
men the Brunswickers and Hessians stampeded.

Of all General Burgoyne's reconnaissance force,
only Pausch's two guns remained in action on the
field. With his gun numbers still working with pre-
cision under the old veteran's tight hand, the Hesse-
Hanau artillery was preparing for a fight to the

muzzle. Discipline kept the gunners at their station; tradition kept the old captain from abandoning his sacred guns while they could still fire a shot. And it was tradition and discipline and loyalty that ultimately saved them. Out from the trees at the northern end of the wheatfield the limbers came at a gallop, the quirts of the drivers flaying their teams. Down the hill they came, swinging wide through the field in a curve cut to bring each limber close to the trail of its gun. The gun crews fired, to clear their guns with a parting shot, hooked up quickly, and as the drivers slashed down at their off-horses, they grabbed a stirrup leather and ran free and wild, in great bounds, beside the running horses.

At the log cabin, which less than an hour before had borne upon its roof four British generals, Captain Pausch unlimbered for another stand. Learned's brigade was reforming at the rail fence, which they were pulling to pieces to make a way through for Mattoon's guns. Coming up from out of the woods behind them was a fresh regiment, still marching in column of route, led by a senior officer in full uniform, riding a big chestnut horse. Some men of Poor's brigade, to the east, had drifted over and were poking about among the Hesse-Hanau dead at Pausch's old gun position down the hill, where the wheel tracks through the wheat came to an end.

In the woods behind the cabin, Pausch could find no line of resistance forming up. There were still plenty of German soldiers, but they were individuals, some of them without weapons, who, recognizing him as an officer, skulked away into the bush as he approached them or called out to them. Without an infantry line to support, it was foolhardy to stand with the guns and waste such good men as remained to him. Pausch ordered up the limbers, hooked up again, and continued his retreat with honor, down the narrow track through the woods. He followed it eastward toward the Freeman's farm road and the redoubt, but he did not get far down the crooked, narrow trail. Saplings snarled the wheels, stumps seemed to rise up from the ground to foul the axletrees, and when the gunners rushed forward to clear them, the standing horses grew fractious under the taut reins held by uneasy drivers. Rifle fire was drawing nearer, as Morgan's men infiltrated the woods. The end of Pausch's guns came when a hidden rifleman shot a wheel horse in the leading gun's team. Its driver leaped free, but the lead team took fright and bolted, dragging the squealing beast with it for a few feet, until all ended in a hopeless tangle of horses, harness, limber, and gun. More rifle fire broke out, now aimed at the horses, and Pausch and his gunners ran. The old captain rested for a time behind a rail fence, trying to catch his breath. It was then that he saw one of his ammunition wagons, abandoned, its team quietly nibbling among the leaves on the ground. Almost gratefully, Pausch climbed up onto the driver's seat, and with one of his gunners beside him, drove off. At least he had saved something of his pride.

At the eastern corner of the wheatfield, where the

road from Neilson's farm entered the wood on the north side of the field, Simon Fraser was making his last stand. He had found his own regiment (the 24th) intact, its morale still high, retiring under orders with Balcarre's light infantry. He had led the men out onto the corner of the field, and, sitting high and proud on his gray horse, had watched while the rest of the reconnaissance force passed around behind him, bound for the redoubts. The Yankees, too, were keeping their distance, though rifle fire was chipping into the solid wall of the company fronts. Suddenly, the American rifle fire concentrated on the conspicuous General Fraser. A ball creased the cruppers of the gray horse. For a moment the animal danced in surprised pain, then Fraser quieted him. The riflemen held their fire. Once more, horse and rider were motionless. A second ball passed through the horse's mane, then a third took the general in the stomach, doubling him over as though he were executing an awkward bow from the saddle. Soldiers rushed to steady the stricken officer before he fell. An aide leaped to the bridle, and before the general could protest, led horse and rider away. With two men to hold him in the saddle, and the aide leading his horse, Fraser began the long, agonizing ride to the hospital, far away on the banks of the Hudson.

For a short distance, Gentleman Johnny rode beside his wounded friend. Behind them followed the 24th Foot. The reconnaissance in force was at an end. Burgoyne turned off at the Balcarres redoubt, to organize its defenses — for the rebels were following closely behind the rear guard. General Fraser rode on, one of a long line of wounded men finding their way through the late afternoon shadows to the camp beside the river.

Heavy firing could be heard inland at the redoubts, as the two soldiers eased the wounded general from the blood-flecked gray horse. They carried Simon Fraser into the cool, quiet darkness of Baroness Riedesel's new house, and there, on the table at which he had been invited to dine, they gently laid him down.

19

Prisoners of Hope

The sorely wounded Sir Francis Carr Clarke found himself in the most unusual situation for a prisoner of war, of all the distinguished British officers captured on 7 October. Major Acland, who had been overrun while helpless in the angle of the rail fence, was cared for with proper consideration. Captain Money and Major Williams, being less seriously wounded, were held politely but firmly by the American provost guard. But Burgoyne's knighted aide came to rest in Horatio Gates's own camp bed, with the rebel general giving him as much attention as did the headquarters physician.

While Gates was occupied with his august prisoner, Benedict Arnold escaped the restraint of his virtual arrest. He had gone forth to fight with the men of his old division. Arnold had ridden forward with the last regiment of Learned's brigade, and by going up to the firing-line had put himself beyond reach of the exquisite aide sent by Gates to fetch him back.

Arnold, whose enemies referred to him as a "horse jockey," rode extremely well. He had need of his skill,

as he brought his big red horse pounding after
Learned's leading regiments, up the hill and through
the wheat. The bodies of the dead — first those of the
Americans and then of the Germans — and the
wounded of both sides caused the big animal to start,
leap, and swerve. But Arnold's strong hands and self-
possession quieted the nervous horse into a useful
charger.

The charge over the rail fence had hardly ended
and the last of Burgoyne's men had just retired under
the rear-guard action of Fraser's 24th Foot when
Arnold rode over the field. He was cheered by the
regiment, and he was seen reining in for an instant
to shout a gay word to a company officer, or to com-
mend a flush-faced colonel. At a time when the elation of victory might well have dampened to the
flaccid content of physical exhaustion, Benedict Arnold spread his own unquenched lust for battle over
all the well-won field. Soldiers stopped their aimless
looting of the enemy dead and ran back to their
officers. Drummers beat the call, and colonels shouted
the rallying cry of their commands. The haphazard
fire of Morgan's riflemen and the marksmen of regiments concentrated and held on the old British general mounted on his handsome gray horse. The
Americans saw him sag in his saddle, and they saw
him led away. Many a Yankee claimed that shot!
The noisy Irishman, Tim Murphy, vowed it was his
own. So did an old man in a full-bottomed wig and
a greasy big hat, with a long-barreled musket which,
according to his claim, had never been known to miss.

Arnold was not there to see the shooting of General Fraser. He was off to the captured 12-pounders, where Morgan and Poor and Learned had gathered at his summons. The three leaders, whose measured blows — one, two, three — had beaten out the shape of the British defeat, now turned expectantly to the former division commander for the plan to complete the afternoon's success. Benedict Arnold's order was simple: "Follow me!"

General Gates's aide, Major John Armstrong, also followed Arnold, but he trailed along at a distance, contentedly busy as he snuffled at the cold track through the wheatfield, at the cabin door, and in the angles of the rail fence, while Poor's and Learned's men streamed down the road in the direction of the British redoubts, and Morgan's corps re-entered the enveloping forest. The hesitant major was prowling through the shambles of the abandoned gun batteries as the New York militia of Abram Ten Broeck's brigade hurried past. For the most part they were Albany County Dutchmen, who marched loosely in village groups or together with their neighbors of the valley. They were untried troops, though there were some who had fought with Herkimer, and others who had been with Arnold on the road to Fort Stanwix. The latter, as they marched across the clearing and down the road the Continentals had traveled before them, looked with interest at the British dead. The green men looked away as they came past where Acland's big grenadiers lay huddled all around. From the walking wounded, Ten Broeck's men knew that

Arnold had gone ahead; from the sound of firing further on, they knew where they would find him.

Lieutenant General Burgoyne himself commanded in the Balcarres redoubt, where the outflanked, outnumbered, overwhelmed remnant of the reconnaissance in force had now reformed. Gentleman Johnny had been lucky. A horse had been shot from under him, his waistcoat had been ripped by a rifle ball, and at one point during the battle at the wheatfield he had been obliged to remove his hat and rearrange the plume cut by an aimed shot. Everyone had been under fire in the clearing. Behind the walls of the redoubt the soldiers would have shelter, and beyond the loopholes and the gun embrasures lay a clear field of fire over open ground. The woods were a long rifle-shot away. In front of the redoubt, two small earth-and-log barricades were positioned to cover some dead ground beyond an outcropping of gray rock. Into the southern and larger of these barricades, the Earl of Balcarres had gone with his light infantry and a complement of cannon. The men were composed as they leaned against the log walls of their barricade, occasionally interrupting their talk to peer through the loopholes in which their muskets lay. A gunner sergeant blew softly on his slow match and watched the glow as it brightened.

The sun was dropping quickly toward the undulating line of the tree-tops. Black shadows, gathering in the deep spaces between the marginal trunks of the trees, spilled out onto the clearing. The British

watched the approaching dusk and awaited the coming of the enemy.

Suddenly the enemy was there, dark figures running out from the sheltering shadows into the reveal-
ing light of the cleared field. As if startled, the British
guns roared and pranced back on their wheeled carriages. The guns fired again. A light infantryman saw
his chosen target drop his musket and fall into the
low scrub. Balcarres's man selected another Yankee,
waited for him to come within range, and fired.

Once triggered, the fire from the British field works
became measured and purposeful. The artillerymen,
loading, aiming, firing to a long-rehearsed rhythm,
beat out their bass note in a recurring sequence of
emphasis; the musket fire quickened or slackened
according to the near or distant approach of the
attacking rebel infantry.

The first rush had carried the American charge up
and into the British abatis. For a moment, the attack
had hung there while the Yankee soldiers furiously
wrenched and clawed and pulled at the mesh of
branches that kept them from the raw-faced walls of
earth and logs beyond. Then the British fire had
driven the Continentals away, into fire positions in
the scrub, among the stumps, or wherever a slight
fold of the ground offered shelter in concealment. All
up and down the long, twisting line of the Balcarres
redoubt, small American attacks were now developing. Out of the Yankee firing line, a group of shouting men would rise up and charge forward in a new
attempt to come to grips with the enemy beyond the

abatis. Each time a group came on the British or the Germans at the threatened part of the redoubt would drive them back. As the battle developed into a long fire-fight, a pattern in the local attacks became apparent. First, the British at the loopholes would see an American officer gallop up on a big, chestnut horse; the Yankees would rise slowly out of their hiding places surrounding the figure astride the prancing horse; then they would charge. By the time the attack had been beaten back, the big horse was far down the line, and wherever he was, another charge could be expected.

But even the fury of Benedict Arnold (who was the mounted figure) could not lift up the whole Continental line and hurl it forward en masse. The sun was down, the day was dying, and the passing minutes were sliding the balance of victory over to the side of the defense.

Then Arnold, changeable, unpredictable, never constant, totally unreliable but instinctive in battle, abandoned the frontal attack on the Balcarres redoubt. He left his own troops in their fire positions and he left the British at their loopholes, their guns agape at the embrasures. He was off and away on the impulse of a new idea. In his urgency, the fact that the direct way to his new objective — the Breymann redoubt — was across the front of the two firing-lines, was of no consequence. He gave spur to his chestnut horse. American marksmen withheld their fire as the swarthy major general galloped by in front of their leveled pieces. British and German infantrymen forgot to shoot, as they watched the horse with the flowing black mane and tail dash past them.

It was almost a mile to the American left, where fresh regiments were coming onto the field. Unscathed, Arnold reined in at the head of the Massachusetts regiment, where Lieutenant Colonel John Brooks was waiting for orders. Arnold did not tarry long. He made a sweeping motion of his arm in the direction of the two log houses in the gap between the two redoubts, Brooks and his men understood their orders. A touch of the spurs and again Benedict Arnold was away, to meet the militiamen of Ten Broeck's brigade, who were running toward him from the west. Here, too, there was no need for words. Arnold had but to wheel his mount to draw the whole brigade after him in a march, the direction of which would turn the open end of Breymann's log redoubt. The big horse was walking now, to allow the foot soldiers to catch up with him. Many of them reached out to touch Arnold's stirrup as they hurried by, and, looking down at them, he saw that some of Dearborn's and Morgan's men had joined him for the final assault. From all over the field they came to him: men in buckskin and in civilian clothes, boys with their fathers' hunting guns, old men with muskets as old as their fathers before them. Even a dog joined the parade. He came out of the cabins from which Burgoyne's Canadian troops were now fleeing. Although the boy, Monin, tried to call him back, he was irresistibly drawn by the shouting Yankees.

Within the redoubt, Colonel Heinrich Breymann

was in a frenzy. His men had grown sullen as the acid of their fear ate into the core of their discipline. There was little firing over the log wall at the oncoming mass of rebels; the grenadiers were watching over their shoulders for a chance to cut and run. One man *did* run, but Breymann, snarling like a Hartz Mountain cat, slashed viciously at him with his sword.

The rebels had passed the open southern end of the redoubt and were slanting in on the German flank and rear when Breymann's grenadiers broke. The raging colonel stood, his legs apart, cutting and jabbing at his own men. In the rush for safety, he struck three of them; a fourth, a big man with waxed mustaches and a mad look of panic in his wide blue eyes, shot Breymann dead, then calmly turned to meet the enemy now entering the works. For a wild moment it was hand to hand, clubbed gun against bayonet, sword against musket. In the center of the melee, the big chestnut war horse stamped and slashed with his hooves, as the rider on his back shouted and whooped. A wounded German on the ground saw the great beast bearing down on where he lay. The man's gun was still unfired. He raised it, aimed at the wide red chest and let loose the charge. It pierced the animal's great heart.

Arnold felt the horse go slack between his knees. He kicked free of one stirrup, but the leg wounded and then broken at Quebec was awkward. On it fell the dead weight of the horse. Once more, Benedict Arnold had broken his leg.

It was all over in the Breymann redoubt. Amer-

icans guarding them, a long line of Hessian prisoners sat, their backs to the wall that they had built.
The Yankees had rolled the dead horse from their
general's leg, and, having given his orders, Arnold was
resting. It was almost dark. The salmon-colored sunset glow was fading quickly. Breymann's redoubt was
firmly in American hands. Burgoyne's whole defense
line had been turned.

It was then, and in such circumstances, that Gates's
aide, Major John Armstrong, at last caught up with
Benedict Arnold. He had been too late to prevent
Arnold from acting "rashly." Only the last part of
Gates's orders to him remained to be carried out.
Standing before the wounded and prostrate hero general, the bright boy aide requested Arnold to put himself under the major's escort, to be returned to his
quarters at once. Arnold complied and so left the
field of his battle, borne on a litter high on the shoulders of four of his veterans.

With the coming of darkness all musket and cannon fire ceased. In front of the Balcarres redoubt,
Private Soldier Ephraim Squier sat up, put his back
against the white birch stump which, for the duration
of the fire fight, had been his fortress, and waited for
the sergeant to come and tell him what to do next.
Ephraim was tired. As he figured it, the Continental
Army owed him a full night's sleep. The night before
— Monday night — he had been one of a patrol
whose leader got lost and did not bring the men in
until ten o'clock in the morning. Sunday night,

Ephraim had stood the middle guard. On Sunday he had heard the parson preach from the text, "Return to the stronghold, ye prisoners of hope." On Tuesday the British and their hirelings certainly had returned to their stronghold! The sergeant, calling the company in a low-pitched voice, roused Ephraim from his reverie. Stiffly he levered himself up from his stump and shuffled off toward the voice he hoped would lead him back to Fort Neilson and his blankets.

There was no sleep that night for William Digby. At first dark, carrying a lantern, he had searched the Balcarres redoubt for the scattered remnants of the company of grenadiers, which, since the death of Captain Wight in the wheatfield, Digby had commanded. Of the twenty men who had marched out that afternoon, he could find only four. He knew that there were others: some wounded who might recover, some sick who would return, and a few who had been left out of the battle for valid reasons of administration, were still on the rolls of the company. But for duty that night of 7 October, Lieutenant Digby had but four men out of the fifty who had sailed so gaily up Lake Champlain only three months before. Digby's succession through survival scarcely seemed a promotion.

The duties of seniority, however, kept him up late. He had organized his command, set guards (like a sergeant), sought food and water for his men, searched without success for a commander of grenadiers in Major Acland's stead, and finally had reported to Balcarres, the new commander of the ad-

vance corps. If Digby had hoped for a few hours'
sleep, he was quickly disabused of the notion. Balcarres had just returned from General Burgoyne, with
serious news and urgent orders.

When John Burgoyne had received no report from
Colonel Breymann as to the light firing heard from
his key redoubt, a contact patrol had been sent out
at dusk. It returned with the news that, not only had
the Brunswick colonel been killed and his grenadiers
captured, but that the Yankees, who now held the
redoubt in force, were bringing up their own cannon
to add to the three pieces taken in the works from
the Hessian gunners there. The loss of two hundred
additional men was a blow to Burgoyne, but the loss
of the vital corner of the defense line was cata-
strophic. In the morning, a bombardment followed
by an attack such as had been seen on the 7th would
roll up the Balcarres redoubt like a map. Disheveled,
gaunt, and in the lantern light looking all of his fifty-
five years, Lieutenant General Burgoyne gave the
order to evacuate the Balcarres redoubt.

It was one o'clock in the morning of 8 October before the retreat to the new position on the heights
above the hospital could begin. Horses had to be sent
up from the camp beside the river to draw off guns
and their ammunition and the wagons with the tents.
Tending a watch fire, kept to deceive the Yankees in
Breymann's old redoubt, Digby heard his own men,
and the other Britishers, mutter as the German infantry marched out first. Silent and chastened, the
blue-coated soldiers quick-marched past their red-

coated comrades. His head held high, Captain Pausch, who had fought the good fight, stamped off at the head of his proud gunners.

It was the dark before the dawn when the Earl of Balcarres entered the gully behind his redoubt, and the last of General Burgoyne's army quit Freeman's farm.

20

The Highland Lament

Only three hours of the night remained when the surgeon who was attending General Fraser crossed the room to speak to Baroness Riedesel. She was sitting bolt upright on a bench with her small daughters sleeping beside her. The surgeon told her that, despite all efforts to save him, the general was dying. The baroness roused her children and was attempting to slip quietly out of the room when Fraser himself spoke to her. He apologized for the inconvenience he was causing. Friederika Riedesel spent the rest of the night sitting on the floor of the corridor, while her children slept peacefully nearby.

The old Highlander had prided himself on his mastery of the difficult military maneuver of withdrawal and retreat. The British army during the hours and days following his funeral was in sore need of General Fraser. Burgoyne had given the order for a general retreat to Saratoga — to Fort Edward — down Lake George to Ticonderoga: a sixty-mile climb back down the ladder of his success, without pause on the rungs of his delays.

John Burgoyne was the dashing cavalryman of the "hell-for-leather" charge, the gambler who always expected his high cards to win, the politician in debate who was always impatient to make his rebuttal. He saw no glory or merit in retreat, however bold or reckless, from an unbreached wall. To discard a court card was dishonorable, even though such a move might develop a whole line of lesser trumps, and, in debate, to concede was to admit defeat. Now, Burgoyne had no plan for retreat. He had only the hope that his luck would turn and that he could yet reach Albany.

A few necessary preparations were made, however, during the daylight hours of 8 October. At the British camp, carts and boats lay, as on any other day, under the watchful scrutiny of rebel scouts on the east side of the Hudson River. The increased activity around the hospital, where the surgeons worked to prepare the sick and wounded for the Yankees to whose care they must be left, could well be attributed to the previous day's battle. The guns could not yet be removed from the redoubts, as a renewed American attack was expected, even hoped for, by the British troops imbued with their general's infectious determination. Only the men of the fighting regiments, by resting quietly behind their strong redoubts, could prepare for the secret night retirement.

During the morning there was a general alarm, when the tired, underfed troops stood to and watched the Americans deploy in front of their lines on the flat river plain. But the guns and howitzers of the

Royal Artillery kept the Yankees at their distance, while the foot soldiers, wrapped in the blanket of near exhaustion, resumed their interrupted sleep.

In a hiding place that he had made beyond the picquet post, a *Jäger* private, alert because of the danger in which he found himself, caught a glimpse of blue and buff among the trees, a long rifle-shot away. As a huntsman on the ducal estate, the *Jäger* had often watched the wild boars drifting, ghost-like, through the forest. Now he raised his rifle, waiting for his quarry again to expose himself. In the instant before pulling the trigger, he saw the biggest and fattest man to come before his eyes since last he had seen His Grace's baker, at home in Wülfenbutl. In the German's aimed shot General Fraser was avenged.

Major General Benjamin Lincoln took the *Jäger* bullet in his leg. Though not fatal, the wound seriously affected the future course of the American campaign. In immobilizing the great bulk of the man, it removed the weighty influence of the general. Benjamin Lincoln's value as a soldier had been proven on the northern frontier under both Schuyler and Gates. He it was who had roused the militia, who had placated John Stark sufficiently to prevent his returning home; he had organized the telling raid on Fort Ticonderoga, leaving it be carried out by men more agile than himself. During the action of 19 September Lincoln had been in Vermont, but he soon returned to keep his level head, and his command of the right wing of the Continental Army and of the militia,

while the Gates-Arnold controversy raged. He had
taken Benedict Arnold with him when he went forward to estimate the situation created by Burgoyne's
reconnaissance in force. General Gates had listened
to his report, and at Lincoln's urgent instigation had
sent out Morgan and the brigades of Arnold's former
command. Although he was the only available major
general on duty at the time, Lincoln had made no
attempt to take over the disgraced Arnold's men for
the battle of 7 October. He had returned to his right
wing command, where he readied Glover's and Pat-
terson's brigades to exploit any breakthrough that
might be achieved on the left.

With Lincoln down, as well as Arnold, Major General Horatio Gates stood alone in the high place of
his rank and his command. He demonstrated no need
for a deputy; he had never sought one. None of his
seven brigadier generals was permitted to approach
him. Content with the working out of his own
schemes, he remained in every way aloof. From
Gates's headquarters, all contact forward was made
through that "bright lad," James Wilkinson. General
Gates saw his troops and their battles only through
the eyes of the young lieutenant colonel and adjutant
general, who rode here and there as he felt inclined,
a platoon of couriers trailing him.

Now, on 8 October, undisturbed by the bold inter-
ruptions of Arnold or by the necessity for showing
courtesy to the able and amenable Lincoln, Gates
could continue with his plan for holding the diminish-
ing British army within its contracting lines. If Bur-

goyne retreated, as now appeared likely, Gates would follow, as inevitably as the cart follows the horse, into the marketplace of victory and reward.

But as the day after the battle wore on, Gates was reminded again and again of one administrative detail which had been overlooked — 7 October had been the beginning of a new four-day ration period. Because of the battle no individual issue of food had been made. The Americans had been sustained by the excitement of victory and by the anticipation of a second day's harrying of the British. But inaction had kindled fires of hunger in the soldiers deployed on the river plain and in the captured redoubts. Gates ordered the issue of rations on 9 October, and called the troops back into their fieldworks so that in the day-long ceremony of weighing, apportioning, and recording of the rations, each man might draw the issue to which he was entitled.

At sunset, when the Americans had not yet returned to their lines, a group of British soldiers was spotted on a hilltop, only a cannon shot away. Before it limbered up, a rebel battery fired on this target of opportunity, its round shot falling short by only a few yards. It was close enough to throw a shower of dirt and sand over the black coat of Chaplain Edward Brudenel. But the interruption failed to halt the flow of his words, nor did General Burgoyne, or Phillips, or Riedesel, or young Captain Alexander Fraser, raise his bowed head until the remains of General Simon Fraser had been committed, with all ceremony, to the grave.

At nine o'clock on the evening of 8 October, with
Captain Fraser's marksmen leading, the retreat of
Burgoyne's army began. General Riedesel followed
with his Germans. Then came the British contingent,
with the guns and wheeled transport sandwiched in
among the regiments. Before the rear guard, under
Balcarres, had begun to march, Riedesel, at the head
of the column already four miles forward on the road
to Saratoga, received the order to halt. A light rain
was falling when General Riedesel climbed into his
family's *calash* to await the order — expected momentarily — to resume the march. Three hours later,
he awoke with a start of bewilderment which quickly
changed to anger at his wife, who had pillowed him
in his heavy sleep. Rain beat on the canvas cover of
the wagon, and gusts of the northeast wind flapped
the sodden cloth against the taut bows holding it
away from the passengers and baggage that it pro-
tected. Still in a rage, the general left its shelter and
strode off through the mud to get to the bottom of the
cause for the delay.

The cause was all too apparent. It was visible in
the drawn white faces of the men who sat by the
roadside, wet and cold and seemingly heedless of
their misery. Like the baroness herself, the German
women were with their men, instead of at the wagons.
They looked at him boldly, and the general's anger
softened into indignant compassion. It was the transport which had caused the delay. Whereas the will
of the men could be revived by encouragement, the
dumb beasts pulling the guns and the wagons

through the mud could only be driven until they died. Yet they struggled on. In one of the carts, Riedesel saw Major Harnage, wrapped in blankets; he had refused to be left behind. With one hand on the tailgate, Mrs. Harnage walked beside the cart, smiling at Major General Riedesel as she passed.

From across the Hudson River, a single shot was fired. It was directed at a provision bateau which, in its struggle upstream, had worked its way too close to the enemy, dogging the east bank of the river.

At a point where grooms were holding a large herd of saddle horses, Riedesel found General Burgoyne, who was rejecting the plea of Colonel Sutherland to release his regiment (the 47th) for an attack. On the previous day, 8 October, Sutherland had been sent ahead to see if the way was clear. He had reported that the road was unobstructed through Saratoga. Beyond that place, Brigadier General Fellows of the Massachusetts militia lay in such a loose, carelessly organized camp that Sutherland felt sure he could attack with the two hundred and fifty men left in his regiment and have every expectation of success. Burgoyne, however, refused to detach any part of his force. He remained throughout the day in the rainy bivouac at Dovegate, and at four o'clock in the afternoon the march to Saratoga — the first leg of the retreat to Ticonderoga — was resumed.

Earlier in the day a group of German soldiers had eluded their officers long enough to desert into the woods. There, without their own Indian allies to hunt them down like rabbits, the "hirelings" found mercy

from the Yankees. That evening Lady Acland, too,
quit the army. With her she took her maid, her husband's wounded valet, and, for consolation and to
row the boat, the Reverend Edward Brudenel. The
little party went downriver to a safe landing behind
the American lines. Her pass from General Burgoyne
was respected, and soon she was reunited with her
wounded husband, whom she nursed back to health.

The evening was still young as the head of the
British army crossed Fish Creek and spread out into
the old positions, made in mid-September. Scouting
north of the old camp, Fraser's marksmen saw the last
of Fellows's brigade splashing across the ford to the
east bank of the Hudson. A few shots in the dark
hurried them along.

Burgoyne himself did not cross Fish Creek that
night. Always reluctant to give in, he ordered three
British regiments, under Brigadier Hamilton, to keep
a bridgehead on the south side of the stream. Wea-
rily, he then permitted himself to turn in at the gate
of Schuyler's house. The wife of his commissary had
preceded him, and already lamps had been lighted
in the downstairs rooms. As Burgoyne crossed the
threshold, a champagne cork popped with a noise like
a pocket pistol. Gentleman Johnny headed instinc-
tively toward the familiar sound.

In the morning, rested and refreshed, General Burgoyne moved all his troops north of the Fish Kill.
Regretfully, he gave the order to burn down the
graciously hospitable Schuyler house. It had to go,
overlooking as it did the stream crossing and the
British defensive positions on the other side.

On 10 October General Gates finally moved out of his fortified camp and with his whole army went in pursuit of Burgoyne. During that day, Fellows's brigade held the British to the west side of the river by harassing fire, preventing Burgoyne's pioneers from building a bridge over the Hudson at the old crossing place.

In the dense river fog of the autumn morning of 11 October, Daniel Morgan and his grizzled riflemen crossed Fish Creek on improvised rafts, disembarking on the bluffs three-quarters of a mile west of the Hudson. To men at home among the close, solid, friendly trunks of great trees, the vast emptiness of the thick blue mist hanging over the open fields was a disconcerting thing. As if drawn by a magnet, their northward advance inclined to the west, where the deep woods began again. Thus they missed the strong redoubt where Balcarres's advance guard stood at arms, marking the rangers' passage by their eerie, though all too familiar, call of the wild turkey gobbler. Nearer to the river bank, Brigadier General John Nixon had crossed the creek with his brigade of Continentals. Though a town man from near to Boston, Nixon, like Morgan's woodsmen, also moved warily through the fog. Uncertain of his true position and mistrusting the report that the British had gone on to Fort Edward, he called a halt. It was well that he did so, for with the rising sun the mist burned away to show his whole brigade under the muzzles of a British battery. Promptly and without hesitation, Nixon, in whom the keen edge of vainglory had been dulled on many battle grounds, brought off his bri-

gade at a run, not stopping until he had recrossed
Fish Creek to its south shore. There he fell into line
of battle beside John Glover, a Marblehead man.
Only Ebenezer Learned sprang forward on discovering that the fog had hidden all of Burgoyne's army in
a position of defense. As on 7 October when Benedict
Arnold led, he sought out Morgan and prepared to
mount a charge. He was stopped only by the arrival
of the ubiquitous Wilkinson, who, in the name of
General Gates, ordered him back. Reluctantly, and
muttering strange biblical quotations, Learned withdrew.

Gates's artillery came up in the afternoon, and
from positions along the line of Fish Creek began the
bombardment of the British entrenchments. Using
captured British bateaux as ferries, Yankee artillerymen moved guns and ammunition over to the east
shore of the Hudson, where men from Fellows's command pointed out gun sites to enfilade Burgoyne's
camp. On 12 October, the first gun of the east-shore
batteries fired on a house that was known to belong
to Peter Lansing, which, from the activity surrounding it, the American gunners believed to be British
army headquarters.

It was on that day, too, that Gates completed the
encirclement of Burgoyne's army. Morgan shifted his
line northward until it overlapped the British positions on the west. Again crossing Fish Creek, Learned
lined up to the right of the riflemen. That night, Massachusetts men of Fellows's brigade crossed on rafts
to the west shore of the Hudson. Pushing boldly

westward through the darkness and rain they cut
the forest road up the west bank of the river to Fort
Edward, Burgoyne's only clear way to the north.
Patrols continued westward through the sodden underbrush until they were challenged by the picquet
of riflemen holding Morgan's suspended left flank.
By dawn of 13 October, twelve thousand American
guns, rifles, and muskets ringed around Burgoyne's
scant four thousand men and bayonets.

Since the fog had lifted on the morning of 11 October, the British troops on the high ground had
learned every angle and nook of their redoubt. They
knew every spot where a Yankee rifleman perched
high in a tree could reach in with his murderous small
shot. They knew where they could crouch and where
they could lie in reasonable safety from the American
cannon. Men quickly grew wise in judging the sound
of an oncoming shell, and learned by a glance at a
distant puff of smoke whether to duck for safety or to
continue their wretched waiting in the rain.

Baroness Riedesel had seen the first shot fired from
the east shore of the river. With the shrewd judgment
of a veteran, she had guessed that it was intended for
the Lansing house, in the cellar of which she and her
children, with the other women, were taking refuge.
For the remainder of the siege, the house was under
constant and accurate bombardment, but there, in
the vaulted arches of the cellar, she ruled as she had
ruled in her stately Brunswick home. After thoroughly fumigating the smelly quarters by burning

vinegar there, she apportioned the available space. In
the deepest vault she placed the wounded; the
women she assigned to the middle room; and in the
room from which the stairs climbed to the outer door,
she curtained off her own corner of luxurious privacy.

In the outer room, which she shared with Mrs.
Harnage and Mrs. Reynell, Baroness Riedesel received her callers and turned away all those whom
she deemed "skulkers." She saw but little of her husband, though he sent his aides from time to time to
reassure her. On one such errand, Captain Willoe
silently handed his wallet to her for safe-keeping.
She was already holding Captain Geismar's wallet,
with his watch and ring. One day, after a particularly
heavy bombardment, during which those in the cellar
could hear the cannon balls rolling across the plank
flooring above them. Captain Green came to have
his old wound dressed by the surgeon. Before leaving, he told the baroness that he had made arrangements with three officers, each of whom would take
one of her children on his saddle-bow, and that, when
the time came, a horse would be brought for her to
ride.

At headquarters the generals were talking flight. In
the lines the men talked of food, of a bayonet charge,
of old campaigns: Ticonderoga, Hubbardton, Fort
Anne, Fort Edward, even of Bennington. All these
were now only places in the distant past.

21

The World Turned Upside Down

At all the councils of war, Major General the Baron
Friederich von Riedesel — though himself a "hireling" and his men but chattels of their respective
dukes — spoke out in favor of any plan which was
in any way of benefit to his troops. In doing so, he
risked incurring the disapproval of those same Dukes
of Brunswick and of Hesse-Cassel, who stood to gain
if their soldiers were killed, wounded, or taken prisoner. Of the former, three wounded subjects equaled,
in cash to the duke, one dead subject. Perhaps the
baron's concern for the common soldier was the
result of his own long years in the army, and his con-
sequent knowledge of, and respect for, those men he
deemed true soldiers. General Riedesel recognized
the investment in training, experience, and loyalty
represented by the men, both British and German,
who had fought from Ticonderoga to Freeman's
farm, and considered them to have a greater value
than the guns and stores.

At the council of war held on 12 October 1777,
in the all but encircled camp at Saratoga, General

Riedesel's views finally prevailed. His proposals were accepted and the necessary orders issued by General Burgoyne. At ten o'clock that night, guns, wagons, stores, boats — everything but small arms — were to be abandoned, and the men and women of the expedition, carrying their food on pack-horses, were to march by the west road to Fort Edward. They were to fight for the crossing there, and proceed to Fort Ticonderoga.

But at Saratoga the plan, which might have succeeded four days earlier, no longer served its purpose. The drag of the wheeled vehicles in the rain and mud, and the northeast wind which had delayed the provision boats forcing their way up against the current of the river, killed all hope of the troops being able to save themselves. Had the delay not rendered the plan unfeasible, in all probability General Burgoyne's hesitancy would have done so. He still saw his duty and loyalty in faithful adherence to "The Plan," and he was honor-bound while he yet had guns and battalions, to hammer the enemy pending the arrival of Sir Henry Clinton and his army, still confidently expected by Burgoyne.

Even in this desperate situation John Burgoyne could not quit. Before the appointed hour on the night of 12 October he cancelled the order to retreat. By accepting the decision of a council of war, a commander in chief gains friendly witnesses at the inevitable court of inquiry. By overriding the decision and going against the advice of his senior officers — Phillips, Riedesel, Hamilton, and von Gall — General Burgoyne accepted full responsibility for the consequences.

By the morning of 13 October any attempt to get away by the west road was futile. The road was dominated by Fellows's Massachusetts men, from a strong hill position with marshy ground in front. In the afternoon, Burgoyne called a general council, to which came the generals, the colonels, and the majors. The captains, too, were summoned, some of them coming from exposed company positions, darting across open spaces, under the watchful eyes of Morgan's riflemen, and crawling through underbrush so as not to be seen by the Yankee gunners. After brushing their uniforms with grimy hands and straightening their rumpled stocks, with some embarrassment they entered the presence of their general.

Burgoyne rose to speak. He accepted all blame for the situation in which they found themselves. He reported frankly that there remained but five days' rations in all the camp. Eloquently, he cited comparable examples in history of armies that had capitulated. The officers listened in silence as their general made his case for surrender. Then Burgoyne posed two questions: Would a surrender on advantageous terms be disgraceful? The solemn answer was an unhesitating "No." Under existing circumstances was such a capitulation necessary? Speaking, first, as is the custom, the most junior captain shyly and unemotionally offered his life and pledged the loyalty of his men in a "do or die" attack. Others followed

his lead, and on up through the grades of ascending
rank, General Burgoyne heard out his tribute. In the
reaction of his officers John Burgoyne regained
reason and found wisdom. He entered into negotiation with Horatio Gates.

Early in the morning of 14 October a drummer in
a yellow coat marched boldly to Fish Creek, where
the bridge stringers still reached over to the south
bank. He was busy for a moment as he tightened the
soggy head of his drum. Then, posing with the tips
of the drumsticks just touching the down on his
upper lip, he sensed that unseen Yankees were watching him. He beat out the parlay.

At ten o'clock, James Wilkinson rode past the
burned-out ruins of the Schuyler mansion, dismounted, and strode to the south end of the broken
bridge. At the north end, a few yards away, Lieutenant Colonel Robert Kingston, Deputy Adjutant
General and secretary to General Burgoyne, waited
in the rain for Wilkinson's invitation to cross, which
came with a polite gesture. Gingerly, the Englishman crossed on the single stringer linking the two
banks of Fish Creek. On the Yankee side, Kingston
accepted the blindfold, and with Wilkinson leading
him set out to open the negotiations with Gates.

All that day and far into the night proposals
and counter-proposals were written, exchanged, discussed, amended, and returned. While the two staffs
worked hard and long and late, the men of both
armies moved about in their positions, secure under
the terms of an armistice.

Compromise by compromise, the negotiations moved toward a still-distant conclusion. Then, with a suddenness that startled Burgoyne into suspicion, Gates agreed to all of Burgoyne's requests, stipulating only that the capitulation be signed by two o'clock that afternoon, Wednesday, 15 October, and that the British and German troops lay down their arms at five o'clock. Such a bullish rush was not in in character for the feline Gates. To Burgoyne, a shrewd player at cards, Gates appeared to be pushed from behind, like a house cat shoved out into the rain. Quite correctly, Burgoyne reasoned that some action on the part of Sir Henry Clinton was the cause of Gates's haste to bring the easy game of negotiation to a close. By every means in his considerable knowledge of the art of procrastination, Burgoyne sought to prolong the discussion of terms. Ever a prisoner of hope, with each passing hour he saw the phoenix of his "Thoughts for Conducting the War" rise from the ashes of his predicament, in the tardily kindled flame of Clinton's advance from Albany.

Burgoyne's spirits soared that night when he was roused from sleep to interview a Tory from the lower Hudson. The man brought word of the capture by Clinton, on 8 October, of the American forts on the highlands. He also reported that English forces, which he had heard were at Esopus, only sixty miles below Albany, probably were now marching into that city.

With this good news, General Burgoyne entered the council of officers that he had called for 16

October. But the temper of the army had now
changed, and the vote held Burgoyne in honor bound
to continue the negotiations with Gates. Even so,
Gentleman Johnny found one more grain of hope in
his larder of desperation. Had Gates broken the
armistice by sending troops from the army encircling
the British to meet the threat of Clinton's northward
march? If so, then Gates himself had broken off the
negotiations. The council of officers recessed while
representations on this point were sent to Gates.
Truthfully the American general could answer in the
negative. In fact, Gates had sent Colonel Peter Ganse-
voort, from the Mohawk Valley, to contain the British
at Esopus. It was these rebel soldiers that the Tory
talebearer had seen on the march below Albany.

When the council reconvened that afternoon the
British officers again saw no legal or moral reason
for failure to sign the surrender. While the officers
waited, Burgoyne sought privately to sway his generals. Phillips, eternally proud, refused comment, as
he had done at the council before the second battle
at Freeman's farm. Riedesel, who had been sustain-
ing himself in his exhaustion with white wine, could
only bemoan the lost opportunity to save such fine
soldiers. Completely alone in all his hopes, opinions,
and determination, Lieutenant General John Burgoyne surrendered his army. With studied careless-
ness, he threw his last card out onto the table: it was
a deuce. Nowhere in the Articles of Agreement should
the word "capitulation" appear; the word, "convention" was to be used in its place.

The British general chose the nicest of words to entitle the script; unexpectedly, the staging of the final scene was a masterpiece of tact, courtesy, and understanding on the part of the American general. The ceremonies were set for Friday, 17 October 1777.

For the first time since the retreat had begun nine days earlier, the sun came out. It rose above the high mountains lining the Vermont horizon. It shone on the wide trace of the Hudson River, where red and gold autumn leaves, riding southward on the smooth, swift flowing current, caught the light. On the western slopes, the trunks and branches of trees that had been hidden by summer foliage now showed a silvery gray.

The day was bright and washed and polished as were the British and German soldiers, forming their ranks in the old redoubts and behind the barricades. Orders were carried out with a crispness matching the clear October air. Closed ranks opened; the dressing was picked up with a shuffling of feet that rustled the dry leaves. Rows and rows and rows of straight, proud figures stood rigidly at attention while the officers made their slow inspection. Not much was left of the uniforms that four months earlier had looked so fine on the banks of the distant Richelieu River, as the royal standard had flapped lazily in the warm June breeze. Now, many miles away on the shores of the Hudson, patches were the soldiers' distinction, and wispy plumes that once had been full and luxuriant marked the fortitude of men on long marches down forest roads. Old muskets, their battered, dented stocks rubbed gleaming with oil, and the burnished steel of bayonets, marked the veterans of General Burgoyne's army as battle-tested troops.

It was their last parade as soldiers. Soon — for the drums had begun to beat — the men would be called upon to lay down the tools of their profession and to march away as prisoners of war. One by one, the regiments came down to the river, the red-coated British and the tall, blue-uniformed Germans. One by one, their colonels gave the order to ground arms, and one by one, the regiments marched off, hands swinging high to the music of the bands. There were no Yankees to witness the shucking of their arms and their pride. Only a few curious civilians watched from the other side of the river. It was for their benefit that the bands played "The World Turned Upside Down," while the tension that had been building up in the waiting troops eased to the sound of the appropriate and familiar tune.

James Wilkinson could hear the sound of the music as, with General Burgoyne riding beside him, he approached the Fish Creek bridge. The stamping hooves of their horses, and of the horses of Burgoyne's four generals who followed behind them, drowned out the saucy music as the party rode across the bridge. On the new side of the world, the young American officer and the old British general he was escorting caught the sound of another air. It was made by the harsh field music of the American Continentals, marching up to line the road to the tune of "Yankee Doodle Dandy," squealed out by the insolent fifes. Once, as Wilkinson led him on, Burgoyne jerked his head up quickly; a wild turkey had called from a copse not far away.

Half a mile from the creek, the cavalcade turned off the Albany road into a field where a large tent had been set up. In front of the tent stood a group of American officers. As the British approached, one of the Americans left the group and mounted his horse. Moving with slow deliberation, the British generals drew nearer. A few yards from the solitary mounted figure dressed in a simple blue uniform-coat, Burgoyne reined in. Wilkinson politely made the introduction. John Burgoyne removed his plumed hat, and in a firm, clear voice spoke the sentence that made him a prisoner of war. Horatio Gates made the appropriate reply, addressing Lieutenant General Burgoyne as "Your Excellency."

The final ceremonies of the "convention" took place beside the straight road to Albany. There, in a cleared space near the road, General Burgoyne tendered his sword to General Gates. Along the road the weaponless soldiers of Britain's northern army marched as prisoners between two silent ranks of solmen-faced Continentals.

To Lieutenant Digby, striding by with all that remained of Acland's grenadiers, the music of their band, though it played their own "Grenadiers' March," sounded dull and lifeless. His face was wet with tears as he stepped out smartly, to pass in style

the place where Gentleman Johnny was taking the
review beside the pudgy little man who was the
conqueror. Company by company they came: light
infantry, artillery, regiments of the British line, *Jägers*
in green, and stolid German infantry. The remnants
of the 62nd passed the motionless ranks of the men
they had met in the bitter fighting at the angle of
the fence at Freeman's farm, a month gone by. The
young Fraser and his moccasined rangers padded
past the riflemen of Morgan's corps, on whom they
had so successfully patterned themselves. The 9th of
Foot, remembering the defile at Fort Anne, marched
along behind its band. In the lead was Colonel Hill,
very conscious of the sudden corpulence showing
under his waistcoat, where his regiment's Color was
safely (he hoped) hidden. The October sun caught
the polished gold and silver of the mitered grenadiers, as they trudged woodenly along behind their
new commander. The sun caught, too, the flourish of
a sword blade as it cut the elaborate arc of a final
salute to the well-loved general it had served with
unswerving devotion. A short distance down the
road, the company commander whose sword it was
turned abruptly and tossed the weapon, now useless
in his hands, to a small American boy who stood,
wide-eyed, in the space between two Continental
soldiers.

Epilogue

Charles Gravier, Comte de Vergennes, was foreign minister to Louis XVI, the young Bourbon king of France. Many people, however, considered him to be little more than a clerk, and it was as such that he was treated by the British ambassador to the court at Versailles when, on 2 September 1777, he brought word to the French court of Lieutenant General Burgoyne's capture of Fort Ticonderoga, the French-built "Fort Carillon." Accompanying this news was a demand by England that the American rebels be treated as outlaws, and that French ports be closed to the Yankee pirates and their prizes. The British ambassador, Viscount Stormont, intimated that failure to comply with this demand might well bring on a formal declaration of war.

For two months after the receipt of the news of Burgoyne's significant victory in the Lake Champlain Pass, Vergennes played the part of procrastinating clerk, while proving himself to be, in fact, an accomplished diplomat, a crafty politician, and a master in the art of devious intrigue. In France, public opinion favored the cause of the Americans in their dispute with England. Since the revolt in Boston had spread so quickly to the other colonies in North America, France had sent supplies to the rebels and had encouraged them in every way short of declaring war on Britain. But in spite of increasing pressures, Vergennes held back from making the ultimate commitment. Actually, he was strengthening his own resources in military preparations and in diplomatic alliances, while watching for a sure sign that the Americans could and would hold fast to their declared independence against the armed might of Britain.

All during September, October, and November, Vergennes was successful in fending off the demands made by the arrogant Lord Stormont, while restraining his own ardent countrymen and following his monarch to Fontainebleau for hunting with the court.

On 4 December 1777, the American commissioners brought to Vergennes's busy private bureau the sure sign for which he waited. General Burgoyne had been defeated in battle, and his whole army had been taken prisoner at a place called Saratoga. Two days later, in a note written in the king's presence and in the king's own apartment, Vergennes gave France's recognition of the new United States as a sovereign nation, and became that nation's ally in war. Scarcely waiting for the ink to dry, Louis XVI approved and dated the simple document which was to assure the victory and independence of the United States of America.

In the office of King George the Third's Secretary
of State for the American Colonies there was another
document, as important to the emergent United
States as was Vergennes's note of alliance and active
participation in the war. But, unlike its French
counterpart, the document in London was unsigned,
undelivered, and in fact, forgotten. This was the
promised letter from Lord George Germaine to General Howe, ordering the latter up the Hudson to complete the grand design of Burgoyne's plan to sever
in two the American colonies along the Hudson-
Champlain Pass.

It was bitterly cold on the March evening in 1777
when Germaine stopped in at the Colonial Office to
sign some letters before continuing his drive into the
country, where he was to spend the week-end. The
important letter he had drafted to Lord Howe was
not yet ready in the form insisted upon by the meticulous Germaine. It was warm beside the fire in the
Secretary's office, but it was *not* warm outside in the
street where milord's coach was waiting. Always a
considerate horseman, Germaine preferred not to
keep his horses waiting in the cold. Besides, his blast
of furious rage over the poorly copied letter would
lose its effect, if he were to wait patiently while the
clerk rewrote the slovenly work. So Lord George
Germaine swept out of his office, his dignity and his
scruples intact, and rode away in his fine coach.
When he returned a few days later, he quite forgot
to ask for the letter to Howe, and no one cared —
perhaps no one remembered — to bring it to his attention.

The letter was never sent, and without any specific orders to co-operate with General Burgoyne, Howe sailed for the Chesapeake to carry out his plan for the capture of Philadelphia.

In the upper Hudson River and in Lake George and Lake Champlain, ice forms in December in quiet bays and backwaters, and between Fort Ticonderoga and Skenesborough, where the water is shallow. On the mountain summits the gathering snows are white along the invasion road from the St. Lawrence to the Hudson. The long silence of winter settles over the land.

By December 1777 all the armies of the long, hot, frenzied days of summer were gone from the northern frontier. Soon after the surrender at Saratoga, Clinton had fallen back on New York. Powell had destroyed and abandoned the British forts at Ticonderoga, and had sailed to Canada. The remnant of Burgoyne's army was beginning its long years of captivity in Cambridge, Massachusetts. Even Gates's army had left the fields it had won. The militia had gone home. The tough Continentals had marched away to join General Washington at the grim camp at Valley Forge, there to watch Sir William Howe wintering comfortably in Philadelphia. No one was left at Freeman's farm, on the Walloomsac, at Fort Edward, Fort Anne, Skenesborough, Hubbardton, Ticonderoga. The softly falling snow covered the debris of Burgoyne's army along all the way of its proud march from British Canada to Saratoga, in New York State.

Chronology

of Lieutenant General John Burgoyne's Campaign of 1777 and of events relating to that campaign.

6 May   General Burgoyne arrives in Canada.

13 June   Invasion army sets out from St. Jean.

20 June   Burgoyne's proclamation to the Americans.

21 June   Burgoyne's conference with the Indians.

1 July   Siege of the forts at Ticonderoga begins.

5 July   British guns arrive on Sugar Loaf, and the Americans evacuate Fort Ticonderoga and Mount Independence.

6 July   British army occupies the forts and Skenesborough.

7 July   Battle on Hubbardton road.

8 July   Battle near Fort Anne.

23 July   General Howe with the main British army leaves New York by sea for Chesapeake Bay.

27 July   Murder of Jane McCrea.

30 July   Burgoyne's army established on the Hudson River at Fort Edward.

6 August   Battle of Oriskany.

9 August   British army advances to the Batten Kill.

16 August   Baum's and Breymann's battles along the Walloomsac River on the road to Bennington.

23 August   Colonel St. Leger raises his siege of Fort Stanwix.

11 September   Howe wins the Battle of Brandywine, Pennsylvania.

13 September   Burgoyne crosses to the west bank of the Hudson at Saratoga.

18 September   General Lincoln's raid on the British-held forts at Ticonderoga.

19 September   First battle at Freeman's farm.

26 September   Howe occupies Philadelphia.

6 October   General Sir Henry Clinton captures the American forts guarding the Hudson highlands.

7 October   Second battle at Freeman's farm.

9 October   Burgoyne's army arrives at Saratoga on its retreat.

17 October   Burgoyne surrenders at Saratoga.

26 October   Sir Henry Clinton returns to New York.

8 November   British destroy and evacuate the forts at Ticonderoga.

British and German Troops

The tables of organization laid down for the three parts of the British army operating in and from Canada for the campaign of 1777 are given in a letter of instruction, dated at Whitehall on 26 March of that year, from Lord George Germaine, Secretary of State for the American Colonies, to General Guy Carleton, Governor General of Canada. The detailed instructions provided for 3770 soldiers to remain in Canada, 675 soldiers plus "a sufficiency of Canadians and Indians" to go with Colonel Barry St. Leger to Albany via the Mohawk River, and 7173 British and German troops to be put under the command of Lieutenant General Burgoyne. In addition, Burgoyne was to have as many Canadians and Indians as might be thought necessary. Both St. Leger and Burgoyne were to be given complete artillery trains. Burgoyne's force was also to include cadres of American Loyalist units to be recruited to full strength in the liberated province. St. Leger's force was to include Sir John Johnson's Loyalist regiment from the Mohawk Valley.

There are several points that should be made about the different kinds of units and their components before proceeding with the table of organization.

In the eighteenth century it was customary to put the best soldiers of a regiment into a single elite company. Originally this company was armed with grenades. Though the weapon itself became obsolete, the assault and shock troops of a regiment continued to bear the name of grenadier company. The overarm motion used to throw a grenade was awkward for a man wearing a wide-brimmed tricorne hat, so special headgear was adopted by the grenadiers. This, with certain other minor deviations from the regular uniform, was carried over as a kind of remnant, though it formerly had served a purpose.

For a particular campaign, the grenadier company of each of the regiments of the force was often removed from the command of the regimental colonel and all the grenadiers assembled as a separate command. Thus, Major Acland's "Grenadiers of Regiments" was made up of the grenadier companies of the seven British regiments of General Burgoyne's army: the 9th, 20th, 21st, 24th, 47th, 53rd, and 62nd. To these were added the grenadier companies of three British regiments which remained in Canada under command of General Carleton: the 29th, 31st, and 34th. Ideally, the strength of a British company was fifty men, giving Acland a potential force of ten companies, or 500 soldiers. After removal of the grenadier company and, frequently, the light infantry company too, the line regiment was left with but eight companies, a total (in theory) of 400 men. In most instances, however, the actual number was somewhat less than full complement, though every effort was made to draft the most able men from the battalion companies into the grenadier and light infantry companies.

When, in the mid-eighteenth century, a need for the employment of ranger-type troops became apparent, the light infantry company of regiments was raised by gathering the youngest and most active men into a second elite corps. Like the grenadiers, this corps also wore a distinctive uniform. Burgoyne's light infantry of regiments, commanded by the Earl of Balcarres, was of the same strength and drawn from the same regiments as Acland's corps of grenadiers.

Burgoyne's forces, including the Indians who joined after the expedition set out from St. Jean, numbered about 8000 officers and men. They were organized, up to the time they quit Skenesborough at the end of July, as follows:

I	Lieutenant General John Burgoyne and Staff	
II	Advance Corps	Brigadier General Simon Fraser
	Grenadiers of Regiments	Major John Acland
	Light Infantry of Regiments	The Earl of Balcarres
	24th Foot	Major William Agnew; Major Robert Grant (killed at Hubbardton); Colonel Fraser, Acting Brigadier General
	Marksmen	Captain Alexander Fraser
	Indians	St. Luc de la Corne and others
	Canadians	De la Naudière and others
III	British or Right Division	Major General William Phillips
	1st Brigade	Brigadier General James Hamilton
	20th Foot	Lieutenant Colonel John Lind
	21st Foot	Major _____ Squire; Acting Brigadier General Hamilton
	62nd Foot	Lieutenant Colonel John Anstruther
	2nd Brigade	Brigadier General Henry W. Powell
	9th Foot	Lieutenant Colonel John Hill

47th Foot	Lieutenant Colonel Nicholas Sutherland
53rd Foot	Lieutenant Colonel Powell, Acting Brigadier General
IV German or Left Division	Major General Baron Friederich von Riedesel
Brigade Specht	Brigadier General Johann Friederich Specht
Regiment von Rhetz (Brunswick)	Lieutenant Colonel Johann Gustav von Ehrenkroock
Regiment von Specht (Brunswick)	Major Carl Friederich von Ehrenkroock; Acting Brigadier General von Specht
Regiment von Riedesel (Brunswick)	Lieutenant Colonel Ernst Ludwig von Spaeth; Major General von Riedesel
Brigade von Gall	Brigadier General W. R. von Gall
Regiment Prinz Friederich (Brunswick)	Lieutenant Colonel Christian Julius Praetorius
Regiment Erb-Prinz (Hesse-Hanau)	Colonel W. R. von Gall, Acting Brigadier
"Reserve" *	Colonel Heinrich Christoph Breymann

* The German "Reserve" were, in effect, the storm troops of the German contingent, as was the advance corps of the British. The grenadiers of regiments were formed in the same way as Acland's grenadiers. However, as the German regiment was composed of five companies only, each with a hundred men, the five companies of Breymann's grenadiers were theoretically of the same numerical strength as their British counterpart. There were no light infantry companies of regiments in the German Establishment.

Grenadiers	Colonel Heinrich Christoph Breymann
Light Infantry Battalion Bärner	Major Ferdinand Albrecht von Bärner
Jäger Company (Brunswick)	Captain von Geyso
Prinz Ludwig Dragoons (Brunswick)	Lieutenant Colonel Friederich Baum
Artillery	Major Griffith Williams

Personnel:

4 companies Royal Artillery

Detachment Royal Irish Artillery

Reinforcement draft of 33rd Foot, destined for their regiment with General Howe's army, attached to Royal Artillery

1 company Hesse-Hanau Artillery	Captain Georg Pausch

Guns:

Siege Train for siege of Fort Ticonderoga 128 guns — cannon, howitzers, and mortars

Guns attached to brigades

Advance Corps	10 guns
Hamilton's Brigade	4 guns
Powell's Brigade	4 guns
German Brigades	4 guns
German Reserve	4 guns

After the fall of Fort Ticonderoga, the siege train of artillery became redundant and was left behind. The army marched off to the Hudson with but 27 guns, which by eighteenth-century standards was a strong complement for the number of soldiers. With the constant problem of securing horses and forage for them, this large train of guns, ammunition tumbrils, tool carts, etc., was a severe strain on Burgoyne's transportation system.

On leaving Ticonderoga, General Burgoyne was forced to detach two regiments: the 62nd (later replaced by the 53rd) and the Brunswick Regiment Prinz Friederich as guards for that important rear link and focus point for the collection of supplies. Two companies of the 47th were left on Diamond Island in Lake George, serving a like purpose when the army severed its supply line to Canada in the march down the Hudson to Albany.

Faced with the necessity of manning and maintaining the posts in his rear, and after the losses suffered at Bennington and by attrition, Burgoyne crossed the Hudson with approximately 6000 men. The organization of the army was altered to fit the reduced size and the anticipated employment and deployment of the troops. At the time of the two battles of Freeman's farm, Burgoyne's army was brigaded as follows:

Advance Corps: Marksmen, Canadians, Loyalists, Indians, Grenadiers, Light Infantry, 24th Foot, Breymann's Corps (Grenadiers and Bärner's Light Troops), Attached artillery (10 guns — varying).

Right Wing (Brigadier General Hamilton): 9th Foot, 20th Foot, 21st Foot, 62nd Foot, Attached artillery (4 guns).

Left Wing (Major General Riedesel): Regiment Rhetz, Regiment Specht, Regiment Riedesel, Regiment Hesse-Hanau, Attached artillery (8 guns).

Rear Echelon: Brunswick Dragoons (remnant as headquarters guard), 47th Foot (6 companies), Gun Park.

Major General Phillips was second in command to General Burgoyne, and in that capacity he took over the supervision of supplies and services while the army was gathering its resources at Fort Edward for the drive to Albany.

The staff appointments at the army level were many and extraordinary:

Adjutant General	Lieutenant Colonel Robert Kingston
Deputy Quartermaster General	Captain John Money
Royal Artillery	Captain Thomas Bloomfield
Chief Engineer	Lieutenant William Twiss
Commissary	Mr. —————— Rousseau
Wagonmaster	Mr. Robert Hoakesly
Provost	Lieutenant —————— Atherton
Department of Civil Affairs	Colonel Philip Skene
Naval Engineer Adviser	Lieutenant John Schank, Royal Navy
Captain of Bateaux	Mr. —————— Munro, Royal Navy
Pioneers	Captain —————— Wilcox
Paymaster	Mr. David Geddes
Surgeon of Hospitals	——————

Almost all of these departments had assistants and deputies, and certain of them, such as quartermasters, commissaries, surgeons, and paymasters, had their counterpart at brigade and regimental levels. The chaplains were attached to regiments. Drummers were carried on the rolls of their regiments, distinct from the musicians of the regimental bands. The former were in effect the signal corps, as they beat the various calls and duties of the camp, as well as giving the pace on the march and in battle. Valets and batmen were also on the regimental lists, as were soldiers' wives, who served as washer-women and hospital attendants, and who had other specific duties for which they received rations.

The final returns of General Burgoyne's brave army at the signing of the "Convention," 17 October 1777 showed a total of 4693 men who entered into the long captivity.

The American Army

General George Washington was the commander in chief of the American army. He was also field commander of the army fighting the British commander in chief, Sir William Howe.

In the summer of 1775, in acknowledgment of the threat of the Hudson-Champlain Pass and the classic scheme of slicing in two the Atlantic Colonies along that geographic fault, Washington created the northern department of the army, command of which was given to Major General Philip Schuyler. It was Schuyler who met the first advance of Burgoyne's invasion in July and August 1777, and it was he who was responsible for the action of his subordinate, Major General Arthur Sinclair, who, with a force of two thousand Continentals, three hundred artillerymen, and about five hundred militia, abandoned the forts at Ticonderoga at the threat of siege by Burgoyne's eight thousand troops and heavy guns. The troops were saved. During Schuyler's rear-guard action, the American army was rebuilt in strength and numbers. However, the loss of the forts at Ticonderoga, symbol of rebel strength, resulted in such a scandal in the Congress that Major General Horatio Gates was appointed to replace General Schuyler and was given almost dictatorial power. Gates assumed command on 19 August 1777.

The American army had two kinds of troops: first, the

Continentals, who in effect were regular army troops, supplied by regiments from the individual colonies to the Continental Congress and to George Washington, its general,
and, second, the militia, who were state or colony troops.
The latter were held in their respective states for local defense, or were called out in a defensive role for a specific
purpose and for a limited time. In the case of the New
England militia at Saratoga, they were on an offensive-de-
fensive mission outside their home states.

Gates took over command of approximately three thousand
Continentals and three to four hundred militia on active
duty. Between 19 August and the Convention of Saratoga,
17 October 1777, Gates's army grew to almost six thousand
Continentals and an undetermined number of militia, estimated variously at from twelve hundred to three thousand
men. At the time of the surrender at Saratoga, the militia
was still pouring in to join the army facing Burgoyne.

The hard core of Gates's army was made up of the Continentals. At the first battle of Freeman's farm, they were
organized into two wings, of which the right was commanded
by Major General Benjamin Lincoln; the left was under the
command of General Benedict Arnold. Gates had five brigadiers of Continentals.* They were, according to seniority:
John Nixon, Enoch Poor, John Glover, John Paterson, and
Ebenezer Learned.

The Continental regiments of Gates's army at the time of
Burgoyne's surrender at Saratoga were as follows:

11th Virginia Regiment (known as Morgan's Regiment of
    Riflemen)

Dearborn's Light Infantry Battalion (under command of
    Morgan's Regiment)

* Brigadier General John Stark held a New Hampshire commission at the time. His Continental commission, an award for his
victory at Bennington in August 1777, was not promulgated until
4 October, so he was unaware of it at the time of the second
battle of Freeman's farm.

1st New Hampshire Regiment	Colonel Joseph Cilley
2nd New Hampshire Regiment	Colonel Nathan Hale
3rd New Hampshire Regiment	Colonel Alexander Scammel
2nd New York Regiment	Colonel Philip van Cortlandt
4th New York Regiment	Colonel Henry Livingston
Livingston's New York Regiment (formerly 1st Canadians)	Colonel James Livingston

1st, 2nd, 3rd, 4th, 5th, 6th, 7th, 8th, 9th, 10th, 11th, 12th, 13th, 14th and 15th Massachusetts Regiments

Warner's Vermont Regiment (The Green Mountain Boys)

Ebenezer Stevens's Independent Battalion of Artillery

Jeduthan Baldwin's Detachment of Engineers and Artificers

Hyde's Continental Light Horse

Seymour's Troop, 2nd Dragoons

The militia was supplied for Connecticut, Massachusetts, New Hampshire, and New York, and for Vermont, a quasi-autonomous territory. The designation of a militia regiment was by the name of its colonel or the county in which it had been raised. The National Park Service has listed fifty-three militia units which either took part in the battles at Saratoga or were present at Burgoyne's surrender. Generally speaking, the militia regiments were brigaded together by states, which gave a great disparity in numbers between the various brigade strengths. Thus, Stark's New Hampshire brigade at the close of the campaign was eight hundred strong, while Ten Broeck commanded three thousand New Yorkers.

Three brigadier generals of the militia, with their troops, took an active part in the Burgoyne campaign: John Stark (New Hampshire), John Fellows (Massachusetts), Abram Ten Broeck (New York).

Two Connecticut militia regiments, those of Colonel Jonathan Lattimer and Thaddeus Cook, were engaged with Poor's brigade of Benedict Arnold's division.

Book List

Anburey, Thomas: *Travels through the Interior Parts of America*, Boston and New York, 1923.

Baldwin, Colonel Jeduthan: *Revolutionary Journal*, Bangor, Maine, 1906 (Limited Edition).

Bascom, Robert: *The Fort Edward Book*, Fort Edward, New York, 1903.

Baumeister, Adjutant General Major Carl Leopold: *Revolution in America: Confidential Letters and Journals, 1776–1784*, translated and annotated by Bernhard A. Uhlendorf, New Brunswick, New Jersey, 1957.

Boardman, Oliver: *Journal*, Connecticut Historical Society, 1899.

Brandow, John Henry: *The Story of Old Saratoga and History of Schuylersville*, Saratoga Springs, New York, 1906.

British Army, Historical Records of Every Regiment in Her Majesty's Service: History of the 8th, 9th, 20th, 21st, 24th, 29th, 31st, 33rd, 34th, 47th, 53rd, and 62nd Regiments of Foot Horse Guards, 1836.

Burgoyne, Lieutenant General John: *The Dramatic and Poetical Works of* ———Vol. I, London, 1808.

—— *Orderly Book*, edited by E. B. O'Callaghan, Albany, New York, 1860.

Cannon, Richard: *Historical Record of the Ninth Regiment of Foot*, London, 1838.

Commager, Henry Steele and Richard B. Morris: *The Spirit of Seventy-six*, Indianapolis–New York, 1958.

Clinton, Governor George: *Public Papers of George Clinton*, Introduction by Hugh Hastings, State Historian (two volumes), New York and Albany, 1899.

Dearborn, Major General Henry: *A Narrative of the Saratoga Campaign*, Bulletin, Fort Ticonderoga Museum, Vol. I, No. 5, January 1929.

Digby, Lieutenant William: *The British Invasion of North America, with the Journal of Lieutenant William Digby of the 53rd or Shropshire Regiment of Foot*, edited by James Phinney Baxter, Albany, 1887.

Duncan, Major Francis: *History of the Royal Regiment of Artillery*, London, 1879.

DuRoi, ——: *Journal of DuRoi the Elder, Lieutenant and Adjutant in Service of the Duke of Brunswick, 1776–1778*, translated by Charlotte S. J. Epping, Philadelphia, 1911.

Eelking, Captain Max von: *The German Allied Troops in the War of Independence, 1776–1783*, Albany, 1893.

Flexner, James Thomas: *The Benedict Arnold Case* (abridged edition), New York, 1962.

Flick, A. C., New York State Historian, and others: *One Hundred Fiftieth Anniversary of the Battle of Saratoga and the Surrender of Burgoyne*, Albany, 1927.

Fuller, J. F. C.: *A Military History of the Western World*, New York, 1955.

——: *Decisive Battles of the U.S.A.*, New York, 1942.

Nickerson, Hoffman: *The Turning Point of the Revolution*, Boston and New York, 1928.

Partridge, Bellamy: *Sir Billy Howe*, New York, 1932.

Pausch, George: *Journal of Captain Pausch, Captain of the Hanau Artillery During the Burgoyne Campaign*, translated by William L. Stone, Albany, 1886.

Pell, John H. G.: *Burgoyne and Ticonderoga*, Bulletin, Fort Ticonderoga Museum, Vol. I, No. 2, July 1929.

Pell, Joshua, III: *Diary of Joshua Pell, III, an Officer of the British Army in America, 1776–1777* (privately printed), Fort Ticonderoga, New York, 1934.

Montross, Lynn: *Rag, Tag, and Bobtail: The Story of the Continental Army, 1775–1783,* New York, 1952.

Morris, Richard B. (see Commager, Henry Steele)

Morton, Doris Begor: *Philip Skene of Skenesborough,* Granville, New York, 1959.

Raddall, Thomas H.: *Canada from the British Conquest to Home Rule: The Path of Destiny,* Vol. III, Canadian History Series, edited by Thomas B. Costain, Garden City, New York, 1957.

Riedesel, Major General Baron von: *Memoirs, Including Letters and Journals Written during His Residence in America,* edited by Max von Eelking, translated by William L. Stone (two volumes), Albany, 1868.

Riedesel, Baroness von: *Letters and Journal,* translated by William L. Stone, Albany, 1867.

Gilby, Thomas (Editor): *Britain at Arms,* London, 1953.

Graves, Robert: *Sergeant Lamb's America,* New York, 1940.

Hadden, Lieutenant James M.: *Journal and Orderly Book,* Albany, 1884.

Hiscock (Hitchcock?), Rev. Enos: *Journal,* Providence, 1901.

How, David: *Diary: An American Private,* New York, 1865.

Hudleston, F. J.: *Gentleman Johnny Burgoyne,* Indianapolis, 1927.

Lefferts, Charles M.: *Uniforms of the American, British, French, and German Armies in the War of the American Revolution, 1775–1783,* New York, 1926.

Lamb, Roger, Sergeant 9th Foot: *Journal of Occurrences During the Late American War,* Dublin, 1809.

Lancaster, Bruce: *Guns of Burgoyne,* New York, 1939.

Lawson, C. C. P.: *The History of the Uniforms of the British Army* (three volumes), London, 1961.

Lossing, Benjamin: *Pictorial Field Book of the Revolution,* New York, 1859.

Murray, Eleanor M.: *The Burgoyne Campaign*, Bulletin, Ticonderoga Museum, Vol. VIII, No. 1, January 1948.

Neilson, Charles: *Burgoyne's Campaign, and the Memorable Battles of Bemis's Heights, September 19 and October 7, 1777*, Albany, 1844.

Roberts, Kenneth: *Rabble in Arms*, Garden City, New York, 1936.

Reid, Arthur: *Reminiscences of the Revolution, or Le Loup's Bloody Trail* (privately printed), Utica, New York, 1859.

"Sexagenary": *Reminiscences of the American Revolution*, Albany, 1866.

Snell, Charles W. and Francis F. Wilshin: *Saratoga National Historical Park*, Washington, D. C., 1958.

Squier, Ephraim: *Journal*, Boston, 1878.

Stanley, George F. G.: *Canada's Soldiers*, Toronto, 1960.

Stanley, George F. G. (Editor): *For Want of a Horse*, Sackville, N. B., 1961.

Roby, Luther: *The Life and Military Services of Major General John Stark*, Concord, New Hampshire, 1831.

Stimson, F. J.: *My Story: Being the Memoirs of Benedict Arnold*, New York, 1917.

Steele, Matthew Forney: *American Campaigns* (two volumes), Washington, D. C., 1909.

Stitt, Edward W., Jr.: *Horatio Gates*, Bulletin, Fort Ticonderoga Museum, Vol. IX, No. 2, Winter 1953.

Stone, William L.: *The Campaign of Lieut. Gen. John Burgoyne and the Expedition of Lieut. Col. Barry St. Leger*, Albany, New York, 1877.

Stone, William L. (Editor): *Washington County, New York: Its History to the Close of the Nineteenth Century*, New York, 1901.

Sylvester, Nathaniel Bartlett: *History of Saratoga County*, Philadelphia, 1878.

Thacher, James: *A Military Journal During the American Revolutionary War from 1775 to 1783*, Boston, 1827.

Trumbull, John: *Autobiography, Reminiscences and Letters*, New York & London, 1841.

Walworth, Mrs. Ellen Hardin: *Battles of Saratoga, 1777*, Albany, New York, 1891.

Ward, Christopher: *The War of the Revolution,* New York, 1952.

Watson, J. Steven: *The Reign of George III, 1760–1815* Vol. XII, Oxford History of England, edited by Sir George Clark, Oxford: 1960.

Watson, Winslow C.: *The Military and Civil History of the County of Essex, New York,* Albany, New York, 1869.

Weeks, William: *Letters of an American Sergeant,* Cambridge, Massachusetts, 1901.

Wilkinson, General J.: *Memoirs of My Own Times,* Philadelphia, 1816.

Wilshin, Francis F. (see Snell, Charles W.).

Index